Palgrave Studies in the History of Economic Thought

Palgrave Studies in the History of Economic Thought publishes contributions by leading scholars, illuminating key events, theories and individuals that have had a lasting impact on the development of modern-day economics. The topics covered include the development of economies, institutions and theories.

More information about this series at
http://www.palgrave.com/gp/series/14585

Matthijs Krul

The New Institutionalist Economic History of Douglass C. North

A Critical Interpretation

palgrave
macmillan

Matthijs Krul
Max Planck Institute for Social Anthropology
Berlin, Germany

Palgrave Studies in the History of Economic Thought
ISBN 978-3-030-06792-2 ISBN 978-3-319-94084-7 (eBook)
https://doi.org/10.1007/978-3-319-94084-7

Cover illustration: SuperStock / Alamy Stock Photo

This Palgrave Macmillan imprint is published by the registered company Springer Nature Switzerland AG
The registered company address is: Gewerbestrasse 11, 6330 Cham, Switzerland

Preface

The present book is the result of a puzzlement, one that began when I was an eager new master's degree student at the London School of Economics. Part of the curriculum at that time was a compulsory methods course, during which various aspects of the prevailing methodological repertoire of economic history were highlighted. Having begun my academic career with the ambition to become a philosopher—something which will be evident in this work—the prospect of such a comparative introduction excited me a good deal. When we came to the qualitative analysis section, I was presented for the first time with the ideas of the New Institutionalist Economic History, in particular in the form expressed in the works of the late Douglass C. North. I fancied myself a critic of 'orthodox economics' at the time and had prepared to be dismayed by the mindless presentation of some *homo economicus* approach, valid for all places and times. In North's work I found instead a combination of theoretical elements that have continued to intrigue me ever since: on the one hand, a thoroughgoing criticism of neoclassical economics, of rational choice theory, of transhistorical reasoning, and of asocial economic models; on the other hand, a strong commitment to the defense of economics, and only economics, in general terms as the exclusive discipline able to provide historians and other social scientists with the means to understand institutional, political, and economic change.

I had never encountered such an approach before. In my memory, it was presented more or less as 'our method' for qualitative and long-term analysis in economic history, but I was far from being immediately convinced. It seemed to me a contradiction in terms, rife with internal tension: How could one be a critic of neoclassical economics and reject what I thought were its basic methods, and yet refuse to simply acknowledge the merits of the 'heterodox' and extradisciplinary critics of the field? What's more, North's theory was hardly modest in its claims and ambitions, seeking nothing less than to provide 'a conceptual framework for interpreting recorded history', as the subtitle to North's final major work, *Violence and Social Orders*, has it. But philosophical tensions and theoretical ambition are both traits that have always attracted me. Besides, as a fledgling critic of economic practice, I felt I should seriously engage with this apparently novel *tertium quid* between neoclassical economics and the hererodox traditions I had familiarized myself with.

The subsequent years of my PhD and part of a postdoc appointment have been dedicated to fulfilling that promise. In the course of researching the nature and origins of North's oeuvre as a whole, I made a happy discovery that it was an ideal case study for engaging with some of my favorite questions and themes in philosophy of social science: the relationship between disciplines and the justification of the boundaries between them, the ways methods from the social sciences can or cannot be applied to historical study, the relevance of natural scientific practices as 'model sciences' for the social sciences and humanities, the role of ideological and political premises in the formulation of method (not just the content of empirical work), and many more. These and related themes will be central to the present work. I also discovered that despite the great richness and the considerable disciplinary, and interdisciplinary, impact of North's work—which ultimately earned him a Nobel Prize in economics, one of only two economic historians to do so—there is a dearth of systematic writing on North's oeuvre. I hope with the present book to contribute to addressing that shortage.

Finally, I became (and remain) fascinated by the tensions in North's theoretical edifice and his conscious endeavors to position himself in some sense between the economic mainstream and the critics of the discipline, trying to give both their due simultaneously. The core purpose of this book is to examine that tension, its origins, reasons, justifications, and consequences, particularly in the most developed stage of North's work. This tension appears, as I interpret North's writings, in two major ways that serve as guiding threads for my analysis. The first are his systematic criticisms of what he saw as the ahistorical, limited, and unrealistic practices of the economic mainstream, and the consequences of these shortcomings for economic history. These criticisms only gained in scope and vehemence over the course of his career. Significantly for the trajectory of his theory, they led him to concede many of the criticisms of economics as a field made by 'external' critics.

As I try to show, it was the criticism of the historical applicability of economic theory propounded by Karl Polanyi that provided North with a way to delineate his intermediate position: accepting many of Polanyi's theoretical objections, but seeing this—unlike Polanyi himself—as an opportunity to rethink what economics as a discipline could accomplish once shorn of its self-imposed neoclassical limitations. This meant he had to find a way to define economics such that he could claim to preserve its disciplinary and methodological core while jettisoning all the premises of the neoclassical paradigm, and without accidentally wandering into the camp of the social scientific critics of the field (whether heterodox economists or critics from history, sociology, and anthropology like Polanyi). From his first encounter with Polanyi, this provided the first productive tension in North's work.

The second such tension is directly related to the nature of institutions in his work. North's great breakthrough was to reformulate economic theory, and especially its application to economic history, in terms of changing institutions designed—or evolved—to compensate for pervasive market imperfections. But the meaning of 'institution' has never been very fixed in the economics literature, nor in the public choice tradition in political science from which North drew much inspiration. North was therefore in a position where he could, and did, reshape New Institutional Economics as a whole by rethinking the concept of an institution. The principle of viewing institutions as 'rules of the game', and individuals and organizations as the 'players of the game', became one of the few consistent methodological premises of North's overall approach.

This has often been praised as one of the great strengths of North's theory, and with good reason, for it allows in principle a clear distinction between structure and agency. Ideally, for North, it would permit him to retain the methodological individualism central to the economics discipline while emphasizing the importance of the institutional variable. Opponents of methodological individualism in economics from the heterodox perspective have, of course, accordingly found fault with his work on this point. But what has not often been seriously studied are the very real difficulties North had in maintaining this approach consistently as the scope and ambition of his theoretical project increased. The concept of ideology and the importance of ideas and moral commitments play an ever-increasing role in North's work, and so does the problem of how societies manage to achieve cooperation instead of violent conflict in the first place, at least sufficient to permit institutions to arise and persist. North's ever-deeper investigation into the *origins* of institutions came to supplant his initial emphasis on developing his fundamental economic analysis, namely viewing society as a set of players in an institutionally constrained microeconomic choice framework ('game'). On the one hand, there is a whole realm of theory in which the development of ideas and experience in the face of uncertainty is primary in explaining institutions and their change. On the other hand, there is a superimposed older theoretical framework which explains institutional change in terms of transaction costs and market imperfection (and incompleteness). Premises of rationality, agency, and incentives are not at all the same in each framework, and this problem persists throughout. In fact, I would argue, he never reconciled the two in a satisfying way, and much of the final stage of his oeuvre—from the 1990s onward—was dedicated to attempting various ways to resolve this problem, usually by reference to biological theory and borrowed anthropology.

These tensions are not just interesting in their own right, to understand North's work and its internal development. Although North's New Institutionalist Economic History is undeniably in some ways an idiosyncratic composite that does not represent the economic historical mainstream in a straightforward way, I think North has contributed as much as anyone to the interdisciplinary popularity of 'institutionalist' approaches and of formulating problems in terms of 'institutions', whether or not other authors adopt his exact framework. The tensions and problems inherent in North's oeuvre have in this way been exported to many works and subdisciplines where the practitioners who invoke him may not necessarily be aware of their origins, or indeed of their existence. But there is more to it than that. On reflection, I think North's work is so interesting precisely because, owing to the immodesty of his theoretical ambitions, he unintentionally laid bare in a very visible way just how difficult it is to sustain such an 'intermediate' position in economics as the New Institutionalism represents.

In a time when it seems to me the New Institutionalism is becoming an essential part of the 'new mainstream' in many social sciences, and when institutional analysis has become something of a silver bullet for any intractable problem of structure and agency in economic analysis, it is worth considering that many of the problems I identify in North's approach in this book are problems confronted by *any* New Institutionalist approach. They are merely drawn out by the admirably ambitious and consistent quest for the next explanatory step that was North's intellectual career. Although I cannot fully prove it in this book, my suspicion is that the tensions here outlined will prove to be present in all New Institutionalisms that seek in some way to be more than just an adjunct to the neoclassical paradigm (however defined). The research underpinning this book therefore gives me reason to suspect that the present belief that New Institutionalist theory has solved many of the old historico-social debates—such as those between 'modernism' and 'primitivism', 'formalism' and 'substantivism', in historical analysis that so concerned Karl Polanyi—will prove to be unfounded.

Since my focus is therefore in this book on North's New Institutionalist Economic History in systematic perspective, both in its own right and as a case study in understanding the theoretical strengths and weaknesses of the more 'radical' wing of New Institutionalism in general, it is worth briefly emphasizing what this book does not do. I have not endeavored to write an intellectual history of the life of Douglass C. North. However worthy such an enterprise would be, I did not see that as compatible with the systematic and philosophical aims of the present work. A proper biographical contextualization of the development of his theory therefore must await a separate treatment, although others (most notably North himself in various interviews and statements) have provided some preliminary materials.

Relatedly, this book also does not place the political context of North's work at the center of the analysis. Certainly, North's concerns about the applicability of his theory for policy purposes, most importantly in development economics, are not ignored. I also draw attention to what I see as the strong classical liberal and contractarian political premises of North's work, actually one of the few consistent elements in the theoretical edifice from the very beginning through to its final form. The heroic intellectual ancestors most frequently and significantly invoked by North are Adam Smith and Friedrich Hayek, and I have tried to give each their due in terms of their influence on, or appropriation by, North himself. I also suggest that North might have added Locke and Hobbes to that pantheon. What I call his 'pessimistic anthropology' of human society and the state, a realm of violence occasionally leavened only by the protection offered by property rights, becomes if anything more evident with time.

But these form the context of discussions about the merits of his theory in his own right, and while I have sought to identify what I view as ideological elements in North's reasoning, I do not here engage in any protracted arguments against them. Neither have I, on this occasion at least, sought to investigate further the role of North's position within a number of liberal-conservative intellectual institutions and endowed chairs (such as the Hoover Foundation and the Luce Professorship). Politics and ideology are important themes in North's own work, and it is all the more justified not to exempt him from analysis and criticism on those points, and I make no secret of my differences of view with his general economic and social outlook. But in this book, philosophy of (social) science is my preferred terrain of discussion, rather than political theory.

The New Institutionalist Economic History has made credible theoretical advances, and its contribution to the changing face of the economics and economic history profession is not to be lightly dismissed. The present trend toward a more socioculturally deep and contextually informed economics, including in its modeling practice, is absolutely a positive one. But it is important to note that at the end of North's winding road some arguments of the critics of economics, from the heterodox traditions of Marxism and Old Institutionalism to the historical economic anthropology of Polanyi, retain validity despite the breakthrough of New Institutionalisms into academic fashion. North began his great project with an admission of the merits of Polanyi's criticisms, perceiving these as a challenge to improve the disciplines to which he was dedicated. The critique of his own approach and its implications for economic thought in the present work will hopefully be received in the same spirit.

As a final note, this book is emphatically a work of *interpretation*. This means I have sought to make sense of North according to my own theoretical knowledge and predispositions, and that I draw connections and attempt to tease out implications that go beyond what is explicit in North's texts. The result is therefore neither just a historical overview of North's work nor a literature review. The critical element in the book consists of both immanent critique, concerned with coherence and consistency, and 'external' critique, concerned with plausibility and validity. While I have at all times endeavored to represent his work fairly, my priorities and opinions may be different from those of many who have made use of North's work, and of North himself. For those reasons, this is only one of many possible books that could be written about North's NIEH, and there are aspects of North's oeuvre that no doubt deserve a fuller treatment than I could provide here.

Berlin, Germany Matthijs Krul

Acknowledgments

A book dealing with the problems of the embeddedness of behavior in a larger social context should not fail to acknowledge the context of its own creation. While academic labor can be a solitary endeavor, I would not be able to perform it without the support, inspiration, and intellectual and emotional environment I have been able to enjoy over the past years. Expressions of gratitude to those who made it possible are therefore in order.

I wish to thank firstly the Economic History Department at the LSE for first setting me on the path to studying the work of Douglass North. In particular, the encouragement and enthusiasm of Paul Strong has been of aid to me. Gareth Dale has throughout played an indispensable role: as my PhD supervisor, as a supporter of my work, as an advisor and therapist where needed, and above all as a comrade. I wholeheartedly thank him again for all the effort and time he has given me. I thank the Department of Politics and History at Brunel University for the opportunity to present and discuss early versions of my dissertation on which this book is ultimately based, and Geoffrey Hodgson and Mark Neocleous for comments on that thesis.

A formative period in the creation of this book was the period I spent as a research fellow at the Max Planck Institute (MPI) for Social Anthropology in Halle (Saale), Sachsen-Anhalt, Germany, where I have benefited greatly from time and resources to give the project its final form. The many people at the MPI who have provided a stimulating intellectual environment are gratefully remembered. Above all, I thank Chris Hann for his patience and advice. Among the other colleagues I want to particularly thank the REALEurasia group for their unstinting friendship and encouragement. As part of my own time in the REALEurasia project was spent on preparation for this book, I also gratefully acknowledge the receipt of funds from the European Research Council under the European Union's Seventh Framework Programme, Grant Agreement no. 340854.

Besides this, I am happy to have been able to present various draft versions of chapters and papers drawn on the material of this book at conferences, including the IIPPE conference in Berlin in 2017, several Historical Materialism conferences in London, the graduate conference at Goldsmiths University in 2013, and the conference on the Eurocentrism debate I was able to organize at the MPI in 2015. I thank the respondents and commenters on these various occasions for their input.

I thank Clara Heathcock and Laura Pacey at Palgrave for helping me navigate the process of publication.

Finally, the irreducibly social and other-regarding element must be acknowledged also. Old and new friends in London, Halle, Leipzig, Berlin, and worldwide have allowed me to survive the slings and arrows of outrageous fortune and the sometimes-arbitrary nature of the academic process unharmed. Without their care, encouragement, and engaging company and discussions, I would not have been able to do it. I am also always grateful for the happy company of my sister, Julia Krul, and my brother-in-law, Maarten Oosten, both great sources of intellectual stimulus in their own right. The love and support of Mika Naylor has defied neoclassical economics by exhibiting no diminishing returns. Finally, my parents have been with me every step of the way, with support, counsel, shelter, and love, and have read my many drafts and always provided valuable commentary. I dedicate this book to them.

Any errors, of course, remain my own.

Contents

1

Introduction: Douglass North's NIEH in Context

Introduction

The concept of the institution has conquered much of the social sciences. Reference to institutions as an explanatory variable, often the primary one, is practically ubiquitous in the social scientific heartlands such as contemporary sociology and political science, and it has even reached the outlying settlements of economic anthropology and ancient history. In short, as the preferred explanatory device in areas that combine economic analysis with a historical dimension, institutions rule (Burki and Perry 1998; Rodrik, Subramanian, and Trebbi 2004). While this turn across a range of disciplines undoubtedly has multiple origins, with dynamics particular to the individual disciplines themselves being one important component, there is little doubt that a major driver of this interest has been the rising popularity of the New Institutionalist Economics (NIE).[1]

[1] Often the approach is called by its practitioners the New Institutional Economics (e.g. North 1986; Alston 2008) instead. However, in the philosophy of social science literature reference to '(new) institutionalism' is more prevalent, and it is also so used in comparative context (Nee 2005). I follow here the philosophical convention (see Mäki 1993), which also has the advantage of distinguishing it from the adjectival derivation 'belonging to an institution'. The terms are in any case entirely equivalent.

M. Krul, *The New Institutionalist Economic History of Douglass C. North*,
Palgrave Studies in the History of Economic Thought,
https://doi.org/10.1007/978-3-319-94084-7_1

This term, coined by NIE pioneer Oliver Williamson (Williamson 1975), has been defined by adherence to two slogans: that "institutions matter" and that "the determinants of institutions are susceptible to analysis by the tools of economic theory" (Matthews 1986). In a more recent consideration of how the NIE has developed since its original coinage, Williamson has emphasized that it is the latter of the two that distinguishes the NIE from the older traditions in institutionalist economics (Williamson 2000: 595). No doubt the prestige of what is perceived as the mainstream of economics in the social sciences at large has thereby helped NIE ideas and concepts achieve a widespread distribution in a way that previous institutionalist traditions did not. In various disciplines the approach has given rise to new research programs inspired by the tools of NIE theory, sometimes distinguished by the use of the 'new' label: for example, the New Economic Sociology (Granovetter 1985; Nee 2008; Richter 2015). It has also converged with public choice theory in political science, owing to mutual inspiration (Buchanan and Tullock 1962; Olson 1965; Mueller 2003; Ostrom and Ostrom 2004).

The result of this 'neoinstitutionalist turn' has been the creation of an interdisciplinary field in economic thought dedicated to the analysis of institutions.[2] As Elinor Ostrom has formulated it, in its broadest sense, it brings together public choice theory, NIE, and game theory into a single framework that "draws inspiration and methods from the other social sciences as well as biology to provide a general framework for the analysis of humanly designed institutions at multiple levels and their consequences" (Ostrom 2007: 240).[3] Where public choice theory is concerned with the incentive structure of individuals in political institutions and organizations and game theory with the analysis of strategic action by individuals under conditions of imperfect information, the NIE provides an economic theory framework to answer the question why institutions

[2] I shall throughout distinguish 'economics' as a discipline from 'economic thought'. The latter will be used for convenience as an umbrella term for all fields of social science concerned with economic structures and behavior as their primary subject matter, including economic history, economic sociology, economic anthropology, and so forth.

[3] Another element she identifies is the debate about public goods and free riding, to which I will also return later in the context of North's NIEH. However, to avoid category mistakes this is best seen as a subject matter rather than a component school of theory.

arise in the first place (Ostrom 2007: 242–243). The central concern of the NIE is to explain the existence of institutions and private organizations in terms of market failure, in other words as the result of limitations of (and on) private contracting. Fundamental concepts of the NIE are transaction costs, which are all costs associated with the process of exchange other than the price of the good in question, and property rights, which are the political and legal constraints on ownership and exchange.

The rise of the NIE in economic thought owes much to the influence of Douglass C. North and his New Institutionalist Economic History (NIEH), the subject of this book.[4] His work is often recognized as one of the main bodies of literature that has contributed to the renewed popularity of institutional analysis, and has done much to refound such analysis on new theoretical foundations.[5] But North's work is neither typical of the neoclassical paradigm nor of the NIE school as such. Where many NIE authors have confined their work to the analysis of firms and market structure in modern capitalist societies, North has—arguably more than any other author—taken the larger framework of the neoinstitutionalist turn to its furthest extent. In so doing, he has made two great contributions to the New Institutionialism: by providing a theoretical foundation for the interdisciplinary project as a whole and by testing the very boundaries of its capabilities to explain.

From his origins in quantitative economic history, North became a prominent advocate of New Institutionalist analysis in every domain of sociohistorical explanation, not limited to the study of modern market societies alone. With North, the NIE has acquired for the first time a systematically historical dimension. He developed his NIEH in a series of stages, each taking him further away from the boundaries of conventional economic analysis and each time extending the scope of his theorizing

[4] Much of the material of this book was prepared before the recent death of Douglass North, on November 3, 2015. In order to emphasize the ongoing relevance of his work, I have not changed the tense used. Discussions of past phases of North's NIEH will be in past tense, while his arguments as formulated in the final phase, most notably his last two monographs, will be in present tense.

[5] As Robert Bates has put it, "If anyone can lay claim to being the founder of the new institutionalism, it would be Douglass North" (Bates 2014).

considerably wider. It is illustrative of North's ambition to fulfill the promise of the neoinstitutionalist turn in economic thought to its fullest extent that the subtitle of his final book, *Violence and Social Orders*, is nothing less than "a conceptual framework for interpreting recorded human history" (North, Wallis, and Weingast 2009). The present book is a study of his work in the context of this larger institutionalist research agenda. It examines how North came to set this agenda, how he developed his approach in response to it, and how ongoing theoretical problems each time led him to reformulate his NIEH in a new direction. It also examines systematically the problems with his NIEH and assesses to what extent North actually succeeded in the aims he set for himself.

Capturing the essence of North's NIEH is less easy than it may seem. Quite likely because of the frequently changing ways he attempted to cohere his many varied insights, he never spent much time on defining his approach as a 'school'. Commentators on his work have therefore tended to focus on different aspects of it as the breakthrough element, depending on their own particular concerns and uses of his theory. A consensus view can nonetheless be distilled. Firstly, North shared with the NIE in general a qualified rejection of the neoclassical tradition, in particular because of its ahistoricity and its inability to explain persistent inefficiencies. Secondly, and this is the qualification, the desire to complement (or, in more ambitious cases like North's, supplant) the neoclassical approach to institutions and their historical development was not to come at the expense of the foundations of economics: price theory and the operation of individual choice within constraints. North, however, went further than almost all other NIE authors in elaborating these constraints. His increasingly strident criticisms of rational choice economics combined with his insistence on historical explanation (path dependence) and the importance of market failures and inefficient institutions to shape his NIEH into something quite different from even neoclassical-adjacent approaches, like those of Oliver Williamson and others.

The central focus of North's NIEH is the study of the formation and change of institutions. The purpose of this explanation is to account for how economies have varied in economic performance over time. In the course of doing so, it also has to study how and why most of economic history has been characterized not by neoclassically efficient markets, but by every possible form of market failure and by wildly differing political economic arrangements, property rights, and allocation systems. In the most fully formed expression of his ideas, North distinguished between these institutional arrangements and the larger 'environment' within which they appear, which consists of a deeper layer of beliefs and ideologies, deep-seated noneconomic logics, and political orders. North's NIEH in its final form is therefore a theory of the interaction between beliefs, institutions, political orders, and economic outcomes.

But this theory has always maintained the economic core of price theory and choice theory: the first three variables in this qualitative model act as constraints on individual action, and this constrained action leads to economic performance (usually rather poor performance, at that) via the operation of markets or quasi-markets. The meanings of efficiency, welfare (Pareto optimality), and rationality are much changed in North's work in comparison even with other NIE theories, let alone neoclassical models.[6] But simultaneously, his NIEH is dedicated throughout to the preservation of what one might call the microfoundations of the modern discipline of economics.[7] His longtime collaborator John Joseph Wallis sums up his attitude well: "North long emphasised the importance of history and of neoclassical economics. He criticised both disciplines for their complacency about the adequacy of the current conceptual and methodological consensus on how history or economics should be done. He always operated within a framework of individuals who act intentionally (neoclassical economics matters) and who perceive the world through cognitive lenses that are part inherited from their culture and part derived from their own experience (history matters)" (Wallis 2015).

As I will argue in this book, this Janus-faced attitude to and within the discipline of economics has its origin in a particular place: his confrontation with Karl Polanyi, standing in for the many criticisms of economics from outside the field. In addressing "the challenge of Karl Polanyi" (North 1977), he was forced to consider the question: If neoclassical economics has only a very limited range of applicability, how can institutional

[6] A lengthier treatment of the origins of the term "NIE" and "NIEH" and their relation to differences between North and other NIE authors can be found in Richter (2005).

[7] For a discussion of this term, see Weintraub (1979).

change in history be explained without giving up on economic orthodoxy altogether? This challenge of Polanyi elevated the need to theorize institutional change from a problem within economics (and economic history) to a problem between disciplines, about the relation between economic theory and other social sciences. To leave it to neoclassical economics would mean losing the historical and institutional dimension; but to substitute a theory from outside established microfoundations would be to give up on the discipline of economics and to cede the field to the likes of Polanyi. Neither appealed to him. On my reading, North's NIEH has throughout its many transformations always been an attempt to solve this puzzle, and to have both the critique of orthodox theory and the preservation of its core at the same time. It should therefore come as no surprise that this has placed his theoretical edifice under considerable intellectual strain, something which only got worse as its dimensions outgrew their initial foundations.

North's NIEH in Disciplinary Context

In the reception of North's work, much of the praise and the criticism have rested on his peculiar relation to neoclassical economics and the economic mainstream, whereby the nature of that reception has often depended for a good deal on what the authors considered to be defining traits of neoclassical economics. North himself had his own definition of it, and provided extensive criticisms of the shortcomings of that school, and yet some have seen his work as preserving core features of the neoclassical tradition. This raises the complex question of the relationship of NIEH and NIE at large to the economic mainstream, and of North's NIEH to the larger NIE tradition and the neoinstitutionalist interdisciplinary research agenda in turn. This question will be a significant theme in this work in understanding North's particular contribution to economic thought. But in order to assess it, we must first have a clearer idea of what the NIE represents and in what way it distinguishes itself from the neoclassical approach. I will therefore first give a brief overview of the development of the NIE at large, concentrating on the most representative or 'mainstream' theoretical work and its relation to the neoclassical school, as defined by the way NIE authors sought to distinguish themselves from that school. I will then discuss the place of North's NIEH in this context.

The notion of social scientific explanation in terms of institutions is itself not new. While the varied and flexible usage of the term in different periods and disciplines makes a general history of the institution a pointless endeavor, the underlying concepts find their origin in the historical economics of the nineteenth century, particularly those authors known as the German Historical School and their American successors, the so-called Old Institutional Economics (OIE). These approaches, however, lost influence with the rise of neoclassical economics in the course of the twentieth century, and institutional analysis faded from prominence with them (Hodgson 2001). As economics rose in prestige within the social sciences, the equilibriating rational choice paradigm of neoclassical economics rose with it, and this left its mark on the methods of other disciplines. During most of the twentieth-century development of the social sciences, those disciplines most sensitive to the influence of economics—notably sociology and political science—looked to it for the provision of a clear theoretical framework that would guide the formulation and interpretation of research. Condemned as lacking in 'theory', after the Second World War few paid any further attention to the descriptive and historically oriented institutionalism of the OIE and the German Historical School (Rutherford 1994, 2001).

The recent revival of institutional analysis therefore owes little to this tradition. Rather, one must look once again to the impact of prevailing economic theory on the social sciences at large. As in recent years the sentiment developed among practitioners of the economics discipline (and allied disciplines such as economic history) that the neoclassical paradigm of rational choice and competitive markets had reached its limits, it was the NIE that was, as it were, waiting in the wings. The strength of the NIE, as I will discuss in more detail in the following chapter, was and is that it offers an enticing promise for interdisciplinary work: having the advantages of rigor that social scientists have sought for in economics, but with a framework considerably less inflexible and narrow in scope than the neoclassical paradigm. The NIE as a body of economic theory allows economics a much greater scope of application and provides more flexibility at once, because it makes less strict assumptions about individual behavior and permits a much greater range of social variables in the analysis. Even so, unlike the OIE or heterodox economic schools of thought, most forms of the NIE have hewed fairly close to the neoclassical paradigm in other matters of assumptions and methodology. This means that, in most cases, the NIE may not require for those used to working with conventional economic theory a systematic change in the fundamental tools of analysis or conceptual apparatus. Most prominent in this domain is the work of Williamson (1975, 1981; Williamson and Winter 1991).

Since the foundational work of Ronald Coase (1937), the central premise of the NIE approach has been to abandon the neoclassical assumption of perfectly competitive markets and rational agents in favor of an (allegedly) more realistic view of market structure. Coase and his successors have sought to address the question why there should be forms of economic organization other than private contracting, if the theory of competitive markets was correct (see Williamson 1973). In other words, the purpose of the theory is to explain the existence and effects of market failure. In the NIE perspective, market imperfections and imperfectly rational agents generate pervasive transaction costs, that is, the costs associated with the process of market exchange itself, including contracting costs, search costs, and so forth. On this view, what Williamson (1975) has defined as the trade-off between markets and hierarchies (such as firms and unions) within a market society arises as an equilibrium optimization problem given such costs.[8]

Thrainn Eggertsson's discussion of his version of the NIE may stand here for this approach in its pure form: "Although NIE widens the scope of neoclassical economics, it does not constitute a new paradigm because the hard core of the neoclassical research program is left intact, particularly the rational choice model… Instead, NIE constitutes a modification of the protective belt of the neoclassical paradigm, primarily by introducing transaction costs and the constraints of property rights" (Eggertsson

[8] Another early contributor to this theoretical line of thought was Allen Barton, who however did not publish it (Harcourt et al. 2016: 271). I thank Geoff Harcourt for this reference.

1990: 450). What for many NIE authors, however, distinguishes their approach from the neoclassical one is the relaxation of the assumption of fully rational individual choice, but not necessarily the principles of self-interested behavior, equilibration, or other aspects of conventional economic (situational) analysis (Heiner 1983; Langlois 1990). But there is a tension between the principles of simple optimizing choice and bounded rationality or limited information models, which has led much of the NIE school to develop an analysis based on rule-following and adaptation. For them, this has shifted the element of maximization one step further: it is the rules themselves that provide optimization and adaptation to changing circumstances (e.g. Vanberg 1988: 9), a view that has also led the NIE to its increasing interweaving with game theoretical approaches (Schotter 1981). This complex of views one might call the 'moderate' wing of the NIE, insofar as it is consciously close to the neoclassical paradigm. The degree of closeness however varies with the extent to which individual choice analysis is constrained solely by transaction costs, property rights, and market imperfections generally, or also by further informational and processual limitations that make rule-formation more important.

Even so, some of the NIE tradition has been dissatisfied with such explanations in terms of rules-as-optimizations, analogous to Williamson's organizations-as-optimizations: an alternative strand of the theory, which one might call the more 'radical' wing of the NIE (in terms of perceived distance to the neoclassical paradigm). This strand has taken inspiration from the work of Friedrich Hayek and Herbert Simon to view norms, rules, and habits as constraints on individual behavior that emerge as the result of evolved cognitive limitations, leading to institutionally guided behavior that is not necessarily in any sense optimizing. Rather, such 'institutionalized' behavior should be seen as part of a framework in which both individual behavior and cultural patterns are subject in some fashion to a process of cultural evolution. A notable early exemplar of this strand is the work of Richard Nelson and Sidney Winter (Nelson and Winter 1982). But the essential distinction between this wing and the 'moderate' wing is, regardless of methodology, more a matter of attitude: whether NIE approaches are seen primarily as a complement to neoclassical rational optimization models or as a different and rival economic theory, for which the neoclassical one is at best a special case, and which does not presume optimization or efficiency.[9]

As will be discussed in more detail in the next chapter, North's work progressed over time from a more 'moderate' form of the NIE, albeit with an unusually strong historical focus, to a direction much more in the 'radical' vein. But it did not stop there: North has gone further than either of these strands had hitherto. At the risk of preempting the discussion in the following chapter, it is worth indicating here how North's NIEH has, by moving through each of these NIE strands, ended up beyond either of them. North did so in two ways that would become foundational for the ultimate form of his theory. Firstly, by redefining 'institution' as rules and norms, and individuals and organizations as agents, he reconceptualized the notion of an institution in such a way as to make the separation between agency and structure in his analysis clear. This has allowed him to attempt in a systematic way to bridge the gap between behavioral microfoundations and macro-level institutional analysis that has been an ongoing problem in the neoinstitutionalist turn (Ostrom 2007: 255–258). Secondly, North increasingly placed at the center of his investigation the question where institutions originate. While some had argued already against the view that rules and norms should be seen as efficient responses to transaction costs, meaning efficient in the neoclassical sense, few had gone beyond taking the rule-like structure of a market's sociocultural context for granted in each individual case. In North's case, however, his role as an economic historian with a primary interest in historical explanation came to the fore. He has sought to provide an explanation for how such institutional orders come about in the first place and how they change over time, providing a dynamic rather than static theory of the effects of institutional variation on economic behavior and outcomes.

A different question is what effect this has had on the mainstream in economic theorizing. In an influential paper on what they call the "changing

[9] The decisive step here for North was the abandonment of the assumption that institutional arrangements are necessarily efficient in some sense, which inaugurated the second stage of his NIEH (North 1981).

face of mainstream economics", David Colander and colleagues have identified a number of trends that have moved what counts as mainstream beyond conventional neoclassical models (Colander, Holt, and Rosser 2004). They helpfully distinguish 'orthodox economics' from 'mainstream economics'. While the orthodoxy is by them equated with neoclassical economics, defined as "optimizing behavior of fully rational and well-informed individuals in a static context and the equilibria that result from that optimization", they suggest the mainstream is (by now) broader than this (ibid.: 490). For the authors, the two are increasingly diverging, so that the mainstream is no longer simply to be equated with neoclassical economics. Rather, owing to changes in attitude among the elite of the discipline, new approaches are now *salonfähig* as long as they remain within the bounds of standard economic modeling: it is this, rather than neoclassical premises, that they identify as the continuing core of the profession's self-perception (ibid.: 496). If true, this would be promising for the neoinstitutionalist turn.

However, even so it is interesting to observe that while they discuss a number of prominent changes in the discipline's method, driven by innovation at "the edge of economics", these primarily concern changes in attitudes to rationality and to the quantitative methods deployed. In the latter field, they emphasize the turn toward more empirical work, complexity theory, agent simulations, and new methods in econometrics, whereas the former is confined to psychological and behavioral economics (ibid.: 496). Institutional economics is only mentioned in the context of game theory, and there is no mention of greater historicizing or a deeper micro-macro integration into a larger social context, outside the brief mention of econometric applications to economic history.

In a separate paper by David Colander in which he has proclaimed "the death of neoclassical economics"—in his capacity as the president of the Economic History Society—the situation is not much different with regard to the NIE (Colander 2000). While Colander's point is clear that 'neoclassical economics', to be a useful term, has to describe an intellectual historical period that has an end, his belief that this end has indeed come does not derive from any observed strength of the NIE in the field. Colander here defines neoclassical economics by 'static allocation', 'utility theory', 'marginal trade-offs', 'perfect rationality', 'methodological individualism', and 'general equilibrium' (ibid.: 135–136). While none of these terms are uncontroversial in the philosophy of economics, Colander argues that in any case "modern economics" (seemingly meaning from the 1990s onward) no longer has any of these attributes as any strong orthodoxy (ibid.: 135–137). What is notable for our purposes is that although from the 1990s onward the neoinstitutionalist turn has rapidly gained steam, and this was also the period of the development of the final instantiation of North's NIEH and its subsequent wide recognition, Colander again does not mention this turn in his pithy list of proofs for the changing nature of economic orthodoxy. Most notably, while institutional economics in general—likely meaning what I have called the OIE—is listed with approaches that are still to be considered heterodox, the New Institutionalism is curiously only mentioned as "being consistently at odds with methodological individualism" (ibidem 136). This is particularly striking since, as discussed below, its alleged methodological individualism is precisely one of the main elements of North's NIEH, and *a fortiori* the NIE tradition in general, that has come under fire from the theory's more heterodox critics.

Whatever the larger impact on economic thought as a whole, therefore, it remains ambiguous from Colander's discussion whether economics itself has been much transformed by the neoinstitutionalist turn. Certainly, there has been no lack of professional recognition. Oliver Williamson won the 'Nobel' in economics as well as a John von Neumann Award, probably the main prizes in economics for advanced career researchers; Daron Acemoglu, another prominent New Institutionalist, won the Neumann as well as the John Bates Clark medal for young economists; and Douglass North himself is, with the Cliometrician Robert Fogel, hitherto the only winner of the economics 'Nobel' for economic historical work. But the large-scale sociohistorical theorizing of the type that North undertook is not, as Colander probably rightly argues, recognized as characteristic of economics proper by most working economists, since it is not wholly or largely expressed in terms of quantitative models.

There have nonetheless been influential attempts to correct the perceived qualitative bias of the NIE tradition: Coase, North, and Williamson founded the International Society for New Institutional Economics in 1996 to support primarily research on empirical work, something North himself occasionally engaged in. Similarly, Avner Greif has applied game theoretical models to explain how informal norms and rules induce economic behavior, as well as multilevel inductive theory, and Acemoglu and colleagues have been influential with combining quantitative analysis with institutional history (see, for example, discussions in Greif 1998, 2006; Acemoglu 2010; Acemoglu, Gallego, and Robinson 2014). To some extent, these authors appear to have consciously developed such approaches to bring the NIE back into this methodological *sine qua non* of economics proper. For Greif at least, this has been an effort to compensate for perceived weaknesses in North's theory in this regard, so that he has reformulated some of North's insights into institutions as equilibrium outcomes of a game (see Greif and Kingston 2011). While I will discuss game theory and its significance in chap. 4, I will reflect on the general viability of such attempts to bring the NIE back into the mainstream fold in the final chapter of this book, where I discuss the implications of my analysis of North's work for other arguments in the NIE tradition.[10]

This should provide some idea of the wider NIE context of North's work. I suspect that while the NIE as a whole is a rising star in the economic firmament, it is not quite yet in the mainstream in Colander's sense. Likely, only those branches of the NIE will become mainstream that are on the opposite end of the spectrum from the Northian qualitative sociohistorical agenda, being rather in the 'moderate' vein of Thrainn Eggertsson's rational choice New Institutionalism or the modeling approach of Daron Acemoglu and others. This need not be a problem for assessing North's work, in particular if one does not—as I do not—attach any particular value to being perceived as part of a mainstream paradigm. Nonetheless, it does draw attention once more to the central problem of this work: how we can understand North's NIEH in the context of his own research agenda, which includes but is not limited to that of the NIE as a whole, and how to do so in a systematic fashion despite all the twists and turns of his own research questions and the continually changing scope of his work and interests. The point is to make sense of how North's work evolved to be a strikingly vast and original paradigm of its own, one that has ended up positioning itself not so much *across* disciplines as *between*

[10] However, the relationship between game theoretical approaches and North's analysis of individual strategic behavior, given rules-as-constraints, will come up again when I discuss North's concept of the 'rules of the game' in depth. See chap. 3.

disciplines, the most 'radical' wing of the NIE tradition so far. With this book, I hope to contribute toward explaining how this came about in despite of North's own ambition to use NIE theory to *rescue* economics from its external critics, and what the costs of its spiraling originality have been in terms of coherence and explanatory value.

The Reception of North's NIEH

However, it would not be just to embark on this quest without acknowledging the paths trodden by predecessors. Turning to the reception of North's NIEH more specifically, and not solely as part of the NIE as a whole, it is striking that the secondary literature is still very scant.[11] For the most part, my impression is that his work has primarily received praise as part of assessments of the NIE tradition and its impact in general, or for having provided a new and clear definition of institutions. As Claude Ménard and Mary Shirley (2014) show, there has been a linear rise in the number of citations of North's work, taking off with the development of the final phase of the NIEH in the 1990s. There is no doubt that his work has been 'received', in that sense. But my own experience leads me to believe that many of these references are cursory, or as part of a larger reference to NIE analysis in general. Also, his 1981 and 1990 books remain popular citations, despite their theoretical supersession by his major publications in book form in 2005 and 2009. Fewer altogether have engaged systematically with the premises of North's theory and the cohesion of its internal argumentation as the general theory of institutional change it sought to become (but never quite achieved).

This may be in part due to the scope and complexity of the whole, but I suspect a major factor has been the awkward status of the theory: both in terms of falling between various disciplines, from economic history to social theory and even evolutionary science, and in terms of the seemingly changing research question in each of North's subsequent works.

[11] The only other book-length discussion specifically devoted to North's work is, by my knowledge, the honorary collection of essays published as Galiani and Sened (2014). I refer to some of its contributions here.

Poor integration is therefore a recurring criticism even from sympathizers. For Greif, North's work failed to integrate the theory of endogenous formation of institutions with the analysis of belief structures (Greif and Kingston 2011); Ménard and Shirley in their essay note difficulties of integrating North's final work with Williamsonian transaction cost economics, the point from which it departed; Robert Bates in the same volume argues that his work lacks an effective theory of politics.

By contrast, for some, the convergence between North's work and that of the OIE and other non-mainstream traditions—rather than integration with the mainstream in Colander's sense—has been a cause for praise and one of the particular strengths of North's approach (see, for example, Groenewegen, Kerstholt, and Nagelkerke 1995; Peukert 2001). This point is significant. As Helge Peukert (2001) following on the work of Malcolm Rutherford (1994) points out, some of the problems that North was confronted with in the course of formulating his NIEH are problems particular to the NIE tradition he inherited and codeveloped, but others are problems confronted by *any* institutionalism. For these authors, institutionalist explanations, from OIE to NIE, have by necessity five methodological dimensions, and a given author in that tradition must take position at some point of the spectrum within each of these dimensions: "The problems [of institutionalism in general] can be formulated as trade-offs between five complementary but dichotomous research strategies and perspectives: formalism vs. anti-formalism, individualism vs. holism, rationality vs. rule following, evolution vs. design, and efficiency vs. reform" (Peukert 2001: 93).

North's struggle to find a satisfactory solution within each of these dimensions is an important part of the story of his NIEH and essential to understanding the problems of internal cohesion it faced. But in this way, this critical interpretation of North's work is not just a matter of Northian idiosyncrasies. It is also a case study in a problematic that applies to institutionalist explanations in economic thought in general. There is inherently a trade-off between hewing close to economic orthodoxy, and thereby limiting the scope and applicability of the institutionalist analysis, and veering toward the anti-formalist, holist, 'substantivist' side of the spectrum, and thereby begging the question why economics should have a privileged position over other social sciences in the explanatory framework to begin with. We must keep this in mind when we come to the confrontation between Douglass North and Karl Polanyi below, as it illustrates this tension perfectly. My argument is that an attempt to find an optimum between these extremes in response to 'Polanyi's challenge' has been a driving force in North's theoretical development. Regardless, on either end of the trade-off critics might be left to wonder what institutions actually explain in the analysis, beyond reformulating existing problems in a particular jargon, and pretending that a suitably adjusted economics can in so doing solve them: a phenomenon often decried as economics imperialism (Fine 2000, 2002; Mäki 2009).

This difficulty of 'placing' North's work in a larger disciplinary context, combined with a concern for his NIEH as a potential juggernaut of economics imperialism, is evident in the reception of his work by his (heterodox) critics. The most notable of these is the systematic critical treatment of his NIEH theory by Ben Fine and Dimitris Milonakis in a series of papers and part of a book (Fine and Milonakis 2003, 2009; Milonakis and Fine 2007). As they are among the few systematic critics of North's NIEH specifically, and moreover their discussion highlights some of the most salient features of his work in an effective way, their arguments are worth outlining in some detail. Their criticisms focus in particular on two dimensions of the five outlined above: rationality and methodological individualism. In their first paper, Fine and Milonakis point out that North's work has been defined by his rejection of neoclassical economic theory in its application to historical cases. By this, North means individual rational choice in the classic sense, which allows for neither stability and altruism in social behavior nor the emergence and persistence of institutions. Instead, North resorts to transaction cost economics and models of bounded rationality to explain these phenomena. North's repeated emphasis on the importance of imperfect rationality and 'ideology' for explaining social behavior, and his argument to take the social-institutional context of markets seriously, all rely on the existence of widespread market imperfections to justify their inclusion into the explanatory framework.

The problem with this, as Fine and Milonakis argue, is that it creates an odd kind of *petitio principii*. All the social-institutional and boundedly rational components of his theory, for them, are only introduced in the first place as it were to fill the gaps left by the neoclassical rational choice paradigm, and thereby broaden its scope of application. As they formulate it: "Having extracted the social from the picture by starting his analysis with the asocial, ahistorical rational individual, he then reintroduces it from without to account for the theoretical lacunae created by the very act of leaving the social out of the picture in the first place" (Fine and Milonakis 2003: 566). The cause of this problem, they argue, is North's methodological approach to institutions. They accuse North of viewing institutions as constraints on otherwise rational, maximizing individual action. His institutionalism is therefore a complement to, but not a systematic deviation from, the canonical choice approach of orthodox economics. This places his criticisms of neoclassical economics in context: North's objections appear less as a fundamental disagreement and more as a regret about its self-imposed limitations. The 'social' being brought back into the picture is, as they put it, "a combination of rational choice theory with irrational choice theory, the latter comprising whatever is left aside by the former" (ibid.: 567).

Their 2007 paper is a more systematic reckoning with North's NIEH as a historical theory. Central to this theory and its influence is, as they rightly state, "his serving as a point of reference for the study of institutions and economic performance, or to put it more generally, the relationship between the economic and the social" (Milonakis and Fine 2007: 27–28). They also note the odd phenomenon that North is primarily cited (as they themselves did in the previous paper) for his 1981–1990 works, rather than his works in the final stage of his theory when he expanded its scope further, introducing cognitive science and evolution into the framework. It is therefore somewhat strange that most of their paper concerns itself with criticizing the empirical historical analyses provided by North and colleagues in the early 1980s. More interesting are the theoretical reflections. Firstly, there is Milonakis and Fine's insight that North's work underwent a series of stages, moving ever further from a (qualitative) model of institutions as creating efficient markets to a (qualitative) model of institutions as inefficient, *sui generis* products of uncertainty and ideology, in no way necessarily 'compensating' for transaction costs. Secondly, there is their observation of the strange way the subsequent literature has treated North's work. As they observe, "Because of the intellectual environment and influences on him, North has felt the need to try to go beyond neoclassical economics, to address the role of property relations, institutions, the state, and ideology." These are "virtues that he brings to economic history, as these are more observed in the breach than his vices by those who appeal to the new institutionalism… North's nostrum that institutions matter has become a conventional wisdom, a point of departure for the (partial) break with neoclassical economics" (ibid.: 53–54).

At this stage of the discussion, discussing the merits or demerits of their critique at length would be getting ahead of the necessary investigation. But Fine and Milonakis' analysis is worth citing in such detail here because they point to a number of insights that are fundamental if one is to make sense of North's enterprise. The first is that North's work has changed in almost every respect since his early days, and yet much of the use of his theory has ignored this, treating his 1981, 1990, 2005, and 2009 monographs as if they are interchangeably part of the same argumentation. This is perhaps convenient for an ad hoc approach to NIE analysis, where only an offhand reference to North is intended, but for applications of North's work it does not lead to a coherent theoretical framework. Moreover, from an intellectual historical perspective it does not contribute to understanding the precise nature and direction of North's trajectory, as I seek to do in this book.

The second important insight Fine and Milonakis offer is that the NIE, and especially North's work, is about reshaping the relationship between the 'social' and the 'economic' in economic thought. But these terms are of course vague and malleable. Their meaning for North's work must therefore be placed in the 'in between' disciplinary context outlined above. The NIE, and *a fortiori* the work of North, is about incorporating 'the social' as the domain of everything not covered by neoclassical economics into the theory. But the aim is to do so without giving up all of what orthodox economics had hitherto seen as defining for its own approach to 'the economic', which is first and foremost its explanation in terms of individual choice in response to incentives. What is being reshaped by North's work is therefore the conception of 'the economic' *only insofar as necessary* for including 'the social', which is simply everything to which neoclassical rational choice economics does not apply. In the process, 'the social' itself is defined by reference to this benchmark. For this intellectual project, the relationship between 'social' and 'economic' then requires the inclusion of the former to be justified as a necessary complement to, but not substitute for, the orthodox conception of the latter.

Phrased in these terms, this may sound unhelpfully abstract. But as we shall see, it provides a necessary philosophy of science framework for making sense of the disciplinary context outlined above: North's NIEH as an attempt to rescue the discipline of economics (in particular as the theoretical anchor for economic history) by subjecting its orthodox core to a process of transformation-with-preservation. Precisely this process is at the heart of the accusation of 'economics imperialism' launched at the NIEH, for example in the work of Fine and Milonakis (2009). In a similar vein, Francesco Boldizzoni (2011) has argued that North's work is as much an attempt to rescue economic history's utility for economists as the other way round. For Boldizzoni, this oeuvre therefore fits in a tradition of economics expansion into social science seeking to "elevate economics over politics, the individual over society, and impersonal interactions over social bonds" (ibid.: 8).

As I share with Fine and Milonakis a concern about the status of rationality and agency in North's theory, I share with Boldizzoni his analysis of some of the main continuities. That is to say: the importance of Polanyi's challenge, North's use of market exchange as a benchmark for understanding nonmarket allocation, and the gradual development of a "Northian anthropology" (26), including its subsequent evolutionary dimension, as will be discussed in detail in the following chapters. In assessments of North's contributions, these guiding threads are often overlooked in favor of a narrow focus on North's bounded rationality approach to the formation of institutions. The present book at various points extends insights that are made in more summary fashion in Boldizzoni's discussion of North (see particularly 2011, chapter 2) and in the work of Fine and Milonakis cited above.

However, I am less certain that—as these and other critics allege—North intended, or ended up, formulating a theory that was fundamentally methodologically individualist and failed to take social integration seriously. Firstly, definitions of what precisely constitutes methodological individualism vary considerably, and North does not qualify under all of them (Hodgson 2007). Secondly, as I will try to show in the course of this book, I think North did intend to provide a theory of institutions as modes of integration (in Polanyian language)—at least some of the time. Rather than seeing North's as consistently individualistic and hostile to the political economic holism of sociology or anthropology, I think we should rather see North as *inconsistently* attempting to find a way out of individualistic rational choice analysis without giving up the aura of 'rigour' and scientificity that this method has afforded economics. It is in this way that we can also make better sense of a habit Boldizzoni identifies, namely North's tendency to give considerable credit to the work of economic thinkers outside his immediate field, from Emmanuel Le Roy Ladurie to Witold Kula, only to dismiss them in the final analysis with some sweeping statement about their lack of understanding of "economic theory" or "price theory" (Boldizzoni 2011: 111, 129). This was also North's attitude to Polanyi, and with this treatment of the challenge of Karl Polanyi, he inaugurated his NIEH and set it on its course.

Looking Ahead

In this book, I want to make sense of North's project as a whole. That is to say, I want to provide an analytical viewpoint from which the huge expansion of scope of the theory, its conscious attempt to cover a vast interdisciplinary range between cognitive science on one end and anthropology on the other, and the sometimes questionable way he 'translated' findings and arguments in various fields into demonstrations of his own principles all appear as necessary outcomes of his train of thought. As I show, in order to 'save the appearances', namely the ability of economics as a discipline to claim a superior ability to explain historical change and economic performance, North had to make historical economics the core of a much larger enterprise. Otherwise, with the decline of neoclassical economics the critics of the discipline would have won the day.

His attempt to forestall the critics by a kind of *Aufhebung* of their criticism, however, took him much further afield from economics than he may initially have expected. It forced him into an ever-deepening institutionalization and socialization of his economic analysis, ranging across vast distances of time and several layers of social abstraction: from the evolved cognitive capacities of the human brain to the development of beliefs and ideologies, then to the level of institutional organization and transaction costs, and finally the upper levels of state formation, political agency, and public choice. As he floated out into theoretical space in this fashion, the lifeline that connected him to what he continued to see as economics proper—the microfoundations of economic behavior in boundedly rational action, the efficiency of price signaling, and incentives—became, if anything, more vital to him.

For my own work, trying to understand the evolution of North's thought and to present it in a way that is comprehensible and coherent, the 'two steps forward, one step back' character this double-mindedness has given North's writings is more than a little frustrating. Add to this the very high level of abstraction deployed in much of his theoretical work, quite remote from the number crunching of most working economic historians, and all this undoubtedly adds to the complexity of the task. The present book therefore operates, indeed perforce operates, largely in a hitherto little explored field one could call 'philosophy of economic history', or maybe 'philosophy of historical economics'. I mean this in the sense that it attempts to apply insights from philosophy of economics, and philosophy of social science more generally, to the specifically economic historical problematic posed by North's NIEH. This does not always make for easy reading, in particular for historians or economists unfamiliar with the more philosophical orientation of this approach, but I have done my best to make it as intelligible and accessible as I can.

The structure of the book will be as follows. In the next chapter, I will provide a roughly chronological discussion of the various stages of development in North's NIEH. One merit of Boldizzoni's interpretation is to emphasize the importance of North's early statements on the relationship between economics and economic history as of programmatic importance for the subsequent development of his theory. For that reason, the chronological discussion of North's NIEH should begin there: with his earliest statements on the relations between economics, economic history, and the social sciences at large, and what the historical dimension of economics meant for him.[12]

If I am right, it was already in this early stage in the 1970s that the foundations for North's NIEH were laid. After North's turn away from Cliometrics, he reformulated the importance of historicity for any methodologically viable approach to economic thought. It was this rethinking of the historical dimension to economics, in particular in his critical engagement with the thought of Karl Polanyi, that gave him a fundamental sense of intellectual direction.[13] This direction would be sustained, albeit through many twists and turns of theory, for the rest of his intellectual career as architect of the NIEH. Following the discussion of Polanyi's challenge, the next chapter will proceed to outline North's rejection of the 'efficiency approach' to institutions, his subsequent growing interest in the role of beliefs and ideology in the formation of institutions, then his evolutionary turn in the 1990s under the influence of Friedrich Hayek, and finally the integration of state theory and a neo-Hobbesian account of violence in *Violence and Social Orders*.

This chronological chapter is followed by a set of systematic chapters focusing on particular themes and aspects of North's work, which provides the main part of the discussion. In it, I subject North's theoretical insights to a critical examination in order to both reconstruct his reasoning in a systematic fashion and make sense of the various (real or apparent) internal contradictions they contain. Throughout, this is done in the context of the larger problematic of the relationship of economics to the other socio-historical sciences and what this meant for North's NIEH, given how he viewed an 'economics approach'—whatever that might mean in any given case—as sine qua non. The first systematic chapter will discuss the contractarian basis of North's approach to institutions. It will reconstruct North's views on the emergence of institutions as something akin to a

---

[12] This means that the present work does not deal in any detail with North's earliest, purely Cliometric work. As it is unconnected to the NIEH project until the point that North becomes dissatisfied with it, it does not properly belong to a discussion of North's NIEH. It should certainly be part of an intellectual biography of North, which I do not here intend to write.

[13] A point also noted by Boldizzoni (2011: 19–22).

social contract process, and how this changed in light of his later interest in institutions as the result of an evolutionary process of discovery.

This also immediately relates to his views on markets and market efficiency, since throughout his work he maintains the viewpoint that, in spite of the significance of market imperfections in practice, in theory at least a well-ordered market has naturally mutually beneficial outcomes. Far from abandoning this view in his later work, he extends it, applying it also to the analysis of states and political institutions. The focal point of this discussion is the frequently invoked concept of the "Smithian result" or "Smithian outcome", a view of markets—insofar as properly 'founded' on clear and enforced property rights and other rules—as maximally efficient forms of social contract to mutual benefit, which he (perhaps dubiously) attributes to Adam Smith. Given the Hobbesian flavor of the importance of mutual violence reduction in his later work, we see therefore that at various levels the "Northian anthropology" referred to by Boldizzoni is one with a strong contractarian basis, and not always internally consistent.

The following systematic chapter is concerned with rationality, choice theory, and individual agency in North's work. Here, the focal point is North's invocation of agents in his theory as 'players of the game', in which institutions are the 'rules of the game'. As I will show, North in fact more often uses a kind of quasi-game theoretical language in order to convey his ideas about the interaction between agency and structure in his approach. But this quasi-game theory is not easily reconciled with his view of individual agents as strongly conditioned by beliefs and ideology, nor with the fundamental role of uncertainty over both process and outcome in his late theory. Given the frequent criticism of North as a methodological individualist, I here examine to what extent that is justified and point to the fundamental and irreparable ambiguities concerning choice and agency in North's model of the interaction between individuals and institutions.

The third systematic chapter goes into more depth on North's theory of cultural evolution, how it came to be, and his use of Hayek's ideas to reformulate the final stage of his NIEH. The focal point here is North's concept of 'adaptive efficiency', which he repeatedly invokes to provide the necessary causal mechanism to hold together his historical model of multilevel economic interaction. Although introduced earlier on, it is in particular in the latest stage of his work that the idea of adaptivity becomes important to North. He develops, in part explicitly and in part implicitly, a macrohistorical evolutionary theory in which evolution plays a dual role. Biological evolution has limited the rational capacities of humans, leading to permanent uncertainty and therefore the need for institutions and conventions. But cultural evolution also plays a major role: influenced by Hayek, North suggests that a non-Darwinian, intentional evolutionary process operates in the long run of institutional change, as certain institutional orders prove more 'adaptively efficient' than others in dealing with changing circumstances. Those adaptively efficient societies subsequently survive. I critically discuss the foundations of this theory of cultural evolution, using literature from the philosophy of biology and from evolutionary economics. I argue that while a cultural evolutionary approach to institutional change has potential, as it stands North's theory is poorly founded in evolutionary theory and serves primarily as a misleading set of metaphors. It therefore also fails at its main task: being the glue that holds together the different layers that form the edifice of North's social theory. This has negative consequences for the theory's ultimate viability.

The final two chapters place North's work in a wider context and discuss its implications. The first concerns itself with North's NIEH as a part of global history, and the importance North himself attached to the implications his work has for development economics and the study of long-run divergence and convergence patterns. To what extent North's NIEH is a suitable vehicle for writing the history of divergence and the developmental policy consequences of such analysis is an open question. The second, and final, chapter returns to the neoinstitutionalist turn as well as Polanyi's challenge, with which themes I opened this book. Here I consider in general terms what the strengths and weaknesses of North's NIEH I have outlined mean for the project of New Institutional Economics as a whole, in its many incarnations in specific sociohistorical fields.

I suspect that many of the problems faced by North's NIEH are faced by the neoinstitutionalist turn as a whole, and that the turn to institutions may end up not delivering on the great expectations that many currently have of it: of reconciling economics and the other sociohistorical sciences. While I am by no means hostile to the NIE and its adjacent theories per se, I think it is due time for a more skeptical note about how much new insight really can be carried by the nostrum that 'institutions matter, and therefore history matters'.

The following chapters will therefore primarily have a critical tone. My purpose in this is neither to denigrate North nor to dismiss the very real contributions made by his NIEH framework. It is also not an exercise in mere nit-picking: one can find inconsistencies or incompleteness in any kind of theory of sufficient scope or ambition. The critical note derives from two concerns. Firstly, that such literature as exists about North's NIEH so far has been largely celebratory, and has considered his work primarily in how it extends and improves on the NIE tradition. This is not wrong, but risks missing some very real problems with it as well, and makes the NIEH look like a more secure foundation for future work than it really is. That leads me to the second point. The criticisms I make of the NIEH's theoretical structure and interdisciplinary positioning are not aimed at North alone, especially since with his demise his own contribution is now finished. Rather, they aim to give substance to my worry that the neoinstitutionalist turn in social science is proceeding rapidly without a due consideration to the very serious methodological problems this paradigm has yet to face. Precisely because North's theory is so sophisticated and so vast in scope, and because North is such a clear and engaging author, his work serves as a perfect case study to elucidate what I think are problems faced by the entire NIE research program at present, in particular as concerns the social and historical dimensions of economic thought.

As I will argue in the conclusion, in many regards the neoinstitutionalist turn is a historic opportunity and a step forward in terms of the unification of the social sciences. But it is not that unification itself, and the advances made threaten to devolve into clichés. We must guard against a 'silver bullet' approach where the mere invocation of the term 'institutions' is thought sufficient to solve long-standing interdisciplinary and philosophical problems. As this book aims to show, those problems are not easily solved. Not without giving up much that economists, including Douglass North, have held dear.

References

Acemoglu, Daron. 2010. *Institutions, Factor Prices and Taxation: Virtues of Strong States?*, NBER Working Paper 15693.

Acemoglu, Daron, Francisco Gallego, and James A. Robinson. 2014. *Institutions, Human Capital and Development*, NBER Working Paper 19933.

Alston, L.J. 2008. New Institutional Economics. In *The New Palgrave Dictionary of Economics*, ed. Steven N. Durlauf and Lawrence E. Blume. New York: Palgrave Macmillan.

Bates, Robert H. 2014. The New Institutionalism. The Work of Douglass North. In *Institutions, Economic Growth, and Property Rights: The Legacy of Douglass North*, ed. Sebastian Galiani and Itai Sened, 50–66. Cambridge: Cambridge University Press.

Boldizzoni, Francesco. 2011. *The Poverty of Clio: Resurrecting Economic History*. Princeton: Princeton University Press.

Buchanan, James M., and Gordon Tullock. 1962. *The Calculus of Consent: Logical Foundations of Constitutional Democracy*. Ann Arbor: University of Michigan Press.

Burki, Shahid Javed, and Guillermo E. Perry. 1998. Beyond the Washington Consensus: Institutions Matter. In *World Bank Latin American and Caribbean Studies: Viewpoints*. Washington, DC: World Bank.

Coase, Ronald H. 1937. The Nature of the Firm. *Economica* 4 (16): 386–405.

Colander, David. 2000. The Death of Neoclassical Economics. *Journal of the History of Economic Thought* 22 (2): 127–143.

Colander, David, Richard Holt, and J. Barkley Rosser. 2004. The Changing Face of Mainstream Economics. *Review of Political Economy* 16 (4): 485–499.

Eggertsson, Thráinn. 1990. *Economic Behavior and Institutions: Principles of Neoinstitutional Economics*. Cambridge: Cambridge University Press.

Fine, Ben. 2000. Economics Imperialism and Intellectual Progress: The Present as the History of Economic Thought? *History of Economics Review* 32 (1): 10–35.

———. 2002. Economics Imperialism: A View from the Periphery. *Review of Radical Political Economics* 34 (2): 187–201.

Fine, Ben, and Dimitris Milonakis. 2003. From Principle of Pricing to Pricing of Principle: Rationality and Irrationality in the Economic History of Douglass North. *Comparative Studies in Society and History* 45 (3): 546–570.

———. 2009. *From Economics Imperialism to Freakonomics: The Shifting Boundaries Between Economics and Other Social Sciences*. Abingdon: Routledge.

Galiani, Sebastian, and Itai Sened, eds. 2014. *Institutions, Property Rights, and Economic Growth: The Legacy of Douglass North*. Cambridge: Cambridge University Press.

Granovetter, Mark. 1985. Economic Action and Social Structure: The Problem of Embeddedness. *American Journal of Sociology* 91 (3): 481–510.

Greif, Avner. 1998. Historical and Comparative Institutional Analysis. *The American Economic Review* 88 (2): 80–84.

———. 2006. *Institutions and the Path to the Modern Economy: Lessons from Medieval Trade*. Stanford: Stanford University Press.

Greif, Avner, and Chris Kingston. 2011. Institutions: Rules or Equilibria? In *Political Economy of Institutions, Democracy, and Voting*, ed. Gonzalo Caballero and Norman Schofield, 13–44. Berlin/Heidelberg: Springer.

Groenewegen, John, Frans Kerstholt, and Ad Nagelkerke. 1995. On Integrating Old and New Institutionalism: Douglass North Building Bridges. *Journal of Economic Issues* 29 (2): 467–475.

Harcourt, Geoff, et al. 2016. *Post-Keynesian Essays from Down Under Vol. III: Essays on Ethics*. Basingstoke: Palgrave Macmillan.

Heiner, Ronald A. 1983. The Origin of Predictable Behavior. *The American Economic Review* 73 (4): 560–595.

Hodgson, Geoffrey M. 2001. *How Economics Forgot History: The Problem of Historical Specificity in Social Science*. London: Routledge.

———. 2007. Meanings of Methodological Individualism. *Journal of Economic Methodology* 14 (2): 211–226.

Langlois, Richard N. 1990. Bounded Rationality and Behavioralism: A Clarification and Critique. *Journal of Institutional and Theoretical Economics/Zeitschrift für die gesamte Staatswissenschaft* 146 (4): 691–695.

Mäki, Uskali. 1993. Social Theories of Science and the Fate of Institutionalism in Economics. In *Rationality, Institutions, and Economic Methodology*, ed. Bo Gustafsson, Christian Knudsen, and Uskali Mäki, 76–109. London: Routledge.

———. 2009. Economics Imperialism: Concept and Constraints. *Philosophy of the Social Sciences* 39 (3): 351–380.

Matthews, R.C.O. 1986. The Economics of Institutions and the Sources of Growth. *The Economic Journal* 96 (384): 903–918.

Ménard, Claude, and Mary M. Shirley. 2014. The Contribution of Douglass North to New Institutional Economics. In *Institutions, Economic Growth, and Property Rights: The Legacy of Douglass North*, ed. Sebastian Galiani and Itai Sened, 11–29. Cambridge: Cambridge University Press.

Milonakis, Dimitris, and Ben Fine. 2007. Douglass North's Remaking of Economic History: A Critical Appraisal. *Review of Radical Political Economics* 39 (1): 27–57.

Mueller, Dennis C. 2003. *Public Choice III*. Cambridge: Cambridge University Press.

Nee, Victor. 2005. The New Institutionalisms in Economics and Sociology. In *Handbook of Economic Sociology*, ed. Neil Smelser and Richard Swedberg, 49–74. Princeton: Princeton University Press.

———. 2008. Economic Sociology and New Institutional Economics. In *Handbook of New Institutional Economics*, ed. Claude Ménard and Mary M. Shirley, 789–818. Berlin/Heidelberg: Springer.

Nelson, Richard R., and Sidney G. Winter. 1982. *An Evolutionary Theory of Economic Change*. Cambridge, MA: Harvard University Press/Belknap.

North, Douglass C. 1977. Markets and Other Allocation Systems in History: The Challenge of Karl Polanyi. *Journal of European Economic History* 6 (3): 703–716.

———. 1981. *Structure and Change in Economic History*. Cambridge: Cambridge University Press.

———. 1986. The New Institutional Economics. *Journal of Institutional and Theoretical Economics/Zeitschrift für die gesamte Staatswissenschaft* 142 (1): 230–237.

North, Douglass C., John Joseph Wallis, and Barry R. Weingast. 2009. *Violence and Social Orders: A Conceptual Framework for Interpreting Recorded Human History*. Cambridge: Cambridge University Press.

Olson, Mancur. 1965. *The Logic of Collective Action: Public Goods and the Theory of Groups*. Cambridge, MA: Harvard University Press.

Ostrom, Elinor. 2007. Challenges and Growth: The Development of the Interdisciplinary Field of Institutional Analysis. *Journal of Institutional Economics* 3 (3): 239–264.

Ostrom, Elinor, and Vincent Ostrom. 2004. The Quest for Meaning in Public Choice. *American Journal of Economics and Sociology* 63 (1): 105–147.

Peukert, Helge. 2001. Bridging Old and New Institutional Economics: Gustav Schmoller and Douglass C. North, Seen with Old Institutionalists' Eyes. *European Journal of Law and Economics* 11 (2): 91–130.

Richter, Rudolf. 2005. The New Institutional Economics: Its Start, Its Meaning, Its Prospects. *European Business Organization Law Review* 6 (2): 161–200.

———. 2015. *Essays on New Institutional Economics*. Berlin/Heidelberg: Springer.

Rodrik, Dani, Arvind Subramanian, and Francesco Trebbi. 2004. Institutions Rule: The Primacy of Institutions Over Geography and Integration in Economic Development. *Journal of Economic Growth* 9 (2): 131–165.

Rutherford, Malcolm. 1994. *Institutions in Economics: The Old and New Institutionalism*. Cambridge: Cambridge University Press.

———. 2001. Institutional Economics: Then and Now. *Journal of Economic Perspectives* 15 (3): 173–194.

Schotter, Andrew. 1981. *The Economic Theory of Social Institutions*. Cambridge: Cambridge University Press.

Vanberg, Viktor. 1988. Rules and Choice in Economics and Sociology. *Jahrbuch für Neue Politische Ökonomie* 7: 1–22.

Wallis, John Joseph. 2015. *Structure and Change in Economic History: The Ideas of Douglass North*. CEPR Policy Portal. https://voxeu.org/article/ideas-douglass-north. Accessed 24 Jan 2018.

Weintraub, E. Roy. 1979. *Microfoundations: The Compatibility of Microeconomics and Macroeconomics*. Cambridge: Cambridge University Press.

Williamson, Oliver E. 1973. Markets and Hierarchies: Some Elementary Considerations. *American Economic Review* 63 (2): 316–325.

———. 1975. *Markets and Hierarchies: Analysis and Antitrust Implications*. New York: Free Press.

———. 1981. The Economics of Organization: The Transaction Cost Approach. *American Journal of Sociology* 87 (3): 548–577.

———. 2000. The New Institutional Economics: Taking Stock, Looking Ahead. *Journal of Economic Literature* 38 (3): 595–613.

Williamson, Oliver E., and Sidney G. Winter. 1991. *The Nature of the Firm: Origins, Evolution, and Development*. Oxford: Oxford University Press.

2

North's NIEH in Historical Overview

Introduction: North's Early Career

As a matter of biographical background, Douglass C. (Cecil) North was born on November 5, 1920, in Cambridge, Massachusetts, to a manager at an insurance company and his wife. According to North, his parents had little educational background, but he was well educated himself and successful at secondary schooling. Although accepted to Harvard, with his family having moved to California he decided to enroll at UC Berkeley instead.[1] There, he became a Marxist and a critic of the buildup to the Second World War, although he was not a member of or associated with the Communist Party of the United States of America.[2] In contrast to the official line of the Communist Party, he continued to oppose American participation in the Second World War even after 1941. When war did come to the United States, to avoid having to kill anyone he enrolled

[1] These and other details about North's early life can be found in Nobel Foundation (2015) and North (2009), as well as in an interview with North published as North, Brown, and Lueck (2015).

[2] It is striking that North as late as 2009 averred that "Marx… was a big influence on my life, and it still is. I'm not a Marxist any more, but still, he had an enormous impact" (North 2009: 160). Yet in his published work, he very rarely referred to Marx. This illustrates how in North's work the explicit references and arguments often hide deeper theoretical concerns and intellectual dialogue beneath the surface.

M. Krul, *The New Institutionalist Economic History of Douglass C. North*,
Palgrave Studies in the History of Economic Thought,
https://doi.org/10.1007/978-3-319-94084-7_2

in the merchant navy. This provided him with plenty of free time to read voraciously. It was this reading that convinced him that he should become an economist, even though his other great passion was photography.[3] On his return, he obtained his PhD in economics from UC Berkeley, writing about the insurance industry his father was involved in. He then decamped to the University of Washington in Seattle, where he worked with Donald F. Gordon. Under Gordon's influence, he shed his Marxist views and became (in his own later words) "a right-wing reactionary" and, more importantly, a strong supporter of neoclassical orthodoxy in economics (North 2009: 164). North observed that the teaching at Berkeley had been largely historical in orientation, while Gordon really taught him the theories and methods of economics as prevailing at the time (Nobel Foundation 2015).

North later reflected on this phase with the pithy observation that "typically, there is nothing worse than when you have lost your way and you pick up the next thing" (North 2009: 164). Even so, this period was intellectually formative for him. It gave his work two attributes that would endure throughout his life: an appreciation for the importance of individual liberty, decentralized decision-making, and strong property rights, an outlook some have rightly referred to as classical liberal (Klein and Daza 2013), and a high esteem for the intellectual accomplishment involved in (neoclassical) 'price theory', which he often referred to and sometimes simply equated with 'economic theory' per se. Already in this period he was more an economic historian than purely an economist. His early work in this neoclassical phase focuses primarily on the history of economic growth in the United States. Besides this he continued his maritime interest in the shape of an influential paper on ocean freight rates and economic development (North 1958).[4]

While this work established him as an economic historian, North really first acquired some degree of fame within the field when he

[3] This remained so throughout his life. One can easily imagine an alternative course of events where North would have become a famous photographer instead—"there but for path dependence go I".

[4] He returned to this topic once subsequently (North 1968); see also below. How North's historical works on maritime trade may have affected subsequent studies of oceanic trade and exchange, a popular topic in global history and related fields, is worth a study in its own right. I thank Laleh Khalili for drawing my attention to their significance.

became involved in the rise of Cliometrics. Cliometrics, also known as the New Economic History, is a product of the postwar period, becoming prominent for the first time in the 1960s in the United States. It arose as a response to two things: firstly, the perceived need to go beyond the traditional economic historical approaches, which were often closer to social history than to economics, with a method that would be based on the best neoclassical economic theory of the time; secondly, the development of new mathematical and statistical techniques in econometrics that would make the application of neoclassical quantitative models to historical cases possible.[5] For this reason, Robert Fogel—one of its most influential practitioners—dubbed it simply "econometric history" (Fogel 1964).

Cliometrics, more than was the norm in economic history up to that point, explicitly drew on what it saw as 'economic theory' (meaning neoclassical microeconomics) as the inspiration for a modeling-based approach to the historical dimension. The implications of this attitude for the relations with the 'traditional' economic historians, whose narrative approaches looked to history as an academic discipline for inspiration rather than to economics, are summed up well by the New Economic Historian Lance Davis (himself a former student of North): "Once terms are defined and the questions framed, an explanatory model must be built. Since the subject is economic history, the models frequently draw on economic theory for their form. These models provide a basis for sorting the useful from the useless, they suggest methods of possible verification, and they provide simplified 'explanations' of a far from simple world. With a model the assumptions are made explicit and it is possible to examine reality in the light of the logical system. Like mathematical economics, the 'new' economic history 'may not be able to say much, but at least the reader is aware of what has been said'. Traditional economic history also has its models, but all too frequently they are implicit, not explicit" (Davis 1966: 658).

Here we find for the first time Douglass North as a major theorist in economic history—but not yet anything like the kind of theorist he would later become. Rather, he appears as, *nota bene*, "chief propagandist

[5] The classic statement is Fogel (1966); a more contemporary perspective is given in Diebolt (2012).

and entrepreneur" of Cliometrics at the meetings of the Cliometrics forum at Purdue University, the first of which was held in 1960 (ibid.: 659). Already early during this period North published what would become one of the pioneering books of the Cliometrics approach, *The Economic Growth of the United States 1790–1860* (North 1961). According to North's own account, it was his shift from American economic history to the economic history of Europe that presaged his equally rapid departure from Cliometrics. As he told the story much later, it was his discovery that neoclassical models could not account for the kinds of social transformations that had happened in European history that made him look for a new approach, one that would be able to explain historical differentiation (Nobel Foundation 2015). His longtime collaborator, John J. Wallis, identifies his 1968 *reprise* of his study of shipping costs as the moment North turned toward institutional analysis; in that study, North argues that shipping costs went down because of declining costs external to the trade itself (e.g. declining piracy), which points to institutional and transaction cost factors (North 1968; Wallis 2015).

While North's Cliometric period is not generally considered terribly significant within either his own career or its lasting influence on economics—it is generally mentioned only in the context of North's shift away from it, toward institutional analysis—it is worth pointing out that it added considerably to his stature. He shared the Nobel Prize in economics, much later, with Robert Fogel, and indeed jointly "for having renewed research in economic history by applying economic theory *and quantitative methods* in order to explain economic and institutional change" (Nobel Foundation 2015). It may be that the Nobel committee intended the former to apply to North and the latter to Fogel, but one should not underestimate how one can buy the freedom to do other types of research in economics by having demonstrated, at some point, mastery of quantitative techniques.

So what made North so dissatisfied with the ability of the neoclassical-econometric approach to explain institutional change, whether in European major transitions or in the more modest area of shipping costs? When in 1974 North gave his address upon having become president of the Economic History Association in the United States, he had already become committed to the New Institutionalism as his favored theoretical base of operations. His paper reflected on what for him in retrospect the limitations of the 'new economic history' were, now seen from that new vantage point. It therefore serves as an excellent summary of the theoretical reflections involved in his turn to NIE: "What the new economic history contributed was the systematic use of theory and quantitative methods to history. The use of a scientific methodology [*sic*] has put a distinctive stamp on this approach, which clearly delineates it from the old economic history, but it is the theory that provides a particular cast to the contribution. It is the systematic use of standard neo-classical economic theory which both has provided the incisive new insights into man's economic past and also serves to limit the range of enquiry" (North 1974: 1).

We see here in a nutshell already what would remain his general attitude toward neoclassical economics in economic history. On the one hand, neoclassical applications are better than any alternative practice that had been developed before, as emphasized by the characteristic identification of price theory and choice theory with 'science' and 'theory' in general. So neoclassical theory isn't, and can't be, wrong. Instead, it is insufficient. As North went on to explain: "Neo-classical economic theory has two major shortcomings for the economic historian. One, it was not designed to explain long-run economic change; and two, even within the context of the question it was designed to answer, it provides quite limited answers since it is immediately relevant to a world of perfect markets—that is, perfect in the sense of zero transaction costs" (ibid.: 2). The problem is therefore a lack of realism and a lack of explanatory scope. Moreover, North specifies that among the problems are a failure to endogenize the role of the state within the model, as well as a general failure to provide what he somewhat vaguely calls "an integrated explanation", "what made the system go" (ibid.: 2). These points will become significant later on.

North followed these criticisms of Cliometrics with a number of suggestions, which constitute a useful summing-up of the theoretical repertoire involved in the first stage of what would become his NIEH. Firstly, he reiterates the continuing importance of choice theoretical microfoundations: "A theory of choice – the self-conscious application of opportunity cost doctrine – is essential to the framing of meaningful questions in economic history" (ibid.: 3). Secondly, he points out how transaction costs form the necessary bridge between neoclassical economics and the widening of scope to include institutions and institutional change. Although it is not explicitly spelled out in this chapter, once transaction costs are included in the analysis, one will immediately want to understand the sources of these transaction costs. Since these lie by definition outside the prices explicit in the exchange itself, they have their origin in externalities—ones imposed by the reality that exchange takes place in a social context and by human individuals. This points to the necessity of understanding the institutional order of the society that determines what kind of costs, and how great, are involved in the process of transacting itself.[6]

Thirdly, North extends this bridge function of transaction costs by arguing that they also allow one to make endogenous to the analysis the study of other forms of choice than via private market transacting. Here, he mentions "households, voluntary organizations, governments, and markets" as part of a mix of different approaches to economic decision-making (although it remains somewhat unclear who exactly is doing this decision-making that encompasses all these categories). Finally, following up on this last suggestion, North points (for the first time) to the need to understand organizations, vertical structures which substitute for individual market transactions. In this chapter, he expresses his expectation that it will be relatively easier to explain why nonmarket economic organization happens in households, guilds, manorial tenure, and so forth, than to explain the role of the state in all this. Significantly, for the latter he suggests one should complement the transaction cost approach with the then emerging subject of public choice theory, a field that would have a lasting influence on North's thought (ibid.: 5).[7]

---

[6] North's argument here refers for this theoretical background to Furubotn and Pejovich (1972).

[7] At this stage of his work, when his NIEH has not yet properly come into existence but is being formulated as a course for future inquiry, it is interesting to note that demographic change and household behavior affecting it are repeatedly invoked as potentially important variables. Unlike the others mentioned above, these factors disappear rather rapidly from view in North's subsequent work. For the sake of a clear explanation, I therefore give them short shrift in the discussion in this chapter. But lest I give the impression of a Whiggish account of inevitable progress to North's project, I want to point to these here as one of various topics that North invokes at different stages in his intellectual trajectory, only to virtually ignore them subsequently. The same goes to a lesser extent for military technology, mentioned in North (1974: 6), which periodically returns in considerations on 'violence'.

As the references to manorialism make clear, at this point North was already in the midst of his new engagement with European economic history, and indeed now on the basis of institutional analysis and transaction cost economics. The study of organizations was in fact the first application of these new ideas, and the medieval European manor—so remote from the modern market economy usually studied by neoclassical economists—seemed an ideal topic for it. Together with colleagues, North wrote two books and some articles which could be described as a merger of neoclassical ideas with institutional analysis, where transaction costs indeed function as a bridge: they explain why organizations other than private transacting come to exist, and persist, in the first place (in particular North and Thomas 1970, 1973; Davis and North 1971). While the structure of the economy and its growth presented in these works is a traditionally neoclassical model, in which Malthusian demographic factors, relative factor prices, and technological change interact, the novelty rests in the idea that one outcome of these mechanisms of neoclassical growth theory was the development of new and historically unique institutions. These institutional innovations and the changes in property rights they entailed allowed the West to shift from the historical virtually zero-growth pattern to one of explosive economic expansion. Put theoretically, the neoclassical Malthusian model gives way to an institutional explanation for historical differentiation in the West in the modern era—here beginning roughly in the eighteenth century, though with its roots in the Middle Ages (North and Thomas 1970).

Yet already in this early, still pre-NIEH stage, North was also aware of the limitations of this approach. As he himself mentions, his 'neoclassical institutionalism' had many of the same weaknesses he had identified in the original pure neoclassical approach in the first place. As he argued already in 1971, "our model is predicated on profit maximization in which the guiding force in the innovation of an institutional arrangement is the private profitability to the primary action group and the model also assumes that individuals will acquire the necessary information to act 'rationally' as long as it is profitable for them to do so… Secondly, people frequently act in terms of general ideological positions rather than incur the costs of acquiring information on a particular issue even when it would pay them to do so" (North 1971: 122). This anticipates the subsequent steps he would take in developing his NIEH: first abandoning the 'efficiency assumption', which saw institutions in the model as rationally chosen and therefore at least locally optimal, and subsequently his increasing interest in the role of beliefs and ideology. But first we must explain how he got there, that is, how the NIEH proper came about. For this we must turn to the challenge of Karl Polanyi.

North's NIEH and the Challenge of Karl Polanyi

In his analysis of the feudal manorial system, North was not just in search of a new theory. He was also in search of a foil for his own thought. Because the neoclassical approach to economic analysis was for his purposes too ahistorical and incapable of institutional analysis, it could not answer questions that became important to North: for instance, why major historical transitions, like from feudalism to the 'free' market economy of the nineteenth century, took place. The only theory that seemed to be available to North at that time was the Marxist one. As we know, North had from the start of his academic career decided that Marxism was incompatible with the choice theoretical microfoundations of economics, the 'economic analysis' he had learned from Gordon and that he found indispensable. Therefore, one of the aims of complementing the neoclassical approach with a focus on the formation and change of institutions was to demonstrate that this approach could rival the Marxist one in explaining historical differentiation, major transitions between institutional orders such as involved in the shift from manorialism to generalized market competition. North and Thomas' paper outlining a neoclassical-institutional model of the manor was intended to provide an explicit alternative, based on "recent extensions of economic theory into the economics of property rights and institutional change" (North and Thomas 1971: 777).[8]

Despite its ambitious tone, the results were not satisfactory. As mentioned, North was already well aware of the theoretical limitations of

[8] These 'recent extensions' refer primarily to the foundational literature on property rights and early public choice theory of the 1950s and 1960s.

the enterprise, even if in his eagerness to provide an (orthodox) economics-based alternative to Marxist historiography he tried to put the best possible face on it.[9] He was not the only one. Within a few years, North and Thomas' model of the manor had come under withering criticism. The critics pointed out that the contractarian approach inherent in the model—in which the manorial system is a neoclassically efficient outcome of a kind of social contract based on private bargaining, exchanging security for tenure—was difficult to justify. Not only did it seem implausible to present feudal society as the outcome of a voluntary and efficient social contract, but it was also far from obvious that transaction costs could really explain the nature of the particular institutional setup involved. Marxist explanations at least had the merit of not presenting feudalism as an efficient and voluntary process (Fenoaltea 1975; Field 1981).

It was therefore no big step to abandon this particular approach and to search for a new one. Institutional analysis was promising in its ability to explain historical change in the long run and to account for major socio-economic transformations of the kind only Marxists had hitherto theorized. That element had to stay. But the neoclassical assumptions were becoming fetters on the analysis. What North needed was an impetus to shed them and to reformulate the whole problem—how to account for institutions, for historical change, for the role of the state, for nonmarket solutions to economic problems—in a new way, without abandoning the commitment to 'economic analysis'. Marxism did not provide this for him. I suspect that a combination of overfamiliarity of the Marxist models and its status as an explicitly heterodox approach within economics played a role. The birth of the NIEH only came about when North was forced to go beyond simply adding transaction costs and contractarian institutionalism to neoclassical economic history. For that, he needed a foil – a theory that sought to interpret long-run institutional change, but

[9] This odd combination of ambition to bypass heterodox explanations and modesty about the actual quality of the alternative offered appears elsewhere too. For example, Davis and North's 1970 paper is described by its own authors as "at some points woefully weak and the explanations at times incredibly simplistic" (Davis and North 1970: 131). This strengthens my interpretation that the point was to develop a theory, *any* theory, that could defeat 'external' challenges to the choice theory-based approach in economics. The difficulty was finding the right formulation of the problem, for which North needed Polanyi's challenge, as described below.

giving a major explanatory role to noneconomic variables, or at least ones not amenable to neoclassical analysis. Such an approach could provide North with means to shed his neoclassical bonds, and yet would leave room for an explicitly economics-based approach to improve on it, proving the ability of economics to really explain institutional emergence and transformation. North found such a theory in the work of Karl Polanyi (1886–1964).

It is not clear precisely when North read Polanyi's work. In fact it is rather remarkable that he did so; not only had Polanyi been dead by that point for over ten years, but North's engagement long preceded the 'Polanyian revival' of more recent times. Probably few scholars outside ancient history read him then, even less so within economics.[10] I suspect that the occasion for the encounter may have been the publication of a posthumous collection of Polanyian essays, edited by Harry W. Pearson under the title *The Livelihood of Man* (Polanyi 1977). However that may be, the subsequent paper North wrote about what he called 'the challenge of Karl Polanyi' contained the fundamental reformulation of his research problem he had been looking for, and thereby inaugurated the NIEH proper (North 1977). It was therefore a pivotal moment in his intellectual trajectory: on my reading of North, the research problems he posed in that paper remained the central 'challenge' for him throughout the NIEH, even as the answers to it changed considerably over time. This will become clearer by a closer look at the paper itself, whose significance has not been realized by much of the later commentary on North.[11]

"Anthropologists, sociologists and historians", North argues in this paper, "have long challenged the relevance of economic theory to the analysis of past societies". However, this theory, defined in this paper as the "wealth-maximizing behavioural postulate", has survived among neoclassically oriented economic historians (such as the Cliometricians)

[10] A recent informal study estimated that only 3% of economists at high-ranking US departments have read Karl Polanyi, according to their own reporting (Grdesic 2016).

[11] Exceptions are Davis (2008) and Didry and Vincensini (2011). However, Davis' paper is much more limited in scope than the present work. Didry and Vincensini's working paper, although apt, rather all too readily assumes that North's NIEH is indeed an effective answer to Polanyi as North claimed. As demonstrated in this book, that assumption is not safe.

nonetheless, because they have generally been unconcerned by the implications of such theoretical background choices: one cannot directly test them anyway; "the proof of the pudding is in the eating" (North 1977: 703–704). But whether or not North had himself been similarly unconcerned before, by this point he had come to be haunted by the presence of a ghost (as he describes it): the spirit of Karl Polanyi. Polanyi, he argues, "cannot be so lightly dismissed, and if his spirit does not haunt the new economic historians, it is because they are probably not even aware the ghost exists" (ibid.: 704). But he does, and his challenge to such economic historians is straightforward: "Polanyi contends that markets have only dominated resource allocation for a brief span of history centering on the nineteenth-century Western world. Before that time… other allocative systems have characterized economic organization and these other systems are not grounded in economizing behaviour" (North 1977: 703).

North is clearly ambivalent about the value of this viewpoint. He explains Polanyi's theory of 'transactional modes', which include—besides market exchange—reciprocity and redistribution, and how for Polanyi these latter two were the dominant or characteristic modes of the economies of premodern societies. Markets dominate only in the most recent historical period, and even then only outside the Soviet-type societies. In this, he rightly notes, Polanyi opposes both the neoclassical and the Marxist approaches. For North, "it is easy to find fault with Polanyi's analytical framework". Indeed, "there are numerous parts of his analysis that show a failure to grasp elementary economic principles", although he does not clarify what those are (North 1977: 707). And yet North is deeply impressed by the significance of this challenge. For "the stubborn fact of the matter is that Polanyi was correct in his major contention that the nineteenth century was a unique era in which markets played a more important role than at any other time in history… To the extent that economic theory was confined to the analysis of markets, the tools of the economist were… irrelevant to an understanding of the ancient world… Economic historians have not even begun to account for such non-market allocative systems, and until they do, they can say very little about societies in which markets had very limited allocative effects" (North 1977: 706).

North first considers Polanyi's own approach to dealing with this problem. Besides defining transactional modes, what North calls 'allocative systems', Polanyi had one other major theoretical tool: a concept that in the subsequent literature would become known as embeddedness.[12] North here refers to it as 'embodied', but is clearly speaking of the same concept. He takes as good a definition of embeddedness as one could wish for from Polanyi directly: "The key to Polanyi's system is the view that economic organization is *embodied* in society in the sense of 'having no separate existence apart from its controlling social integument'... Transactional dispositions of natural resources, labor, produce and services are expressions of socially defined obligation and relationships" (North 1977: 708). The consequence of this is that "the kinship, status, hierarchy and political or religious affiliations which underlie these economic structures are not explicable in terms of economizing behaviour – one can only understand them and therefore the functioning of the economy by 'in depth' studies which are social, cultural, and psychological in origin" (North 1977: 708).

This brings us to North's own solution. To answer the challenge of Karl Polanyi means two things: to shift the emphasis of research to the study of premodern (long-term) economic history—that is to say, the economic history of the period before the dominance of the market as allocation system—and to give an explanation of the nature and functioning of the alternative allocation systems that Polanyi argued dominated in the premodern era. But for such an explanation to answer the challenge, it must be an explanation based in 'economic theory', as North put it, rather than exclusively in the 'social, cultural, and psychological' explanations that Polanyi favored. The NIEH would address the question whether such allocation systems are ultimately embedded in *sui generis* social, political, and cultural (what one could call 'anthropological') causal factors or that they can be causally explained in terms of a general economic theory. If the latter, as North argued, the question as to *which* economic theory is already answered by North's previous economic-theoretical commitments. Although the term 'economizing behavior' remains underspecified, on the basis of his previous statements one may safely assume that this means the combination of orthodox price theory

[12] For discussions of Polanyi's usage of this term, and the contexts in which it appears, see Gemici (2008) and Dale (2010, 2011), as well as the discussion below.

and some form of choice theory familiar in microeconomics. But with a typical added twist, the importance of institutions, and the causes and origins of their formation, is now also explicitly to be recognized. An essential conclusion for North's approach would be the observation that "it is reasonable to assume that the forces that lead to the substitution of firms for markets today may help us to explain the variety of forms of organisation in past societies" (North 1977: 711). In other words, Polanyi's critique can be answered if, and only if, NIE theory can carry the burden of explaining all economic institutions of the premodern past as well—a challenge indeed.

The specificity of Polanyi's challenge does not rest in North's claim to meet it by these means, since, as we have seen, this agenda was already established. Its importance rests in several other elements that would continuously return in North's subsequent work. The first is making explicit the alternative to the explanatory framework of 'economic principles'. Polanyi's challenge means for North that if one does not attempt some explanation of social institutions in terms derived from choice theory, one can only be left with the kind of approach Polanyi himself pursued, namely explanations in terms of concepts derived from anthropology and (to a lesser extent) sociology. For North, this is tantamount to defeat. In this sense, his NIEH after Polanyi's challenge has the character not so much of an optimistic gambit that intractable problems will be easy to solve, as in his neoclassical-institutionalist work, but rather of an *après moi le déluge.*[13]

Second, what would define his NIEH to an ever-increasing extent is first expressed here: the necessity of explaining the (by this definition) 'noneconomic' origins and functions of institutions. While this follows in a sense logically from the use of institutions as variables in an economic model—after all, if institutions are so important, where do they come

[13] There is still an element of optimism in his response that "I wish to make the affirmative point that as yet we have not even tried to see how far economic analysis will take us in explaining institutional arrangements. (…) Transaction cost analysis is a promising framework to explore nonmarket forms of economic organisation" (North 1977: 709). But equally clear is his sense that this is the last lifeline for 'economic analysis' in solving these problems, since neoclassical economics and Cliometrics have failed and the outside critics, like Polanyi, stand ready to provide noneconomic solutions.

from, and can they in turn be reduced to an underlying variable? —it requires abandoning the simple contractarian model he had deployed hitherto. The quest for the origins of institutions and an account of their varying nature and functions, often quite far from being an obvious 'support function' for market exchange, would become a defining one for North's NIEH. Indeed, ultimately Polanyi's substantivism represents a greater challenge than just the question of nonmarket allocation systems for North: "The point goes much deeper than Polanyi realized, and poses a fundamental question to the economist and economic historian. How do we account for substitutes for price-making markets of which families, firms, guilds, manors, trade unions, cooperatives, etc. are organizing institutions which allocate resources instead of markets. Most fundamental of all, how do we explain government" (North 1977: 709)? Beyond the question of government alone, this rhetorical observation cements the shift in North's economic history from the study of markets to the institutions underlying markets. This would over time develop toward a further study of the origins of human sociality, normative and ideological structures, and political formations, that is, the 'non-economic' institutions that codetermine the functioning, embeddedness, and extent of market exchange.

Of course, this interest in nonmarket allocation and its sources is already evident to some extent in North's studies of the feudal manor. But what we see there is an explanation of the manor in terms of what Daniel Ankarloo has called 'as if economic history' (Ankarloo 2006): a method in which such nonmarket allocation systems are interpreted as if they come about through market-like means, a kind of private contracting producing an institutional social contract. In North's comments on Polanyi's challenge, it becomes clear that he realized the problem was more serious than that. For North's hope to be fulfilled, that economics could explain what Polanyi argued it could not, one would need to find an explanation in terms of 'economizing behavior'. But this economizing behavior would need to be defined in a way that would make it plausible why there are, and have been, so many more social institutions and allocation systems than private contracting, and why generalized market exchange constitutes only a relatively small part of economic history in the long run. It would also need to explain why such market societies came about where they did when they did and not elsewhere, and how major social-institutional transformations could happen, such as accounted in Polanyi's own discussions of the 'great transformation' (Polanyi 1944).

Polanyi's challenge made it clear to North, building on his studies of medieval European economic history, that social-institutional orders such as feudalism or the ancient world could not simply be seen as special cases of an optimization problem in reducing costs within a market setting. They really were different forms of society, with different institutions to those of a market society, and those institutions had different purposes, possibly quite remote from facilitating market exchange (like the firm in NIE models does). If the approach based on economizing behavior could not acknowledge this, it would be unlikely to be able to rebut the critics from outside the discipline, such as Polanyi, who argued that (orthodox) economics simply could not be relevant to such questions.

Following Polanyi's challenge, North's NIEH would be pulled in two directions in answering this. On the one hand, his contractarian model never quite went away. There would always remain the temptation to see institutions as the outcome of an optimizing process, a means of saving on some kind of cost—especially transaction costs induced by violence and uncertainty and their effect on property rights. On the other hand, North came to realize more and more the importance of the embeddedness that was the centerpiece of Polanyi's economic historical framework.[14] Earlier, North already had expressed reservations about his neoclassical contractarian institutionalism by stating the caveat that the role of beliefs and imperfect information had yet to be integrated into it. Moreover, he was confronted with a problem of agency: Who precisely was doing the social contracting to determine what the institutional arrangement would be? His reference to the "primary action group" (North 1971: 122) obscures more than it clarifies. Polanyi had been explicit that embeddedness meant noneconomic ideological purposes and functions should explain nonmarket institutions, although he too tended to be vague about agency. Answering his challenge therefore

[14]At least in subsequent interpretations in the recent 'Polanyi revival' it has been the most important concept, even if Polanyi exegesis has been conflicted about its importance in Polanyi's original works. The revival of this concept probably owes much to its use in New Economic Sociology; see Granovetter (1985).

meant finding some way of incorporating beliefs and ideologies into the model, and, moreover, finding in a way that did not simply represent a market-oriented cost saving (rational ignorance), since it was precisely the failure of market-supporting institutions to arise from the beginning that needed explaining.

In answering Polanyi's challenge, North's NIEH would have to steer a safe course between two dangers. On the one hand, there was the circular reasoning involved in assuming market-oriented behavior to explain the emergence of markets, or their failure to do so. On the other hand, there was Polanyi's embeddedness theory: his primitivism and substantivism in economic history, with its rejection of economics as irrelevant to the study of long-term (premodern) economic history and his preferred explanations in terms of *sui generis* ideology (mainly social convention and religious norms) explicitly in lieu of choice theory.[15] The avoidance of both is the story of the NIEH, and therefore from this point I count North's work to properly belong to it. If we wish to judge the success of North's NIEH by its own aims, it must be by this norm: to what extent it succeeded at finding an account of institutional formation and change in the long term, based in some form of choice theory derived from economics that avoided either of these extremes. We must therefore now look at North's NIEH proper, counted from his 1977 paper onward, and the many twists and turns North made in answering Polanyi's challenge. I will focus in particular on the final and most developed stage of his theory, as expressed in his final two books. It represents in many ways the most profound and far-reaching version of his answer to Polanyi's challenge, and one should judge an author especially by their best work.

North's NIEH in Overview

When discussing the birth of North's NIEH in the above terms, this is naturally an interpretative judgment made retrospectively. While the central themes of the NIEH are made explicit to a greater

[15] In his (hostile) review of Polanyi's *The Livelihood of Man* (Polanyi 1977), referred to above as the likely origin of North's encounter with Polanyi, North describes Polanyi's stance as "to attack a choice theoretic approach in societies where custom and tradition eliminate choice" (North 1978: 398).

extent in that paper than any other of North's early works, and the course of development of the NIEH is in some sense embryonically present in it (at least in terms of its overall direction), this naturally does not imply that it was immediately clear to North in what direction his subsequent work would go. Nor was there any immediate sea change in the type of analysis he produced directly afterward. The working out of the implications of the problems discussed in the Polanyi paper took time, several decades in fact, and it happened in fits and spurts.

It has been widely recognized, including by North himself, that a number of stages can be identified in the development of his NIEH. Most identify three (Groenewegen, Kerstholt, and Nagelkerke 1995; Brownlow 2010). I will adopt this view here, but I think these stages are best seen as theoretical constructs; they do not necessarily completely follow a chronological sequence, but overlap at certain points. North's restless mind was rarely at ease with any solution he had found, no matter how confidently elaborated at the time. Each stage, therefore, is in a sense abandoned—or rather subsumed—as soon as it has been achieved. His writing shifts focus and prepares the ground for new ideas, which would ripen into becoming established notions of his NIEH approach in the next monograph. The difficulty of coming to grips with the NIEH's stages is therefore not the way the line of reasoning shifted per se, but rather the complicated process of foregrounding and backgrounding involved: each stage is more characterized by the backgrounding of the theoretical achievements up until that point as by their further development. I define each stage by the theoretical elements held constant, as it were, by that point, because those formed the ground on which North built during each period. But one should not expect these to be the only or even the main topics he discussed during that period: instead, he often quickly moves on to discussing what would end up becoming fixed stars in the NIEH firmament at the occasion of the next major publication.

This also explains why the major publications are best seen as defining each period: they establish the framework, whereas each intervening period sees North fiddling with these results and recontextualizing or backgrounding them in light of new ideas and preoccupations, which then become accepted parts of the method by the next major work. Those major works are particularly his monographs: his 1981 book

Structure and Change in Economic History (North 1981), his 1990 book *Institutions, Institutional Change and Economic Performance* (*IICEP* for short; North 1990a), his 2005 book *Understanding the Process of Economic Change* (*UPEC*; North 2005), and, finally, his collaboration *Violence and Social Orders* (*VSO*; North, Wallis, and Weingast 2009). The NIEH, however, began with such loose exploration—the Polanyi paper in particular, but perhaps also his EHA lecture—rejecting his earlier neoclassical institutionalism, rather than with the 1981 monograph. So I do not count the 1981 book as constituting a major change in outlook. Stage 1 is therefore building up to, and culminates in, two major but closely related publications: his 1981 and 1990 books. Stage 2 runs from his 1990 book to his 2005 book, and stage 3 includes his 2005 book and runs until his death. The 1990 and 2005 books act as major 'hinges' between one stage and the next, as each sums up the theoretical insights of the previous period into a more or less coherent whole, but also presages the direction in which North's NIEH research program would go in the following stage.

The first stage of the NIEH is a case in point. This could be defined as the period between North's Polanyi paper—albeit with prefigurations such as his critique of Cliometrics in his EHA presidential address—up to and including his 1981 monograph and his 1990 book.[16] While most of the institutionalist theory in *Structure and Change* clearly builds on the first NIEH statements discussed above, the purpose is now clearly put in terms of a long-term comparative analysis of institutional structures and the different economic formations that result from them, with an aim to studying the relative '*performance*' of each of these structures. This performance mainly consists of the advantages security of property rights offers for the emergence of efficient markets, which in turn stimulate economic growth. But the purpose is also more explicitly still than in the paper with Robert Thomas to provide a rival theory of long-run historical differentiation in economic systems to existing accounts, here

[16] Intriguingly, at the time this book was seen as heralding a third stage in North's own career—after his neoclassical and then neoclassical-institutionalist phases (Galenson 1983: 188). This merely proves that what counts as a stage can only be a retrospective construct, determined as much by the research interest of the intellectual historian or reviewer as by texts themselves.

(still) mainly identified with the Marxist and the neoclassical (North 1981: 59).[17] Most importantly, in this stage the contractarian nature of institutions, in other words their presentation as the results of some process of market-like bargaining over security versus property rights, moves more to the background (without wholly disappearing). North in this work more clearly perceives feudal elites, as well as those of other allocation systems in the premodern past, as essentially predatory. This is probably in response to the criticisms he had received on this point (as discussed above). But the institutions sustaining their extractive powers undergo change mainly through exogenous factors still recognizably neoclassical in orientation: technological change (including military technology), demographic shifts, and expansion in volume of trade, as well as the more 'neoinstitutional' concern with the costs of measuring goods as a measure of transaction costs.

Effectively, then, his approach in this work is to identify the neoclassical factors normally held exogenous and to propose NIE theory as a means to make these constants into endogenous variables, so that long-term economic change is better understandable. This first stage of the NIEH, in other words, is still close to the neoclassical-institutionalist approach of before. But with one important change: the 'efficiency assumption' of institutions is dropped.[18] There are now political actors, and institutions sustaining them, who are fundamentally predatory and therefore nonefficient from an economic viewpoint. Moreover, he explicitly sets up the necessary components of the NIEH he is building: "A theory of property rights that describes the individual and group incentives… a theory of the state, since it is the state that specifies and enforces property rights… a theory of ideology that explains how different perceptions of reality affect the reaction of individuals to the changing 'objective situation'" (North 1981: 7–8). Together this amounts to the observation that "explaining economic performance in history requires a theory of

[17] An early sign of the noncomprehension of North's new direction is provided by one reviewer of this book, who saw it as *nota bene* a "useful complement to recent attempts… by Perry Anderson and Immanuel Wallerstein" (Millward 1983: 964).

[18] North now explicitly contrasts his view on this point with the NIE tradition of Oliver Williamson and others (North 1981: 7). This underlines that by this point the NIEH has really become something of its own.

demographic change, a theory of the growth of the stock of knowledge and a theory of institutions, in order to fill the gaps of neoclassical theory" (North 1981: 7). But each of these is not yet much developed. It is still transaction costs and the neoclassical factors described above that determine performance, and the rest—ideology, states, agency—indeed act primarily as gap fillers and have little independent theoretical elaboration.[19] The existence of transaction costs makes the invocation of these elements of the analysis necessary, but North has not yet endowed them with life.

For some of the secondary literature even now, this 1981 work is seen as representative of North's approach on the whole, even where reference is made to later works.[20] Perhaps less influential, but nonetheless an important step in the NIEH's history was North's 1990 book *IICEP* (North 1990a). This book could be seen as the hinge between the first and second stages of the NIEH. Through the early 1980s, North's various papers and publications focused for an important part on the problem of government and the effect of governmental policy on transaction costs, still a continuation in many ways of his previous concerns. In the late 1980s, this begins to shift toward a growing preoccupation with ideology and the role of the political process itself (North 1988, 1990b). He moves at this stage even further away from the assumption of efficient institutions. Certainly, transaction costs remain the primary proximate explanatory variable. But underlying the argument for the importance of transaction costs is an increasing realization that in a world of limited information and limited rationality, any political-institutional order or process will not resemble a market model based on rational self-interested agents, as in the public choice tradition North had built on hitherto.

The significance of limited rationality therefore increases considerably in North's explanatory framework by this point, and from this point onward it increasingly overshadows the original analysis based primarily on the more traditionally rational choice-based optimization model in

[19] Something North acknowledges (North 1981: 68).

[20] Oddly, North's John Wallis, who collaborated on North's considerably more sophisticated final work (North, Wallis, and Weingast 2009), considers *Structure and Change* to be North's best book (Wallis 2015).

the face of costs of exchange. Both are still somewhat awkwardly balanced in his paper on the 'transaction cost theory of politics' (North 1990b), but in his book published the same year it is the element of politics and ideology that gets the lion's share of attention. I will first focus on the more compact, and therefore more explicit, argument of the paper and then briefly discuss the book's additions to the theory. The innovations in these 1990 publications are significant enough for the subsequent trajectory of the NIEH that they can be seen, in retrospect, to be the beginning of its second stage.

The centerpiece of the 'transaction cost theory of politics' is North's critique of rational choice analysis of politics. He accepts that politics is like a market and speaks of 'political markets' without further ado. This remains quite in the tradition of public choice and fits both his contractarian approach to political institution formation and his emphasis on choice theory. But he rejects the assumption that such markets are characterized by rational choice or by efficiency: because it is unclear what is actually exchanged in these 'political markets', agreements are difficult to enforce and transaction costs are high (North 1990b: 362). But this begs the question why this is the case. Here, North changes tack. Political rules are heavily biased, he argues, toward compatibility with a larger political-institutional order. Such orders therefore create path dependence and are self-reinforcing. It is when North comes to the origins of these orders that he introduces a number of key new concepts. The institutional order, he argues, consists of (formal) rules, informal constraints, and their enforcement characteristics. These are the "rules of the game and therefore define the way the game is played" (North 1990b: 364). In politics, organizations arise to make use of the opportunities this set of constraints provides, and the interaction between them and the institutional order determines the longer-run trajectory of both.

The role of ideology in this analysis remains a curious mixture of rational and irrational, precisely the kind of melange criticized by Fine and Milonakis (2003): in North's formulation in this paper, ideologies are "subjective models" that nonetheless have "an organized structure that make the models an economizing device for receiving and interpreting information". This organized structure then "plays upon the normative element in individual preferences" in order to sustain collective action and the formation of organizations (North 1990b: 363). Much can be said about this, but I postpone my critical discussion for later. Right now it is important to note that this new emphasis on ideology, and its peculiar combination of rational choice and extra-rational elements in the analysis, is one of the new core ingredients of the NIEH mixture. This is joined with two other essential elements of the subsequent stages of his NIEH. The first is the model of institutional orders as path dependent and possessed of an internally dynamic structure, that therefore endogenously determines its own trajectory; and the other is the model of agency as individuals relating to institutions as 'rules of the game' and themselves (and organizations) as the 'players' of that game.[21]

His 1990 book *IICEP* further develops these themes. As North himself says, the book looks "much more deeply than the earlier studies into the nature of political and economic institutions and how they change. The specification of exactly what institutions are, how they differ from organisations, and how they influence transaction and production costs is the key to much of the analysis" (North 1990a: vii). It is in this book more than anywhere else that North really sets out his celebrated distinction between institutions and organizations. He thereby redefined for the present 'neoinstitutionalist turn' the meaning 'institution' would have, and made it a considerably more tractable concept than it had hitherto been.[22] Quite a bit of the remaining discussion of politics and institutions in the book consists of a lengthier discussion of the themes mentioned above, and I will not repeat them. However, North does here add another important component into the mix: the problem of cooperation. This is a logical step since understanding how an institutional order comes to exist and have stability, as well as understanding how organizations can form to act within it, are both collective action problems that require some form of cooperation to solve. Ideology, as we have seen, was already from early on a suggested 'glue' for the theory, but had until this point not

[21] In this chapter, however, the emphasis is on the role of organizations as agents. The individual 'entrepreneur' in the 'political market' is mentioned, but their role has not yet developed in detail.

[22] It is this distinction that makes Didry and Vincensini (2011), already referred to above, argue that North successfully answered Polanyi's challenge. For them, this distinction makes it possible to see both market and nonmarket phenomena as part of an 'institutional matrix' in a dynamic process, which then gives a theoretical framework for explaining historical change in Polanyian modes of integration. As we will see, I think this judgment is too optimistic and too simple.

had much elaboration. Moreover, North's reliance on rational public choice approaches and his contractarian model of institutions had prevented a clearer examination of this topic. However, the problem of cooperation is not put in radically different terms now.

Characteristically, in *IICEP* North distances himself from the rational public choice approach, but without wanting to give up choice theory or contractarianism. For this purpose, he reformulates the problem of cooperation in terms of an (alleged) theory of Adam Smith, seeing markets—as long as they have the right institutional support structure—as the solution to the cooperation problem. As he puts it: "The central focus is on the problem of… the cooperation that permits economies to capture the gains from trade that were the key to Adam Smith's *Wealth of Nations*. The evolution of institutions that create an hospitable environment for cooperative solutions to complex exchange provides for economic growth" (North 1990a: vii). Far from moving away from a contractarian approach to institutions, North, if anything, deepens this approach here by means of this device. By arguing that the problem of cooperation is that of 'capturing the gains of trade', essentially of making markets work, North then comes to view *all* institution formation, and thereby *all* cooperation problems, as part of this same problematic.

North repeats this view a number of times, as early in the book when he states that "institutions structure incentives in human exchange, whether political, social, or economic", and, subsequently, "the costliness of information is the key to the costs of transacting, which consist of the costs of measuring the valuable attributes of what is being exchanged and the costs of protecting rights and policing and enforcing agreements. These measurement and enforcement costs are the sources of social, political, and economic institutions" (North 1990a: 3, 27). This means all social dynamics are presented as an 'as if' market, again in Ankarloo's terms, which in turn permits complementarity with (not substitution for) orthodox choice theory: "Defining institutions as the constraints that human beings impose on themselves makes the definition complementary to the choice theoretic approach of neoclassical economic theory. Building a theory of institutions on the foundation of individual choices is a step toward reconciling differences between economics and the other social sciences" (North 1990a: 5).

I will go deeper into the meaning and consequences of this argument in the next chapter. With it, in any case, North has introduced all the essential elements of the second stage of his NIEH, which one can count roughly from the period of his 1990 paper and book until the 2005 publication of *Understanding the Process of Economic Change*. However, as in each stage, during this period he had already started laying the foundations of the next. The main focus of his works in the beginning of this stage, so roughly during the early to mid-1990s, was the critique of neoclassical models based on perfect rationality. North on various occasions delved particularly into the argument that institutions arise precisely because people are *not* perfectly rational and because there is no perfect information. By this point North's NIEH was already quite a sophisticated and multisided approach, with theory at the level of economic performance, at the level of transaction costs, and at the level of individual interaction with institutions and the role of beliefs in this interaction. But North continually emphasized that, if it weren't for abandoning the perfect rationality assumption, his work would be essentially just an extension and deepening of neoclassical economics. A particularly clear example is his John R. Commons lecture, where he berates the Old Institutionalists like Commons for not "giving us a theory" and then suggests that "the new institutional economics builds on, modifies, and extends neoclassical theory to permit it to… deal with an entire range of issues heretofore beyond its ken. What it retains and builds on is the fundamental assumption of scarcity and hence competition – the basis of the choice theoretic approach that underlies microeconomics. What it abandons is instrumental rationality" (North 1992: 3).

A separate paper, subsequently published, goes into more detail as to what model of rationality is substituted for the neoclassical one. Building on the work of Ronald Heiner (1983), North suggests that rational choice should be seen as a special case, applying only to problems characterized by "simple problems, complete information, repetitive situations, and high motivation" (North 1993: 161). However, on this occasion he also raises a new topic, one that would become more important as the NIEH developed further. Having established that institutions emerge because of the boundedness of rationality in the face of uncertainty, the next step would naturally be to ask: where do the limits to rationality come from, and how do they operate? This meant a further deepening of North's multilayered approach, by focusing his gaze on cognitive theory and the origins in brain science of what Heiner called the 'C-D gap', the gap between agent competence and the analytic difficulty of the problem.

Concomitant to this developing interest in cognitive science is a shift toward an evolutionary perspective. The emphasis on the importance of cognition and 'local learning' in a given institutional and natural environment pushed North in the direction of theories of cultural evolution. While he did not abandon his contractarian assumptions about the way institutions form, his interest in ideology and the sources of ideology combined with thinking of cognition as local optimization in response to limited information and uncertainty in given, preexisting social environments. This almost naturally produces an approach where institutional orders are (also) local equilibria, given the constraints imposed by our cognitive limitations. This conception would constitute an important further deepening of the NIEH approach as a whole, first tentatively set out in an essay on the historical evolution of polities (North 1994). North's typical use of multiple layers of abstraction and different causal mechanisms between each layer is in evidence here too: institutions are still conditioned for an important part by a combination of ideology and individual or organizational self-regarding incentives, but those ideologies are now in turn the result of a collective learning process. 'Culture' is the residue of past such learning processes, and in turn provides the content for informal norms and conventions, while ideology is both the result of such inheritance and the effect of learning in the face of a changing environment.

In this particular paper, such cultural inheritances are used by North to explain the failure of colonial authorities to impose good—that is, economic growth and private property promoting—institutions in Spanish colonies but the success of doing so in Anglo ones. This also reinforces his generally pessimistic anthropology, in that the ever-growing role of limited cognition and path dependence in his analysis strengthens his tendency to view economic and political 'success' as much more likely to fail than succeed. As he puts it: "The much more indifferent success that the English (and other colonial powers) had in inducing the development of polities and economies when imposed on an already existing culture suggests a fundamental source of institutional failure, and that is the critical role of the informal constraints in shaping the evolution of polities. Imposing a set of formal rules on an existing culture with informal constraints that are inconsistent with the new set of formal rules is a recipe for political and economic failure" (North 1994: 390).[23]

One will notice in these summaries the recurring usage of the term 'constraints', in particular when it comes to the function of institutions. While it is on its face an innocuous enough term, I want to draw special attention to it here because of the role it plays in North's larger framework. I have said earlier on that I think North attempted with his NIEH to have it both ways: to have his choice theoretical microfoundations on the one hand and, on the other, his rich model of agency—mediated by bounded rationality, ideology, culture, learning, uncertainty, institutions, and perhaps altruistic and other-regarding motives too. Clearly, the later stages of the NIEH show an increasing emphasis on the latter, more rich, view of agency and sociality at the expense of the former's emphasis on rationality and self-interest. Yet, as we have also seen, and as North continued to assert, the microfoundations of traditional choice theory were essential to his project. Without them, he could not demonstrate that 'economic analysis', as he understood it, could pass the explanatory tests represented by Polanyi's challenge. For this reason, the word 'constraints' is of great importance to understanding this tension in his later work. In his usage of the term, he attempts to reconcile these two opposing methodological viewpoints. By viewing all the rich, institutionalized aspects of agency at both individual and collective-societal levels as constraints on individual action, he could maintain this richness and yet reduce all these 'embedded' aspects to a case of bounded individual self-

[23] One of the characteristic attributes of the neoinstitutionalist turn in economic thought as well as elsewhere has been the resurgence in popularity of 'culturalist' explanations for economic and institutional divergence. Some new institutionalist (or adjacent) authors have in recent years been quite successful in supporting these old ideas on the basis of new theoretical formulations, and North in turn cited their work. Some examples favored by North are those of Avner Greif (1994) and Timur Kuran (1986, 1997, 2003), as well as older theories about the interaction between ideas and technological change like those of Lynn White (1978). These provide an interesting contrast to recent new institutionalist publications which emphasize institutions *instead* of culture, such as Acemoglu and Robinson (2012). A more thorough analysis of this potential split in the neoinstitutionalist turn awaits a separate publication, however.

regard, a complement to and refinement of the neoclassical rational choice perspective. *Constraints* in this way play an analogous role to the concept of the *rules of the game*: in both cases, all the endogenized institutional elements are in a sense re-exogenized, because they are outside constraints on individual action, not components of that individual action. They constitute the bounds of rationality, but do not change the meaning of rationality itself.

All these elements come together in his 2005 *magnum opus*, *Understanding the Process of Economic Change* (*UPEC* for short; North 2005). As we have seen, over time the emphasis of the structure of NIEH theory has changed, with the more conventional exogenous constraints on growth such as technology and demography fading more into the background and the importance of 'social' phenomena such as ideology, cooperation, cognitive constraints, and the evolution of culture being foregrounded. Where in *Structure and Change* and even in *IICEP*, ideology still lacked content, it has become a centerpiece of the theory itself in *UPEC*. The result is an integration of the various concepts of interest developed over the previous stages of the NIEH into a grand ensemble. The micro-level elements of social learning, cognitive limitations, uncertainty, and so forth ultimately produce differing ideologies or worldviews, which are then inputs into the meso-level system where agents produce, interact with, and change institutions. As North puts it: "The structure that humans create to order their political/economic environment is the basic determinant of the performance of an economy. It provides the incentives which shape the choices humans make… The strength of informal norms and the effectiveness of enforcement play a key part in the story. Where do the rules, informal norms, and for that matter the effectiveness of enforcement, come from? They are derived from the beliefs humans have" (North 2005: 48).

This in turn forms the foundation for the macro-level structure, where the most important concept is that of adaptive efficiency: the ability of institutional orders as a whole—called 'artifactual frameworks'—to be sufficiently flexible to survive in the face of changing circumstances, in a sort of evolutionary process of differential survival at the level of whole societies. Transaction costs and other traditional problems of the NIE still appear, but primarily at the meso-level, where institutions and market behavior co-condition one another. North is therefore not exaggerating when he describes this most developed stage of his NIEH in *UPEC* as "an extension – a very substantial extension – of the new institutional economics" (North 2005: 10).

The basis of this framework rests in the evolutionary pattern at the micro-level. However, North has something particular in mind in using evolution in this context. Although based on evolved human psychology and sociality, this evolutionary process is for North not wholly reducible to Darwinian selection, because of the centrality of intentionality: the beliefs of the 'players' of the 'game' matter. "The selection mechanisms in Darwinian evolutionary theory are not informed by beliefs about the eventual consequences. In contrast, human evolution is guided by the perceptions of the players; choices – decisions – are made in the light of those perceptions with the intent of producing outcomes downstream that will reduce uncertainty of the organizations – political, economic, and social – in pursuit of their goals. Economic change, therefore, is for the most part a deliberate process shaped by the perceptions of the actors about the consequences of their actions" (North 2005: viii).

What matters is that biological evolutionary theory is not enough, but that it must be combined with an economically sound theory of intentionality—for which of course the NIE is the source. If uncertainty and sociality are to be explained in Darwinian terms as the result of our physical limitations and needs, North has no truck with doing the same for the products of intentionality. He rejects the memetic approach famously espoused by Richard Dawkins (1976) in favor of the more traditional economic understanding of 'culture', that is, the domain of human intentional action and its products that cannot be explained in terms of (direct) economic interests. As he explains: "Cultural traits do not possess attributes parallel to those of genes and indeed the growing literature of the new institutional economics makes abundantly clear that institutions must be explained in terms of the intentionality of humans. Informal norms develop that blend the moral inference of genetic origin with the intentional aims of humans, which together provide the backbone of what we should mean by the term culture" (North 2005: 42). I will say more about this approach to evolution and socioeconomic change in chap. 5.

The larger implications for North's approach are about how such learning does or does not contribute, via institutions, to economic performance. This is akin to a system of cultural evolution via a process of social, rather than purely individual, learning: "The focus of our attention, therefore, must be on human learning—on what is learned and how it is shared among the members of a society and on the incremental process by which the beliefs and preferences change, and on the way in which they shape the performance of economies through time" (North 2005: viii). Because both institutions and the belief systems are inherited across generations, the trajectories of societies, insofar as they are shaped by them, are subject to path dependence. This means not just the mere fact of institutional inheritance, but also the slowness and incrementality of changes in their structure. This incrementalism about cultural evolution is to be explained by the fact that institutions give rise to organizations, which then have a stake in existing institutional frameworks and may oppose their change. Moreover, learning is an imperfect process and ideologies may persist in the face of change. Also, institutional changes require extensive reshapings of patterns of cooperation, something difficult to accomplish within a given incentive structure. Therefore, constraints operate at several levels: individuals are constrained in their beliefs by uncertainty, individuals or groups are constrained in their choices by their beliefs and institutions, and societies are constrained by path dependence. Constraints are still the essence of the relationship between agency and structure in North, but now as part of an integrated, multitiered (qualitative) model.

It is the choice of societies as the level at which cultural evolution takes place that determines also North's macro-level analysis of adaptive efficiency, where societies are again the units of differential survival. This macro-level model and its developmental implications—as well as, retrospectively, its implications for understanding economic divergence in historical perspective—are really the lesson of *UPEC* as a whole. It is worth citing this finding more fully, since it doubles as a very good summary of the final stage NIEH and its intended policy implications: "Successful economic development will occur when the belief system that has evolved has created a 'favorable' artifactual structure that can confront the novel experiences that the individual and society face and resolve positively the novel dilemmas. Failures will occur when the novel experiences are so far removed from the artifactual structure of the evolved belief system that individual and society do not have the 'building blocks' of the mind and artifactual structure to resolve the novel problems. If we are going to come to grips with an understanding of the differential performance of different parts of the world both over time and cross-sectionally in the modern world it is here that we must begin… That is what is meant by adaptive efficiency; creating the necessary artifactual structure is an essential goal of economic policy" (North 2005: 69–70).

That leaves us with his last monograph, *Violence and Social Orders* (*VSO* for short), coauthored with John Joseph Wallis and Barry Weingast (North, Wallis, and Weingast 2009). Insofar as *UPEC* was concerned with the emergence of belief systems out of uncertainty and the impact of such cultural frameworks, when joined with bounded rationality, on institutional arrangements, *VSO* puts the state, politics, and formal institutions central. Nonetheless, the argument in this book as a whole is equally concerned with the origins of cooperation—as always, in the sense North attributed to Adam Smith—and of human sociality itself. In *UPEC*, North argued for the importance of a shift from personal exchange to impersonal exchange and for the emergence of an impersonal and limited state power to enforce the formal institutions. *VSO* is in part an elaboration on this suggestion and an inquiry as to how it might come about.

In order to create an origin story for the emergence of human sociality and the 'artifactual framework', *VSO* divides history into a progressive evolution, if not necessarily a linear one, of different types of state. While this contains various categories and subcategories, the most important of these is the distinction between what they call 'natural state orders' and 'open access orders'. The authors describe the former as follows: "The logic of the natural state follows from how it solves the problem of violence. Elites – members of the dominant coalition – agree to respect each other's privileges, including property rights and access to resources and activities. By limiting access to these privileges to members of the dominant coalition, elites create credible incentives to cooperate rather than fight among themselves. Because elites know that violence will reduce their own rents, they have incentives not to fight. Furthermore, each elite understands that other elites face similar incentives. In this way, the political system of a natural state manipulates the economic system to produce rents that then secure political order" (North, Wallis, and Weingast 2009: 18).

The open access order, by contrast, is simply the opposite of this: an order where the state has a monopoly on violence but allows free entry and exit for citizens into political organizations and the economy, and where the state takes on a wholly impersonal character, which ensures equality. The open access order is without further ado identified with the state regimes of the Western world today, whereas the natural state orders characterize all non-Western countries today as well as essentially all state orders of the past. Proceeding from the self-regard of individuals, game theoretical models are used to support the idea that repeated cooperation will be difficult to sustain given the benefits to free riding and cheating, requiring an external enforcer of the 'rules of the game' of some sort. This enforcer then is whatever elite is concocted out of temporary alliances of self-seeking individuals and turns out to be strong enough to transform into a state. The transition from this stage to the open access order is of course the real problem in the book. The answer to this is a situation in which it becomes in the rational interest of the elites to treat each other impersonally, rather than violently, and subsequently to extend access to the impersonal institutions so created to a wider and wider section of the population.

The main thrust of *VSO*, therefore, is this. Because human cooperation is difficult to achieve, a Hobbesian War of all against all is a persistent threat. For larger societies, individual repeated contact and the opportunities for norm enforcement that follow from it—here a conscious reference to the game theoretical literature—are insufficient to ensure cooperation instead of violence and predation. Societies therefore create institutions and political orders to limit competition between groups in the form of violence and to create incentives for peaceful forms of cooperation, of which the market is the paramount example. This requires credible enforcement mechanisms, however, which in turn requires bodies or individuals with sufficient power to enforce the institutional order. These individuals or bodies, however, have an incentive to maintain themselves in power and to predate in turn on society to their own benefit. Virtually all historical societies have been natural state orders, in the terms of this approach. That is to say, they have been governed by elites that restrict the use of violence to themselves, as well as access to their elite body or bodies and their privileges (making them a closed class), in order to find an efficient optimum between rent accrual and economic productivity (North, Wallis, and Weingast 2009: 16–20).

The joy of the open access order, by contrast, is that in such orders competition is maximally channeled through market-like structures, at the level of both economics and politics. Free peaceful competition, with low barriers to entry and exit, guarantees that rent-seeking at the political level can be minimized while the presumed productivity and desirable 'capturing of the gains of trade'—the 'Smithian result' of a well-ordered market—can be maximized. The echoes of public choice theory are evident in the concern with rent-seeking as a concomitant of state-building in cases where the market is not allowed, or supported, to do its job. In some ways, the argument of *VSO* resembles a more historical and sophisticated form of Mancur Olson's model of most states as 'stationary bandits' (Olson 1993).[24] The social contractarian structure of the argument is also quite explicit, owing as much to Locke and Hobbes as to Smith.[25] In the next chapter, I will return to this point in more detail and critically examine the contractarian structure of North's NIEH and his invocations of the 'Smithian result' to justify the role of markets in his overall framework. At its heart is what I call the 'pessimistic anthropology' underlying North's analysis, which is also in evidence on the rare occasions that in *UPEC* and *VSO* anthropological research is directly discussed (examples are North 2005: 45–47; North, Wallis, and Weingast 2009: 51–54).

Also important is the quasi-game theoretical structure, evoked by the importance of alignment of incentives and the view of agency as the pursuit of payoffs within an institutionally given incentive structure. This has been in evidence since the 'rules of the game' were introduced in North's approach, and grew in significance over time. In this, the elaborate structure

---

[24] *VSO*'s approach builds on a model developed first in North and Weingast (1989). The authors mention Olson's model, but differentiate themselves from it, in that they view 'the state' as composed of multiple internal agents or organizations, rather than being a single actor as in Olson's model (North, Wallis, and Weingast 2009: 17). The sophistication of *VSO* rests in depicting the state as the equilibrium *outcome* of elite action, rather than as simply being the actor itself. Another comparable model is Barzel (2000).

[25] Indeed Hobbes is explicitly invoked (North, Wallis, and Weingast 2009: 13), but the point is made that the analysis in *VSO* offers a way out of Hobbes' state of nature.

of interaction between beliefs or ideology and institution formation as described in *UPEC* is not abandoned here. The emphasis has shifted, but the two books are clearly complementary. The view of beliefs as developed in *UPEC* and the role of institutions and enforcement structures as described in *VSO* jointly form a model of agency and rationality. It is one that simultaneously owes much to game theory and public choice theory as well as to cognitive science, anthropology, and critiques of rational choice. A good example of how the different points of emphasis of the two books are integrated is when, invoking the work of Avner Greif, the authors state that "a supportable set of beliefs can develop within an institution if the beliefs are consistent with the behavior the institution induces. Successful public institutions create common knowledge, and therefore common beliefs, about how the formal or informal rules will be implemented. The common beliefs can sustain an institution that would otherwise not work. These shared beliefs become focal points, as described by Schelling" (North, Wallis, and Weingast 2009: 44n13). I will elaborate on these observations later in this book. In chap. 4, I will discuss how agency, rationality, and North's critiques of neoclassical approaches cohere—or fail to—in his NIEH, and what the consequences are for his overall framework.

Conclusion

After his turn away from neoclassical and Cliometric approaches, North had the notion that transaction cost economics could explain the long-term institutional dynamics of economic history that those approaches could not. Initially, however, he was unable to quite get away from the neoclassical framework he was used to. Only the encounter with Polanyi's challenge provided him with the necessary material to formulate his NIEH. At the heart of this formulation is to prove the criticism of Polanyi (and other heterodox 'outside' views, like the Marxist one) wrong. The critiques they leveled are right, North's NIEH argues, but only for neoclassical economics and then only insofar as they do not touch on choice theory itself. The NIEH seeks to rebuild economic history on the basis of a combination, or perhaps juxtaposition: on the one hand, choice theoretical microfoundations, on top of which is built a vast and expansive framework of institutional analysis, where limited information, uncertainty, transaction costs, mental models, and cooperation and coordination problems are central to the analysis.

In so doing, North has always sought to answer Polanyi's challenge by proving that an institutionalist form of economics could explain the kind of phenomena Polanyi's substantivism was meant to address: nonmarket allocation systems, persistently inefficient institutions, 'uneconomical' ideologies, and the limits to rational market action. But over time, his NIEH moved further and further away from its origins in the forms of New Institutionalism that still hew closely to the neoclassical framework. From the efficiency model of institutions he has moved to an elaborate multitiered interactive model, one with few constants and many degrees of freedom. The theory spans cultural evolution and social learning to the formation of beliefs and ideologies, to the creation of institutions and the ways individuals and organizations interact with them in a market-like way, and to the overall impact of such institutional orders in terms of adaptive efficiency and path-dependent development patterns.

Throughout, however, the core of North's NIEH remains the attempt to prove that the formula 'traditional choice theory plus untraditional institutionalism' can do better in long-term economic historiography than approaches from outside economics, such as Polanyi represents, can do. In the following chapters, I will delve deeper into a number of major components or concepts in North's NIEH and subject them to a systematic critical analysis. The purpose of this exercise is ultimately to evaluate this *raison d'être* of North's work, both externally and (especially) in its own terms. Has North really demonstrated that his approach can coherently and convincingly address the challenge of Karl Polanyi? The next chapters will seek to answer this question.

References

Acemoglu, Daron, and James A. Robinson. 2012. *Why Nations Fail*. New York: Crown Publishing.

Ankarloo, Daniel. 2006. *New Institutional Economics and Economic History: A Case of Economics Imperialism*. Paper Presented to Historical Materialism Conference, London, 8–10 December.

Barzel, Yoram. 2000. Property Rights and the Evolution of the State. *Economics of Governance* 1 (1): 25–51.
Brownlow, Graham A. 2010. Structure and Change: Douglass North's Economics. *Journal of Economic Methodology* 17 (3): 301–316.
Dale, Gareth. 2010. Social Democracy, Embeddedness and Decommodification: On the Conceptual Innovations and Intellectual Affiliations of Karl Polanyi. *New Political Economy* 15 (3): 369–393.
———. 2011. Lineages of Embeddedness: On the Antecedents and Successors of a Polanyian Concept. *American Journal of Economics and Sociology* 70 (2): 306–339.
Davis, Lance. 1966. Professor Fogel and the New Economic History. *The Economic History Review* 19 (3): 657–663.
Davis, Ann. 2008. Endogenous Institutions and the Politics of Property: Comparing and Contrasting Douglass North and Karl Polanyi in the Case of Finance. *Journal of Economic Issues* 42 (4): 1101–1122.
Davis, Lance, and Douglass C. North. 1970. Institutional Change and American Economic Growth: A First Step Towards a Theory of Institutional Innovation. *The Journal of Economic History* 30 (1): 131–149.
———. 1971. *Institutional Change and American Economic Growth*. Cambridge: Cambridge University Press.
Dawkins, Richard. 1976. *The Selfish Gene*. Oxford: Oxford University Press.
Didry, Claude, and Caroline Vincensini. 2011. *Beyond the Market-Institutions Dichotomy: The Institutionalism of Douglass C. North in Response to Karl Polanyi's Challenge*. HALSHS-00601544.
Diebolt, Claude. 2012. Where Are We Now in Cliometrics? *Historical Social Research* 37 (4): 309–326.
Fenoaltea, Stefano. 1975. The Rise and Fall of a Theoretical Model: The Manorial System. *The Journal of Economic History* 35 (2): 386–409.
Field, Alexander. 1981. The Problem with Neoclassical Institutional Economics: A Critique with Special Reference to the North/Thomas Model of Pre-1500 Europe. *Explorations in Economic History* 18 (2): 174–198.
Fine, Ben, and Dimitris Milonakis. 2003. From Principle of Pricing to Pricing of Principle: Rationality and Irrationality in the Economic History of Douglass North. *Comparative Studies in Society and History* 45 (3): 546–570.
Fogel, Robert W. 1964. *Railroads and American Economic Growth: Essays in Econometric History*. Baltimore: Johns Hopkins University Press.
———. 1966. The New Economic History: Its Findings and Methods. *The Economic History Review* 19 (3): 642–656.

Furubotn, Eirik G., and Svetozar Pejovich. 1972. Property Rights and Economic Theory: A Survey of Recent Literature. *Journal of Economic Literature* 10 (4): 1137–1162.

Galenson, David W. 1983. Structure and Change in Economic History. Douglass C. North. *Journal of Political Economy* 91 (1): 188–190.

Gemici, Kurtulus. 2008. Karl Polanyi and the Antinomies of Embeddedness. *Socio-Economic Review* 6: 5–33.

Granovetter, Mark. 1985. Economic Action and Social Structure: The Problem of Embeddedness. *American Journal of Sociology* 91 (3): 481–510.

Grdesic, Marko. 2016. *What Do Economists Think of Karl Polanyi?.* Orgtheory.net. https://orgtheory.wordpress.com/2016/04/02/what-do-economists-think-of-karl-polanyi/. Accessed Feb 2018.

Greif, Avner. 1994. Cultural Beliefs and the Organization of Society: A Historical and Theoretical Reflection on Collectivist and Individualist Societies. *Journal of Political Economy* 102 (5): 912–950.

Groenewegen, John, Frans Kerstholt, and Ad Nagelkerke. 1995. On Integrating Old and New Institutionalism: Douglass North Building Bridges. *Journal of Economic Issues* 29 (2): 467–475.

Heiner, Ronald A. 1983. The Origin of Predictable Behavior. *American Economic Review* 73 (4): 560–595.

Klein, Daniel B., and Ryan Daza. 2013. Douglass C. North. *Economics Journal Watch* 10 (3): 525–532.

Kuran, Timur. 1986. The Economic System in Contemporary Islamic Thought. *International Journal of Middle East Studies* 18 (2): 135–164.

———. 1997. Islam and Underdevelopment: An Old Puzzle Revisited. *Journal of Institutional and Theoretical Economics/Zeitschrift für die gesamte Staatswissenschaft* 153 (1): 41–71.

———. 2003. The Islamic Commercial Crisis: Institutional Roots of Economic Underdevelopment in the Middle East. *Journal of Economic History* 63 (2): 414–446.

Millward, Robert. 1983. Review: Structure and Change in Economic History. *The Economic Journal* 93 (372): 963–965.

Nobel Foundation. 2015. *Douglass C. North – Biographical.* https://www.nobelprize.org/nobel_prizes/economic-sciences/laureates/1993/north-bio.html. Accessed Feb 2018.

North, Douglass C. 1958. Ocean Freight Rates and Economic Development 1730–1913. *The Journal of Economic History* 18 (4): 537–555.

———. 1961. *The Economic Growth of the United States 1790–1860.* Englewood: Prentice Hall.

———. 1968. Sources of Productivity Change in Ocean Shipping, 1600–1850. *Journal of Political Economy* 76 (5): 953–970.

———. 1971. Institutional Change and Economic Growth. *The Journal of Economic History* 31 (1): 118–125.

———. 1974. Beyond the New Economic History. *The Journal of Economic History* 34 (1): 1–7.

———. 1977. Markets and Other Allocation Systems in History: The Challenge of Karl Polanyi. *Journal of European Economic History* 6 (3): 703–716.

———. 1978. The Livelihood of Man. By Karl Polanyi. *Business History Review* 52 (3): 398–399.

———. 1981. *Structure and Change in Economic History*. Cambridge: Cambridge University Press.

———. 1988. Ideology and Economic/Political Institutions. *Cato Journal* 8 (1): 15–28.

———. 1990a. *Institutions, Institutional Change and Economic Performance*. Cambridge: Cambridge University Press.

———. 1990b. A Transaction Cost Theory of Politics. *Journal of Theoretical Politics* 2 (4): 355–367.

———. 1992. Institutions and Economic Theory. *The American Economist* 36 (1): 3–6.

———. 1993. What Do We Mean by Rationality? *Public Choice* 77 (1): 159–162.

———. 1994. The Historical Evolution of Polities. *International Review of Law and Economics* 14 (4): 381–391.

———. 2005. *Understanding the Process of Economic Change*. Princeton: Princeton University Press.

———. 2009. Interview with Karen Ilse Horn. In *Roads to Wisdom: Conversations with Ten Nobel Laureates in Economics*, ed. Karen Ilse Horn, 153–172. Cheltenham: Edward Elgar.

North, Douglass C., and Robert Paul Thomas. 1970. An Economic Theory of the Growth of the Western World. *The Economic History Review* 23 (1): 1–17.

———. 1971. The Rise and Fall of the Manorial System: A Theoretical Model. *The Journal of Economic History* 31 (4): 777–803.

———. 1973. *The Rise of the Western World: A New Economic History*. Cambridge: Cambridge University Press.

North, Douglass C., and Barry R. Weingast. 1989. Constitutions and Commitment: The Evolution of Institutions Governing Public Choice in Seventeenth-Century England. *The Journal of Economic History* 49 (4): 803–832.

North, Douglass C., John Joseph Wallis, and Barry R. Weingast. 2009. *Violence and Social Orders: A Conceptual Framework for Interpreting Recorded Human History*. Cambridge: Cambridge University Press.

North, Douglass C., Gardner Brown, and Dean Lueck. 2015. A Conversation with Douglass North. *Annual Review of Resource Economics* 7: 1–10.

Olson, Mancur. 1993. Dictatorship, Democracy and Development. *The American Political Science Review* 87 (3): 567–576.

Polanyi, Karl. 1944. *The Great Transformation*. New York: Farrar & Rinehart.

———. 1977. *The Livelihood of Man: Studies in Social Discontinuity.* Ed. Harry W. Pearson. New York: Academic Press.

Wallis, John Joseph. 2015. *Structure and Change in Economic History: The Ideas of Douglass North*. CEPR Policy Portal. https://voxeu.org/article/ideas-douglass-north. Accessed Feb 2018.

White, Lynn T. 1978. *Medieval Religion and Technology*. Berkeley: University of California Press.

3

Markets, the Social Contract, and the 'Smithian Result'

Introduction

In his scathing criticisms of the New Institutionalist approach to markets, Daniel Ankarloo has accused North—among others—of practicing what he calls "as-if economic history" (Ankarloo 2002a, 2006). Ankarloo and Palermo (2004) used this phrase to describe what they saw as a widespread practice in the NIE of excessively theory-driven formulations of historical phenomena, which in this way become mere illustrations of some already-assumed putative economic principles. As they put it, "The story does not start with 'once upon a time…', but with 'let us assume that the world is as if it were coherent with our theory…'. (…) In NIE at large, history is treated as if it did not matter to the conception of the model; rather, history is 'as-if' to the validity of the model" (Ankarloo and Palermo 2004: 419).

For Ankarloo, North's treatment of the market—both what a market is and what its historical function has been—is a paramount example of this type of historiography: "The disturbing problem with North's economic history is all the same that the decisive institutions and human characteristics that are specific to capitalism have to be assumed to exist even when

M. Krul, *The New Institutionalist Economic History of Douglass C. North*,
Palgrave Studies in the History of Economic Thought,
https://doi.org/10.1007/978-3-319-94084-7_3

he admits capitalism is not at hand… But, if he acknowledges that markets and the institutions of capitalism originate from somewhere, and evolve, he cannot assume them to have existed from the start " (Ankarloo 2002a: 25). Even though North acknowledges even in his early work that in much of premodern history markets have been absent or very limited in their functioning, for Ankarloo he treats these observations in an 'as if' manner: it is as if markets should have been there, but weren't, and their absence is therefore the thing to be explained. Ankarloo calls this the yardstick—"the market in North's explanations remains the universal yardstick – the eternal reference point" (Ankarloo 2002b: 18)—although one might perhaps better think of it as a benchmark against which historical performance is measured.

Ankarloo's criticism is interesting for two reasons. The first reason is because he identifies a serious issue in North's work, namely the applicability of the NIEH framework to cases where market or market-like institutions are not in evidence. As the discussion of Polanyi's challenge in the previous chapter makes clear, the very purpose of the NIEH was this: to show the relevance of economic theory based on microfoundations plus transaction cost analysis to the long run of economic history, not just to well-established modern market economies. Even if the economic theory in question was much revised in the process, this remained the goal. If however the NIEH explains these premodern economic phenomena by reference to concepts that are in turn only applicable to market-like institutions, it is assuming what it needs to prove, and there is a serious logical deficiency in the approach. In other words, if Ankarloo's criticism is correct, North can 'account for' long-run institutional change only by assuming that nonmarket institutions come about through some form of market failure, like the effect of transaction costs. Otherwise, markets would have emerged as they eventually did. This would mean naturalizing the market by assuming it 'naturally' appears *unless constrained from doing so*, and that therefore concepts relevant to markets can be applied straightforwardly to explain nonmarket institutions.

But this is precisely what Polanyi's criticism amounted to: that economists and economic historians could only explain away nonmarket phenomena by subsuming them under theories that were irrelevant to them, that is to say by denying any substantive difference between market and nonmarket societies. This is the second interesting aspect of Ankarloo's criticism: unlike many critics of North, he explicitly contrasts North's approach to markets with that of Polanyi and argues that this *petitio principii* on North's part comes about because of his inability to answer Polanyi's challenge (Ankarloo 2002b).

In order to see whether Ankarloo's criticism is justified, we need to understand better how North's NIEH actually understands 'the market' and what role it plays in the analysis. This is difficult for a number of reasons. North rarely makes his theoretical assumptions and definitions explicit, and therefore some degree of interpretative digging is required in order to excavate the underlying framework. This goes particularly for those aspects of North's NIEH that touch directly on unexamined assumptions that are part of the microfoundations. The way North thought about concepts such as 'choice', 'exchange', 'transactions', and 'markets' all directly touch on fundamentals of his way of thinking and require careful treatment to interpret. They operate as it were below the visible level of theorizing. (This is of course neither unique to North nor a criticism of him: the same can undoubtedly be said for any social theorizing of sufficient complexity.) Another difficulty arises from the need to disentangle two aspects of the problem: on the one hand, how North uses concepts like 'the market' and 'the Smithian result' in general, and on the other hand how he applies his ideas to the study of premodern economic history where, as Polanyi pointed out, their applicability is not immediately obvious. Finally, understanding how these aspects interrelate in North's NIEH also requires a better grasp on his evident, but equally unexamined, contractarian view of social institutions. It is not a large conceptual leap from the social contract to interpreting social phenomena as a type of contracting.

Certainly, North abandoned the overly simplistic view of the manorial system as a kind of implicit collective contract of rents for security, providing optimal welfare for all (North and Thomas 1971). What came in its place is less obvious. As he abandoned the efficiency assumption of institutions, he also abandoned any explicit discussion of his contractarian framework. But it did not disappear. On the contrary, it was, if anything, strengthened: North came increasingly to rely on the idea of the 'Smithian result' to explain the desirability of institutionally supported markets, while also defending the notion of 'political markets' as a viable framework for institutional analysis. Moreover *VSO*, North's final work of theory, presents social orders as the outcomes of negotiations among elites, and between elites and societies, over how violence might be limited in a way that satisfies the interests of those parties with power to enforce rules. This is both reminiscent of his early analysis of the manor and of the social contractarian conception of Thomas Hobbes. There is a potential tension here: on the one hand, there is Adam Smith, famous for his moral and institutional account of markets and of their limits on the basis of sympathy, and on the other hand there is Hobbes, famous for his stark social contract theory where society is hardly more than an efficient protection racket. In this chapter, I will discuss to what extent North resolved this potential tension and what the consequences are for his NIEH theory in light of Ankarloo's (and Polanyi's) critique.

Defining the Market: The Problem of Transaction Costs

In his 1977 paper on Polanyi's challenge, North observes: "It is a peculiar fact that the literature of economics and economic history contains so little discussion of the central institution that underlies neoclassical economics: the market" (North 1977: 710). North points out that one implication of Polanyi's argument is that exchange and trade must not necessarily imply 'economic motivation', by which he appears to mean a profit motive. He points to Polanyi and George Dalton's famous arguments regarding administered trade in ancient Babylonia and the *kula* trade of the Trobriand Islanders—a set piece of economic anthropology taken from Bronislaw Malinowski—as illustrations of this argument (North 1977: 708). In that paper's approach of maximally conceding to Polanyi's economic historical 'primitivism', North goes out of his way to accept this premise. In fact, for him this is even true in the post–Industrial Revolution economies of the modern world: firms and governments also undertake economic activity in modern market societies, so that even there price-making markets do not fully dominate all transactions (North 1977: 709).

Polanyi importantly distinguished markets per se from what he called 'price-making markets', one in which supply and demand act as independent forces to determine the relative prices of goods and which is integrated, or tends to integrate, into a larger system of market exchange (Polanyi, Arensberg, and Pearson 1957: 255). As North points out, this seems to apply to markets with "a large number of buyers and sellers, a variety of goods, an agreed-upon medium of exchange and an enforced set of property rights" (North 1977: 710). For North, as one might expect, it is the latter that is decisive: the property rights arrangements (and their enforcement) determine transaction costs (information costs, measuring costs, etc.) and thereby the viability of such markets compared to other forms of exchange. The salient point is that "the costs of defining and enforcing property rights… lead to non-price allocation of many goods and services today… transactions costs in the ancient past would have been an insuperable barrier to price-making markets throughout most of history" (North 1977: 710). As we have seen in the previous chapter, this leads to his conclusion that "it is reasonable to assume that the forces that lead to the substitution of firms for markets today may also help us to explain the variety of forms of economic organization in past societies" (North 1977: 711).

Here, then, is the market benchmark in evidence: a working assumption that nonmarket (or at least, non–price-making market) allocation systems can be explained by the same causes that explain substitution for private contracting (a favored topic in the NIE literature from Ronald Coase to Oliver Williamson) in modern market societies. The difference between the case firms and other vertical or hierarchical organizations as substitutes for individual contracting and the premodern social phenomena Polanyi discussed is, however, considerable. In the former case, price-making markets in Polanyi's sense already exist: there is widespread private contracting and price-setting mediated by money and a very large part of society is commodified in some form with a market orientation. The formation of firms is explained in the Coase-Williamson tradition with that social fact as a backdrop.[1] The Polanyian case however concerns

[1] Indeed, Williamson in his pioneering book famously declared in biblical tones that "in the beginning there were markets" (Williamson 1975: 20). In a subsequent interview, however, he saw the issue more agnostically: "You could start with the neoclassical theory markets and market failures and interpret hierarchies as a response to market failures. But a sociologist might start with hierarchies

societies in which, according to the primitivist economic historical tradition to which Polanyi belonged, no such context existed to begin with, a claim North explicitly conceded. For both Polanyi and North, an important challenge is to understand the (partial) emergence or existence of markets when they are embedded, in the Polanyian sense, in a largely nonmarket society, again in the Polanyian sense. The problem is therefore whether one can equate this with an investigation of the causes of the emergence of *nonmarket* phenomena in a society where markets are the dominant allocation form. The questions seem at first sight too different, and yet North conflates them into a single research question: Why was there ever anything other than markets? In this fashion, North transforms the nature of the problem Polanyi posed, simply by changing the *explanandum*.

One way in which this transformation of the research question into the market as benchmark manifests itself practically is in the way transaction costs are actually used in the historical analysis of the long run. While there is no doubt that North was sincere in his efforts to apply transaction cost economics to new problems, he did not much engage explicitly with the problem of how such an application can be relevant in cases where market prices have only limited significance. In the Williamsonian framework, these transaction costs account for the existence of vertical or hierarchical structures, but that is explicitly within the context of widespread price-making markets as Polanyi defined them. What is less obvious is that that reasoning can be extended to premodern history as well. The measurement of transaction costs is a significant conceptual problem: by definition they are not immediately measurable in the market, and if institutions and organizations are said to arise to compensate for them in some form, then that would render their nature and quantity even more opaque. The risk is therefore that transaction costs become a kind of shadow explanation, something which is *deduced* from the existence of nonmarket allocation while simultaneously having to play the role of *explaining* such social institutions.

and hierarchical failures and interpret markets as a response to hierarchical failures. I think… that the literature on markets and market failures is in a lot better shape than the theory of hierarchies and hierarchical failure… [but] if the literatures on both sides develop equally and symmetrically, then it is a toss-up" (Hodgson and Gindis 2007: 378–379).

This is precisely one of the main issues the heterodox critics of North have held against his explanatory framework as well. Ben Fine and Dimitris Milonakis observe that "in North's hands, transaction costs has become a catchall phrase to be used as an explanatory tool in almost any historical or theoretical context… it becomes possible in principle to explain the existence of any institution in history by invoking the high transaction costs of some other theoretically possible institution" (Milonakis and Fine 2007: 49–51). They argue that "in the absence of markets, explaining the (historical) existence of another institution (labour services) through a cost/benefit analysis in relation to the market is historically meaningless" (Milonakis and Fine 2007: 50).

Much of the import of this problem depends on how one defines transaction costs and why they are considered to be important. One influential viewpoint within the NIE tradition sees transaction costs as primarily applicable to capitalist market society, where they are relevant precisely *because* in such a society there must be many economic phenomena other than private contracting: one could otherwise not account for money, firms, public regulation, and other such things (Furubotn and Richter 1991: 11). However, this already assumes an equilibrium framework of perfect competition and attempts to explain phenomena at variance with it by reference to the nonexistence of this perfectly competitive benchmark, which is not the most analytically convincing maneuver. The same goes for defining transaction costs as the cost of market exchange itself. As Ankarloo (2002a) points out, this entire approach has to veer between Scylla and Charybdis. If one takes the mainstream NIE approach cited above, then if transaction costs are the price of the price mechanism—the costs of information within the market—there must be a price of the price of the price mechanism, namely the costs of finding out the level of transaction costs, and so forth ad infinitum.

The alternative course steers to Northian formulations. North at various stages defines transaction costs as "the underlying costs of exchange" (North 1989: 661), "the costs entailed in the measurement and enforcement of agreements" (North 2005: 53), and "resources devoted to the process of exchange" (North 2005: 65), and he insists that "the costliness of information is the key to the costs of transacting" (North 1990: 27). Although the last formulation has the problems of regression mentioned, the other formulations can be taken to imply that transaction costs are rather to be measured as the cost of the institutional apparatus necessary to sustain and enforce property rights. This has the advantage of not being self-referential. But then, as Ankarloo points out, one falls into the other problem: in that case, institutions cannot be explained by transaction costs, because nonmarket institutions do not carry market prices, and it is not obvious therefore how they are to be quantified or how individual agents are supposed to know what they are, especially in a world of costly information. If transaction costs act as a sort of 'shadow prices' of institutions, we can of course assume that agents will have perfect knowledge of what those costs are in a given case. The consequence is however that as rationality is assumed to be bounded in the NIEH framework, the explanatory power of modeling behavior as responses to transaction costs has to be limited accordingly (Ankarloo 2002a: 17–18, 2006: 8–10).

Certainly, North made serious attempts at estimating transaction costs empirically (most notably in Wallis and North 1986). But such efforts have not had the long-term comparative historical aspect that they require to really sustain the NIEH argument, whatever their merits for understanding the modern, capitalist market societies to which they have been applied. While some inspired by New Institutionalism have sought to measure 'non-market transaction costs', this has generally come in the shape of studies measuring the costs of obtaining government licenses or of finding trading partners, again as information and regulatory costs within the wider sphere of the market in market societies themselves (De Soto 1989; Benham and Benham 1998). There is no general consensus about how well these kinds of measurements reflect the concept of transaction costs generally. As Ning Wang points out, generally "what is measured or indexed in these studies is not transaction costs per se, but the cost of institutional inefficiency or poor governance" (Wang 2003: 8).

What is necessary for the Northian framework would be to find some quantifiable and historically and cross-culturally comparable measure of objective 'shadow costs' of institutions themselves, such as those that would have been known and knowable to the agents of those societies or, in North's terms, to the 'players of the game'. The arguments of critics like Ankarloo do not prove that this is impossible, but it is far from clear that much headway has been made into achieving such a measure, or that there is sufficient conceptual clarity to even render this aim achievable. Should it not be possible then that the NIEH's transaction cost framework falls afoul of the critiques of Milonakis and Fine and of Polanyi alike: the explanation of institutions by transaction costs is then a purely arbitrary, deductively imposed theoretical construct, one that rather serves the purpose of making the market benchmark relevant transhistorically than of explaining institutional variation.

Defining the Market: The Scope of the Market Concept

Another important aspect of thinking about markets in North's NIEH is his generalization of the concept beyond the economic sphere. An oft-repeated phrase in his later work is 'political and economic markets', invoked as a single conceptual phenomenon. This is important insofar as North's attitude toward markets is to understand how they can be made to function in an efficient manner, in other words, so as to minimize transaction costs and 'capture the gains from trade', in that curious formulation we have seen earlier. Especially in the last two stages of the NIEH, from *IICEP* onward, North is quite explicit that an important aim of his entire project is to explain "how, and under what conditions, humans create the conditions that make for markets with low costs of transacting and increasing material well-being" (North 2005: 15).

North does however distinguish the welfare implications of both types of market, even while seeing efficient markets as one of the most important policy aims within his NIEH outlook: "As I use the term efficiency throughout this work I mean a condition in which, given the state of technology and information costs, the market has the lowest production and transaction costs attainable. In economic markets efficiency would coincide with improved material well-being, in political markets the welfare implications are more ambiguous" (North 2005: 15–16n3). The difference is for North that political markets are structured so as to inherently have high costs of information and a relationship between voting and welfare returns that is opaque (North 2005: 54). One cannot realistically hope to achieve efficient political markets, therefore; and even if one did, it is less clear that this would be positive in welfare terms. On previous occasions, he had already doubted that we would know what a Pareto-efficient governmental structure would mean (North 1984: 256).

Even so, on certain occasions North also clarifies what he thinks that type of efficiency in the 'political market' would look like (if we did have it): "Just as the efficiency of an economic market can be measured by the degree to which the competitive structure, through arbitrage and efficient information feedback, mimics or approximates the conditions of a zero-transaction-cost framework, so an efficient political market would be one in which constituents accurately evaluate the policies pursued by competing candidates in terms of the net effect on their well-being; in which only legislation (or regulation) that maximized the aggregate income of the affected parties to the exchange would be enacted; and in which compensation to those adversely affected would ensure that no party was injured by the action" (North 1993: 66–67; see also North 2005: 53). This is the standard Pareto efficiency criterion from mainstream economics. The main issue for North does not therefore seem to rest in any significant methodological distinction between the study of politics and economic exchange, but rather in the difficulty of removing the barriers to efficiency in the political case.

In *VSO*, this extension is taken further. The distinction between natural state orders and open access societies, the main topic of the book and its most important theoretical innovation, rests for an important part on the idea that open access societies are more competitive and that this competition takes place in an institutionally well-organized way, emphasizing low barriers to entry. North and colleagues however speak very generally of terms like 'exchange' and 'competition' in this book, so that the attributes they ascribe to such competition in the open access order—invariably positive ones—appear to apply to those societies as a whole. A case in point is the discussion of impersonality in the book, by which is meant the treatment of individuals as essentially equal and interchangeable (one might say as consumers) rather than on the basis of personal status, dynasty, patronage, and so forth. Impersonality is positive because of its effect on competition in society. The authors write: "Competition in an open access order, therefore, differs from competition in natural states for another critical reason beyond limitations on competition through violence… Impersonality fundamentally changes the nature of competition. Impersonal markets and impersonal exchange are not just a theoretical ideal in economics; they are a feature of open access societies. Individuals and organizations pursue rents as vigorously in an open access society as they do in a natural state, but impersonal economic and political competition result in the rapid erosion of rents" (North, Wallis, and Weingast 2009: 23).

With markets and exchange being here distinguished, one is left to wonder what this exchange may be that is apparently also market-like. Although elsewhere in the book it appears to refer sometimes to market transactions,[2] in this case it may refer to his earlier concept of 'human exchange', which is bound up in turn with the idea of agents (individuals or organizations) as 'entrepreneurs', both concepts found already in *IICEP*. Not only are agents players of the game, where the game consists of the institutional rules and norms of the society, but they are also entrepreneurs when acting (usually as organizations) to change that institutional rule set to their own benefit, "at some margin" (North 1990: 8). Institutions in turn give shape to 'human exchange', which in this way becomes a quasi-market covering all aspects of human society: "[institutions] structure incentives in *human exchange, whether political, social, or economic*" (North 1990: 3, emphasis added).

Note that this market benchmark operates for him independently of motive, as is clarified in *UPEC*: "It is something else again exactly what the intentions of the players are. The overall direction of economic change will reflect the aggregate of choices made by political and economic entrepreneurs with widely diverse objectives, most of them not concerned with the consequences for overall performance" (North 2005: 79). These entrepreneurs need not have economic performance at the macroeconomic level in mind. Rather more likely, North seems to suggest, their aim is "lining the pockets of the players"—individual self-regard in a market or market-like process (North 2005: 79). But insofar as this entrepreneurialism regarding institutions—constrained by the usual bounded rationality—generates economic competition in an efficient market, it will have efficient consequences: "The Smithian result ensues" (North

[2] For example, North, Wallis, and Weingast (2009: 114).

2005: 80). The open access order is, in this sense, merely the outcome of that entrepreneurial process if it goes right.

From a norm about markets, the characteristics of efficient competition have here been transferred firstly to 'political competition', and then to open access societies in general. Similarly, North's terminology of 'entrepreneurship' that operates 'at some margin' according to 'incentives' in 'human exchange' is all designed to suggest an equation at the methodological and ontological level between major domains of past and present societies and market-like exchange relations. This gives the rhetorical effect of dissolving different aspects of a social-institutional order into the institutional framework of markets specifically. After all, entrepreneurs are in economic parlance individuals who in a market setting pursue arbitrage opportunities to obtain profit (Endres and Woods 2006: 191–192). Similarly, 'at some margin' invokes a marginalist approach to market equilibrium and incentives apply to the self-regarding behavior of individuals given a particular set of payoffs over a range of different choice possibilities.

All these terms are not only directly derived from mainstream economic theory and carry no particular new institutional content to distinguish them from neoclassical approaches, but moreover are normally applied to cases of consumers, traders, or other agents in market settings. Normally, such terminology is not worth noting by itself, as all are common and well-established concepts in economics. But in this specific context, the picture changes. North had to demonstrate in the first place that nonmarket phenomena, in market societies and *a fortiori* in nonmarket societies in the past, can be analyzed by methods normally applied only to market exchange. In this way, North fails to establish the relevance of his terminology. One is inclined to conclude that far from making that case against Polanyi's challenge directly, he achieves it by rhetorical sleight of hand.

However tiresome the scare quotes may be, it is important to draw attention to North's discourse in this regard. Where he does not offer explicit theorizing, often his rhetorical usages reveal the underlying preconceptions. There we find precisely those that suggest North resorts time and again to reimagining the institutional organization of society transhistorically as an (as if) market structure—the very phenomenon

Polanyi had criticized, and the NIEH is therefore not supposed to simply reproduce. Such a conflation is pervasive in North's later works. While the micro-level of his theory is concerned with cognition and beliefs, and the macro-level with adaptive efficiency, the meso-level is the realm of the interaction between individuals their institutional environment. It is at this level that the distinction between what is market and what is not market becomes difficult for him to maintain, despite the importance of the distinction between institutions, agents, and economic behavior for the coherence of his overall framework. The market benchmark returns with a vengeance, now not at the level of history, but at the level of theory. Where Polanyi saw markets as embedded in society, North suggests society is embedded in markets.

The Smithian Dimension

As we have just seen, in the more developed stages of his NIEH theory, North recurrently makes use of the concept of the 'Smithian result' (or equivalent phrases). This term serves him as shorthand, it seems, to describe the efficiency and coordination results one can expect from well-functioning—that is to say, institutionally well-supported—modern markets. The Smithian result is supposed to emerge from the market-like entrepreneurial behavior of the political entrepreneurs, at least if their institutional entrepreneurship manages to bring about the prerequisites of efficient markets. This concept requires further examination if we are to understand North's market theory. What is this result, and what does Adam Smith have to do with it?

The full quotation in *UPEC* states that "when economic markets are so structured that the players compete via price and quality rather than at non-productive margins then the Smithian result ensues" (North 2005: 80). This seems to capture a rather more neoclassical-institutionalist insight, one that has affinities with the public choice literature: not the trade-off between markets and hierarchies, but more that between rent-seeking through nonmarket means and the pursuit of marginal advantages within the market. North is more specific when a little later in *UPEC* he points to a number of problems with the neoclassical model that reduces it, and the Smithian result with it, to this special case status. As we shall see, there are four such problems. First, the 'movement from personal to impersonal exchange' is necessary to obtain the Smithian result. This requires 'fundamental rethinking at odds with our genetic heritage', namely by shifting from small-group cooperation to large-group noncooperative coordination (more on this in the following chapters). What one needs is therefore for markets to become general and large in scale, so that the necessary 'impersonality' is the result.

Second, "Adam Smith's specialization and division of labor—the necessary condition for achieving such markets—is really specialization of knowledge" (North 2005: 84). This, North argues, cannot be done by a 'price system' alone, and requires institutional support to coordinate and achieve public goods. Third, and perhaps most importantly, there is a direct relationship between market competition and the 'Smithian result'. And this is not easy: for "all well-functioning factor and product markets must be structured to provide incentives for the players to compete at those margins, and those margins alone, that induce growing productivity. Only then do we realize Smith's beneficent result. Moreover, in a dynamic world with changing technology, information costs, and politics there is nothing automatic about the structure changing in response to these changing parameters to continue to produce efficient markets". Fourthly, achieving all this requires strong political support, perhaps even initiative, and this in turn demands political institutions strong enough to generate and sustain public goods, but weak enough not to interfere with market efficiency or individual property rights (North 2005: 84–85).

What we are told about the 'Smithian' view of markets is then this: that with his name is associated a 'beneficent result', the nature of which is not stated, if and only if markets are structured in a competitive way such that they foster productivity increases. But this beneficent result is a matter not just of channeling competition through markets, but also of having as general a market structure as possible: only by politically and institutionally providing for scale and scope in market exchange does one achieve "the potential envisioned by Adam Smith when he viewed the wealth of nations as being a function of the size of markets" (North 2005: 84). But one additional problem for achieving Smith's result is a Hayekian problem of ignorance of these advantages of the market, so that they fail to translate politically: people do not sufficiently realize the correctness of this Smithian analysis of markets, and this prevents a structuring of political and economic institutions favorable to it. As North suggests, "It is more than two hundred years since Adam Smith explained the underlying sources of the wealth of nations but the extent to which such views are embedded in the decision-making process of those shaping political/economic change is problematic… Adam Smith's wealth of nations was a function of specialization and division of labor. But the logic of specialization and division of labor implies a world in which individuals know a great deal about their specialty but in consequence know less about the rest of their world. Hayek emphasized the crucial additional point that in consequence individuals can have only a very imperfect understanding of the overall character of the political/economic system" (North 2005: 156, 162).

Although on other occasions North does refer more explicitly to Adam Smith's actual writings on the eighteenth-century commercial economy,[3] the strong impression generated here is that Smith is not really invoked as an economic thinker, but rather as a shorthand for a particular model of the capitalist market. Smith stands for the belief that competitive and well-structured markets are ultimately both beneficial in economic terms and have the capacity to coordinate individual actions and desires in a society large enough that most interactions are impersonal and noncooperative. North simply uses Smith to represent an assumption about the overall desirability of competitive markets, but to also point to the difficulties of achieving and sustaining such markets at the level of institutional and political support. Using Smith to make the neoclassical analysis of efficient factor markets (perfect competition) a special case of a more general—and considerably less optimistic—institutionalist framework allows North to take the desirability and efficiency of classical competitive markets for granted and to shift the subject of contention to a deeper level 'beneath' the market, namely the so-called artifactual structure.

One may wonder how much this view really has to do with Adam Smith's own work; indeed, North seems singularly unconcerned with this question, despite the extensive literature on the complexities of Smith's

[3] North, Wallis, and Weingast (2009: 205).

writings and the degree to which the view of Smith as the founder of 'free market economics' is a misrepresentation (Lamb 1974; Brown 1997; Kennedy 2009). I would argue that this use of Smith serves a triple purpose:

1. 'Smith' stands for the way markets can turn coordination problems into mutually beneficial solutions, an attribution that not coincidentally has a pedigree in game theoretical approaches in economics and public choice theory.
2. 'Smith' stands for the ability of markets to promote the division of labor, distribute scarce knowledge, increase productivity, and other economic behavior that is beneficial for economic growth and thereby for general well-being (this is clear from North's references to the 'wealth of nations').
3. Smith's 'two faces'—his emphasis on the way markets enable cooperative solutions to strategic games and his interest in their background in personal sympathy and moral values—represent each of the two aspects of North's own approach to markets: the special case (perfect competition with ideal results) described by neoclassical theory and the general case for which the emphasis must be on social institutions (norms and values as rules of the game). In both cases, Smith can be said to stand for the suggestion that society works best when both the market itself is relatively free, competitive, and impersonal, *and* the normative institutional order is oriented toward market exchange.[4]

To substantiate this reading, an illustrative passage can be found where North argues that "the central focus is on the problem of human cooperation – specifically the cooperation that permits economies to capture the gains from trade that were the key to Adam Smith's *Wealth of Nations*. The evolution of institutions that create an hospitable environment for cooperative solutions to complex exchange provides for economic growth" (North 1990: vii).[5] That trade has such gains, and that they can be captured by institutional arrangements that allow an approximation of

[4] See Smith (1998) for an argument along these lines.
[5] See also North (2005: 62).

competitive, open, and nonrent-seeking markets, is taken as given. In the background of such an assumption seems to be North's commitment to what one might call a classical or ordoliberal perspective on society, something which comes to the fore in his contractarian approach to the formation of institutions. North made little secret of his fundamental political sympathy with the classical liberal tradition (Klein and Daza 2013). Although in this book I am not primarily concerned with the political-intellectual biography of North, it cannot be avoided when discussing the policy elements of his work, and it seems to me relevant here in his peculiar invocation of Smith. His classical liberalism can be seen as one of the two sides of his intellectual coin, his overall worldview of how society works, which in this social scientific context I call his anthropology.

North certainly was not a believer in zero or minimal government, and always emphasized the importance of the role of the state in enabling and enforcing positive, market-sustaining institutions. To say that North's politics have classical liberal influences is not to reduce his theory to his political views, or to say that it stands or falls with it, nor is it to simple-mindedly accuse North of being a *laissez faire* enthusiast in the style of pseudo-'Smithians' associated with the Adam Smith Institute and similar bodies. For North, as for the actual Adam Smith, the institutional-normative context of markets is at least as important for what markets do as the degree of *laissez faire*. But he equally was not a supporter of a large distributional role for the state or intervention beyond that necessary for achieving the Smithian result.

In an essay for the American rightwing magazine *National Review*, he made clear that "from my perspective, individual liberty is inextricably entwined with the options—the alternatives—available to individuals in a society. By this definition individual liberty has been seriously eroded. The choices of occupations, the decision to hire, fire, or promote employees, the exploitation of natural resources, the establishment of new enterprises, the determination of quality standards for products, the disposition of one's earnings all are increasingly more circumscribed than in the past...What have we obtained in return—greater economic security for individuals, a more desirable distribution of income, the reduction of environmental deterioration? Aside from the difficulty of agreeing about what is a desirable distribution of income, the assessment of these benefits (particularly as compared to hypothetical alternatives) would differ widely… the cost in terms of my definition of individual liberty has been substantial" (North 1983: 812).

This same classical liberal anthropology is everywhere in evidence: we have his sanguine view of the benefits of free markets, his attachment to strong rules of private property, his belief in the Western market order as it has emerged since the nineteenth century as a model 'open access order' that has—in his schema of state orders—virtually exclusively positive traits, and his striving, where it can be achieved, for a free market with a sharply circumscribed sphere of government combined with a high degree of individual liberty. This is one side of North's anthropology, and one that perhaps best explains the rather underdeveloped and underargued attachment to the inherent benefits of well-ordered markets in his work. Certainly, he sometimes buttressed the development economics implications of his argument with observations about the benefits of such market societies for economic growth or 'economic performance', and to that extent provided some support for this view. I will discuss these arguments in more detail in chap. 5, when focusing on the implications of his NIEH from a global development perspective. On the whole, however, the point is left implicit. That capturing the gains from trade is good for everyone and that the Smithian result, should it be achieved, is obviously desirable is taken for granted in most of his work. In that regard, there always remained traces of the "right wing reactionary" economist, learning his basic lessons about the virtues of the market in order to dispel his original Marxist notions, as he late in life portrayed his younger self (North 2009).

Smith, Hayek, and the Classical Liberal Social Contract Tradition

Now let us consider North's contractarian view of institutions and his emphasis on gradual reform as ways of thinking about how social institutions emerge and change. An important role in strengthening this classical liberal perspective is played by the thought of Friedrich Hayek, the famous liberal theorist and economic thinker. Hayek's influence on North's work cannot be overstated, and I will discuss it in more detail when I broach the topic of cultural evolution, one of his main concepts. But additionally he served, among other things, as the lens through which North viewed the meaning of Smith and his liberal institutionalist tradition in social contract thinking. His contractarianism and his interest in institution formation and the role of beliefs in the functioning of markets all converged in North's adaptation of another central Hayekian concept, spontaneous order.

North was quite explicit about the influence Hayek and his intellectual genealogy had on his own work. On one occasion, he declared Hayek to have been the "the greatest economist of the twentieth century, and by a long way" and even "if you look for people who really want to try and understand the world, Hayek came closer to that ideal than anybody who has ever lived".[6] On one occasion, North discussed at greater length the contribution of Hayek to his own understanding of the process of economic change (North 1999). His discussion of Hayek focuses in particular on how Hayek has helped us understand how intentionality and institutions contribute to generating economic change as well as constraining such change within the boundaries of inherited belief and normative systems. Moreover, in this paper North himself suggests a union of Hayek's insights with the 'Smithian' concept of expanding market exchange as driver of increases in productivity. This forms for him the basis of his approach to the study of economic transformation.

Deriving from the thinkers of the Scottish Enlightenment in particular, such as Adam Smith (at least as invoked by North), as well as David Hume and Adam Ferguson, the concept of spontaneous order suggests the aggregation of the actions of very many individuals in such a way that society can avoid the doom—as invoked by Thomas Hobbes—of a *bellum omnium contra omnes*. The notion of spontaneous order suggests an alignment of norms, beliefs, and practices such that a cooperative order ensues in which the whole is more than merely the conflict between its parts. In the classical liberal interpretation of this approach, in particular in the tradition of Herbert Spencer and Friedrich Hayek, this idea is

[6] Cited in Klein and Daza (2013: 531).

further specified. In this tradition, it is economic coordination through the market that enables cooperation, and to be precise, cooperation through the economic action of self-interested individuals.

It is this conception of social cooperation as an essentially exchange-like phenomenon, and one best coordinated by an explicit market process, that connects Smith, Hayek, and, ultimately, North. For Hayek, it was specifically the problem of limited information, implying the ubiquity of tacit and local knowledge, that made cooperation only possible through market coordination. As Peter Boettke sums up Hayek's interpretation of the Smithian legacy: "The voluntary action of thousands of individuals, each pursuing their own interests, generates and utilizes economic information that is not available to any one individual or group of individuals in its totality… Smith's case for economic liberty amounts to an argument and demonstration that individuals pursuing their self-interest can, and will, produce a social order that is economically beneficial… It is this emphasis on the use of contextual knowledge that underlies the critical defense of the liberal order from Smith to Hayek" (Boettke 1990: 64–65). This, then, is the Smithian social contract, via Hayek: even given cognitive limitations, the pursuit of self-interest by individuals in market exchange will create a form of cooperation that creates order instead of violence and has desirable economic effects. Agents do not need to be perfectly rational for this to occur; if anything, it is rather their *lack* of information and their uncertainty that spurs them toward creating order out of chaos.

In this liberal contractarian tradition one can trace through Spencer and Hayek, and then we find two vehicles of such coordination: the free market, as seen above, and the sphere of social institutions. The latter coordinates the psychological or cultural propensities or norms of individuals in much the same way that the market, through the price mechanism, coordinates their local information (beliefs) and preferences. Institutions constitute the 'order' implied in spontaneous order, a social arrangement that can be more or less favorable to the operations of decentralized market exchange. As Boettke summarizes the Hayekian view: "The key question for the social theorist is how the various and diverse images of reality that individual minds develop could ever be coordinated to one another. The social institutions that arise through the voluntary association of thousands of individuals serve to guide individuals in the process of mutual accommodation" (Boettke 1990: 69). Through the spontaneous formation of institutions, and through the process of market exchange, a spontaneous order—a form of collective cooperation—arises. Not coincidentally, this emphasis on *order* as the (desired) outcome of collective action, either as the form taken by cooperation or as the preconditions for it, is found also throughout *VSO*. Order as in safety from violence is a precondition; order in the sense of a (more or less) stable set of institutions with welfare-enhancing properties (welfare-enhancing, that is, relative to the Hobbesian state of nature) is the result.

Hayek's ideas in *The Sensory Order* (Hayek 1952) and elsewhere are also the foundation of North's shift toward cognitive science and the centrality of how beliefs are formed, which frame the discussion in *UPEC*, arguably his most developed theoretical monograph. Equally, his NIE analysis in terms of institutions and path dependence is, for North, "complementary to and in the spirit of his framework" (North 1990: 84). Ultimately, for North "our economic history can be rendered intelligible in a Hayekian framework", joining an evolutionary approach to cognition and trial and error to the New Institutionalist conceptual toolset and the argument, shared by North and Hayek alike, that getting the institutions right is a question of fulfilling the promise of "Smith's happy conclusion" (North 1990: 95, 86).

North's Pessimistic Anthropology

The difficulty with this perspective is the question of how desirable results should come about by means of coordination, and indeed whether this leads to desirable results at all. In the Spencer-Mandeville tradition, the outcome of the process of spontaneous order is often depicted as optimizing, so that ours is the 'best of all possible worlds', or would be if we let the process do its work. In the Hayekian tradition, such optimization and efficiency is explicitly disavowed: for Hayek, there was nothing about coordination neither through the market nor through social institutions that necessitated any kind of optimality about the result, only the impossibility of improving on it by any form of *pre-planned* coordinating action, especially by the state (Boettke 1990: 75–76). For David Ramsay Steele, this claim—particularly strong in Hayek's work of the 1980s, such as *Knowledge, Evolution, and Society* (Hayek 1983)—entails a change in Hayek's own relationship to the classical liberal tradition of spontaneous order: from a liberal claim that the resulting order would be one characterized by desirable traits of cooperation to the conservative claim that however undesirable the order, it simply is as it is and cannot be consciously improved upon (Steele 1987).

Although whether or not this entails a shift within Hayek's own perspective is disputed, it is perhaps illustrative for Hayek's influence on North that the latter has followed a somewhat similar trajectory: from the efficiency contractarian approach, where the medieval manor was as it was because it was optimal that way, to an explicit disclaiming of such optimality, preferring to see—as Hayek did—the process of institutional change as an often-decidedly *inefficient* process. Like Hayek, he reorients the discussion away from the efficiency characteristics of a particular economic order to the evolution of institutional orders in general, where any optimality is at best local and temporal, but where the evolutionary characteristics of institutions and market exchange join together to form *some* spontaneous order, even if it is from the viewpoint of neoclassical economic efficiency a bad one. However, as Viktor Vanberg has noted for Hayek's case, this leaves open the question of why it is that the evolution of institutions should be such that it favors cooperative outcomes, as the idea of spontaneous order being represented by the free market suggests (Vanberg 1986: 83).

That North's theoretical inspiration, and indeed often normative standpoint regarding what form of institutionalized cooperation is most desirable from an economic point of view, derives much from Hayek, and his interpretation of the larger classical liberal contractarian tradition ('Smith') is therefore beyond doubt. But for North, this has been an impetus to study precisely the *problems* of coordination, with an emphasis on the frequent failure of the 'right' combination of institutions and market exchange to come about. North's comparative economic historical research gives it a decidedly more pessimistic cast. In a Hayekian vein, North excoriates the unrealistic nature of assuming optimizing forms of rationality and complete information. But the more he does so, in other words the more restrained individual reason is posited to be, the more difficult it becomes to see how a spontaneous order emerging from such reason could have the desirable properties associated with cooperation that the Smithian tradition (as interpreted by North) implies. This applies in particular when such reason is assumed to be self-interested.

The spontaneous pursuit of self-interested action therefore can have decidedly undesirable outcomes, which is a major challenge to the more 'Panglossian' version of the spontaneous order tradition. As Vanberg notes, the problem here is that this tradition needs to distinguish between coordination problems, which are self-enforcing once individuals can be brought together to pursue collective action, and those kinds of problems, exemplified by the prisoner's dilemma, where "there is no 'natural' harmony between constitutional and action interests, even if there is perfect agreement on the former between all members of the community" (Vanberg 1994: 65).[7]

For North, moreover, one cannot ultimately expect the decentralized free market to do the work of coordinating, so as to make the 'Smithian' cooperative result possible, if one does not have the proper institutional structure. This proper structure therefore needs to come about, not only despite coordination problems, but also despite prisoner's dilemma type situations. We can therefore read North as putting on the research agenda the integration of the two into a single account of how institutions and the state (or 'elites') mediate between both sets of problems. To do this, he must sustain a flexible and in a sense pessimistic account of the limits to individual rationality and the suboptimality or inefficiency of many real-life historical orders. Simultaneously, he argues for an account of market exchange that legitimates the assumption that, given the 'right' institutional order, in this kind of situation the problem will be mainly of the coordination type, and not of the prisoner's dilemma type.

Cooperation in the normative sense depends then on the evolution and 'spontaneous' emergence of the right norms and rules (as well as psychological states such as trust and the right beliefs), such that they

[7] I will discuss the underlying game theoretical argument concerning the 'players of the game', and the significance of the prisoner's dilemma and other coordination and cooperation problems for this aspect of North's approach, more fully in the next chapter.

become self-enforcing; 'right' being defined as being favorable to the 'Smithian' process of mutual advantage through market exchange. The payoffs in the prisoner's dilemma game will be changed so that the results are a coordination problem, one for which the Hayekian tradition of markets and spontaneous order has already established a solution. In short, in this tradition one can say the cooperative outcome first and foremost *is* the 'Smithian result'. But it is not easy to see how it can be achieved, if one does not trust too much in the inherent success of 'spontaneity'.

Therefore, to return to the two sides of the Northian coin, the verso side of his anthropology—or worldview—is also important in the context of the Smithian result. This is what I call his 'pessimistic anthropology'. Characteristic of North's intellectual two-steps-forward, one-step-back pattern is how he combines his insistence on the merits of the institutionally supported free market with an equally strong pessimism about the likelihood of achieving it. Pessimism is indeed generally a characteristic of his work, and one that increases in visibility over time. One could even summarize the main lesson of *VSO*, and to a lesser extent also of *UPEC* and his work in the second stage of the NIEH, as this: it's not the market itself that is at fault, but the difficulty of getting the institutional infrastructure to make it work, that is the problem. The importance of the concept of constraints on choice in North manifests itself because, again, the consequences of choice are not the issue but the limits on our abilities and cooperation are. North's description of institution formation and its problems is larded with negatives: uncertainty, lack of information, failure of incentives to align, failure of beliefs to correspond to reality, failure to adapt in the face of change, inability to form lasting agreements, selfish elites, selfish individuals and organizations, and, ultimately, the manifold inborn limitations of our human mind.

North sums up his viewpoint well at the end of *UPEC*, when he intones: "The way in which beliefs → institutions → organizations → policies → outcomes evolves has led to unparalleled economic well-being and to endless disasters and human misery… We have now come to understand enough about institutions to be able to pinpoint the sources of poor performance. They have their origins in path dependence. We inherit the artifactual structure—the institutions, beliefs, tools, techniques, external symbol storage systems—from the past. Broadly speaking this is our cultural heritage and we ignore it in decision making at our peril—the peril of failing in our attempt to improve economic performance. The degree to which such cultural heritage is 'malleable' via deliberate modification is still very imperfectly understood. At any time it imposes severe constraints on the ability to effectuate change" (North 2005: 155–156). In other words: we know that the Smithian result is what we want to obtain. We also know what institutions are needed, namely a classical liberal society, with the right rules of the game, such as strong private property, limited but strong states, and the right belief systems that promote free market(-like) competition in economics and politics. However, we simply cannot get there, because there are too many interlocking obstacles in the way.

The mind is willing, but the flesh is weak. So North argues throughout his final works, and to think one can simply impose the right framework and get the expected results is futile.[8] He has set up his own system so as to endogenize as many social-institutional elements as possible to understand the emergence and performance of markets. Now he has too many mutually dependent variables and, so, despairs of anyone's ability to get them all lined up in the proper way. This is the shadow side to the Smithian result: it may be that open access orders have all the desired traits to bring it about and to provide sufficient robustness to keep doing so in the face of a changing environment. But as North and colleagues lament in *VSO*, most societies today are not open access orders by their definition, and show few signs of becoming so. Never mind the societies of the premodern past.

Viewed from the *longue durée*, therefore, things do not look good for the feasibility of the desired classical liberal society with its Smithian properties: that ideal social contract—based on low barriers to entry, open competition in all spheres, and the Hobbesian violence of natural states sublated into the peaceful process of economic and political entrepreneurship—turns out to be one rarely agreed to by any historical social formation. The operation of path dependence, in which each historical step has irreversible consequences for the next, turns out to be so severely

[8] As emphasized at the end of *VSO*: North, Wallis, and Weingast (2009: 271).

restricting that even the slightest misstep of a society on the road to open access orders and their "world of plenty" (North, Wallis, and Weingast 2009: 272) spells doom for a society's adaptive efficiency in the long run, and therewith its ability to achieve that cornucopia of happiness.

Conclusion

Is North then guilty of Ankarloo's charge, that his NIEH is an 'as if' economic history—that is to say that it is a theory that treats nonmarket phenomena *as if* they are markets, and explains their existence and function by reference to limits on markets? By and large, the answer must be yes. North in fact maintains a market benchmark, by which I mean a tendency throughout his work to explain social phenomena in a 'Whiggish' way as if all social institutions are only explicable in terms of their constraining or enabling effect on 'the market'. Polanyi's point, that one must first investigate whether market exchange, large-scale commodification, and private property in factors of production actually play the dominant role in a given society, is ignored in practice, despite North's evident rhetorical willingness to accept the historically limited role of markets. North does this not by contesting the latter claim, but by changing the question: he throughout investigates social phenomena according to the benchmark that he would come to call the 'open access order', and asks why societies did not get there at a given point in time. Whereby, moreover, he often does not sufficiently clearly distinguish between the desirability of efficient markets as a normative criterion and an explanation in terms of market failure as an analytical instrument. The weakness of such a negatively formulated question is that there can always be any number of reasons why something did not happen at a given time, while it requires a much more tightly knit causal account to explain why something did. This opens the door to a great deal of speculative, 'just-so' stories.

As I have argued, North derives and justifies this market benchmark via his concept of the Smithian result, which stands in for a series of beneficial, even ideal, properties of well-supported free markets in terms of social cooperation and economic performance. This idea appears to find its origin in the Hayekian tradition of viewing markets, and market-like calculation, as the spontaneous coordinator that enables social order. But North gives to the Hayekian formulation also a pessimistic coloring. Hayek initially assumed that spontaneous orders mediated by the market would lead to desirable results, and later in life appears to have argued that even where they did not, they could not be improved upon. North accepts his general view, but disputes the spontaneity: for him, institutions are always created rather than born. This leaves him, however, with a very pessimistic view of the human capacity to create such orders as would bring about the Smithian result. The relevance and applicability of this result is never in question, and North's politics are thoroughly committed to the classical liberal 'open access order' as the ultimate *desideratum*. Consequently, North's historiographical response to Polanyi's challenge ends up being a tale not of a 'great transformation' from non-market to market society—as Polanyi's was (Polanyi 1944)—but of an overwhelming and repeated failure to transform. The history of all hitherto existing institutions is, with a few happy exceptions in the developed West, the history of human failure.

This puts one more in mind of Edward Gibbon than of the quantitative rigors of mainstream economics or the anthropological history proposed by Polanyi: "history, which is, indeed, little more than the register of the crimes, follies, and misfortunes of mankind" (Gibbon 2003 [1776]: 53). As I will discuss later in this book, North did intend his work to have usable policy prescriptions for development economics, as well as historiographical significance for understanding the 'great divergence' between rich and poor nations. But the market benchmark remains an obstacle to the NIEH's ability to really work as *history*. Firstly, it is not sufficiently theoretically justified in its own right unless one accepts the Smithian-Hayekian political and ideological framework from the beginning. This contrasts with Polanyi's approach, which although in various ways is incomplete and deficient in clear analytical structure, bases its approach on a much more historically anchored concept of institutional differentiation via the notion of embeddedness.[9]

[9] Similarly, a much less sanguine view of the operation of 'the Smithian result' of the market itself, showing the negative effect increasing market exchange has had on social institutions in various historical settings, can be found in the pioneering work of Van Bavel (2016).

Secondly, there is historiographical dispute about to what extent negative questions—why something did not happen—are productive frameworks for inquiry, in particular in the history of science where they tend to most frequently appear. Although some have argued for their necessity (e.g. Brush 2007), this is mainly to support a systematic comparative approach, of the kind Polanyi also undertook. North, however, never undertakes such an approach: as his critics have argued, he tends to use historical cases exclusively for illustrative purposes and his willingness to cross time and space in selecting them has the character of cherry-picking.[10] Without such a systematic comparative framework, a negative question is to my mind at much greater risk of imposing extraneous and irrelevant assumptions onto the subject matter than a simpler positive causal question would.[11] Much of the larger framework of North's NIEH has, I suspect, actually no need for the market benchmark or the Smithian-Hayekian assumptions about it. It is only his scientific commitment to defending the discipline of economics by extending transaction cost economics and his political commitment to classical liberalism that make it so. Shorn of these, one would certainly lose much of the remaining connection with NIE and adjacence to more orthodox economics. But there would also be much to gain.

References

Ankarloo, Daniel. 2002a. New Institutional Economics and Economic History. *Capital & Class* 26 (9): 9–36.

———. 2002b. *Using Karl Polanyi as a Stepping Stone for a Critique of the New Institutionalist Orthodoxy.* Paper presented to CRIC Workshop 'Polanyian Perspectives on Instituted Economic Processes: Development and Transformation', Manchester, 23–25 October.

[10] A case in point would be the way *VSO* freely roams from the Aztec empire to the Carolingians, Napoleonic France and Norman Britain, or the use of the Soviet case to demonstrate the preconceived argument concerning adaptive efficiency in *UPEC*.

[11] To some extent of course, the one can be reformulated as the other. But Cohen (2010) is an excellent example of a study that asks why a major transformation (the Scientific Revolution) did occur when and where it did, based on a comparative study of cases where it did not. The negative provides the benchmark; the positive the question.

———. 2006. *New Institutional Economics and Economic History: A Case of Economics Imperialism*. Paper presented to Historical Materialism Conference, London, 8–10 December.

Ankarloo, Daniel, and Giulio Palermo. 2004. Anti-Williamson: A Marxian Critique of New Institutional Economics. *Cambridge Journal of Economics* 28 (3): 413–429.

Benham, Alexandra, and Lee Benham. 1998. *The Costs of Exchange*, Ronald Coase Institute Working Paper no. 1.

Boettke, Peter. 1990. The Theory of Spontaneous Order and Cultural Evolution in the Social Theory of F.A. Hayek. *Cultural Dynamics* 3 (1): 61–83.

Brown, Vivienne. 1997. Mere Inventions of the Imagination: A Survey of Recent Literature on Adam Smith. *Economics and Philosophy* 13: 281–312.

Brush, Stephen G. 2007. Suggestions for the Study of Science. In *Positioning the History of Science*, ed. Kostas Gavroglu and Jürgen Renn, 13–25. Dordrecht: Springer Netherlands.

Cohen, H. Floris. 2010. *How Modern Science Came into the World*. Amsterdam: Amsterdam University Press.

De Soto, Hernando. 1989. *The Other Path: The Invisible Revolution in the Third World*. New York: Harper & Row.

Endres, Anthony M., and Christine Rachel Woods. 2006. Modern Theories of Entrepreneurial Behavior: A Comparison and Appraisal. *Small Business Economics* 26 (2): 189–202.

Furubotn, Eirik G., and Rudolf Richter. 1991. The New Institutional Economics: An Assessment. In *The New Institutional Economics*, ed. Eirik G. Furubotn and Rudolf Richter, 1–34. Tübingen: J.C.B. Mohr.

Gibbon, Edward. 2003 [1776]. *The Decline and Fall of the Roman Empire*. Ed. Hans-Friedrich Mueller. New York: Random House.

Hayek, F.A. 1952. *The Sensory Order*. Chicago: University of Chicago Press.

———. 1983. *Knowledge, Evolution, and Society*. London: Adam Smith Institute.

Hodgson, Geoffrey M., and David Gindis. 2007. An Interview with Oliver Williamson. *Journal of Institutional Economics* 3 (3): 373–386.

Kennedy, Gavin. 2009. Adam Smith and the Invisible Hand: From Metaphor to Myth. *Econ Journal Watch* 6 (2): 239–263.

Klein, Daniel B., and Ryan Daza. 2013. Douglass C. North. *Economics Journal Watch* 10 (3): 525–532.

Lamb, Robert. 1974. Adam Smith's System: Sympathy, Not Self-Interest. *Journal of the History of Ideas* 35 (4): 671–682.

Milonakis, Dimitris, and Ben Fine. 2007. Douglass North's Remaking of Economic History: A Critical Appraisal. *Review of Radical Political Economics* 39 (1): 27–57.

North, Douglass C. 1977. Markets and Other Allocation Systems in History: The Challenge of Karl Polanyi. *Journal of European Economic History* 6 (3): 703–716.

———. 1983. Private Property and the American Way. *National Review*, 805–812, July 8.

———. 1984. Government and the Cost of Exchange in History. *The Journal of Economic History* 44 (2): 255–264.

———. 1989. A Transaction Cost Approach to the Historical Development of Polities and Economies. *Journal of Institutional and Theoretical Economics/Zeitschrift für die gesamte Staatswissenschaft* 145: 661–668.

———. 1990. *Institutions, Institutional Change and Economic Performance*. Cambridge: Cambridge University Press.

———. 1993. Toward a Theory of Institutional Change. In *Political Economy: Institutions, Competition, and Representation*, ed. William A. Barnett, Melvin Hinich, and Norman Schofield, 60–70. Cambridge: Cambridge University Press.

———. 1999. Hayek's Contribution to Understanding the Process of Economic Change. In *Freiheit, Wettsbewerb und Wirtschaftsordnung*, ed. Viktor Vanberg, 79–96. Freiburg: Haufe.

———. 2005. *Understanding the Process of Economic Change*. Princeton: Princeton University Press.

———. 2009. Interview with Karen Ilse Horn. In *Roads to Wisdom: Conversations with Ten Nobel Laureates in Economics*, ed. Karen Ilse Horn, 153–172. Cheltenham: Edward Elgar.

North, Douglass C., and Robert Paul Thomas. 1971. The Rise and Fall of the Manorial System: A Theoretical Model. *The Journal of Economic History* 31 (4): 777–803.

North, Douglass C., John Joseph Wallis, and Barry R. Weingast. 2009. *Violence and Social Orders: A Conceptual Framework for Interpreting Recorded Human History*. Cambridge: Cambridge University Press.

Polanyi, Karl. 1944. *The Great Transformation: The Economic and Political Origins of Our Time*. Boston: Beacon Press.

Polanyi, Karl, Conrad M. Arensberg, and Harry W. Pearson, eds. 1957. *Trade and Market in the Early Empires*. Glencoe: The Free Press.

Smith, Vernon L. 1998. The Two Faces of Adam Smith. *Southern Economic Journal* 65 (1): 2–19.

Steele, David Ramsay. 1987. Hayek's Theory of Cultural Group Selection. *Journal of Libertarian Studies* 8 (2): 171–195.
Van Bavel, Bas. 2016. *The Invisible Hand? How Market Economies Have Emerged and Declined Since 500 AD*. Oxford: Oxford University Press.
Vanberg, Viktor. 1986. Spontaneous Market Order and Social Rules. *Economics and Philosophy* 2 (1): 75–100.
———. 1994. *Rules and Choice in Economics*. New York: Routledge.
Wallis, John Joseph, and Douglass C. North. 1986. Measuring the Transaction Sector in the American Economy, 1870–1970. In *Long-Term Factors in American Economic Growth*, ed. Stanley L. Engerman and Robert E. Gallman, 95–162. Chicago: University of Chicago Press.
Wang, Ning. 2003. *Measuring Transaction Costs: An Incomplete Survey*, Ronald Coase Institute Working Paper no 2.
Williamson, Oliver E. 1975. *Markets and Hierarchies: Analysis and Antitrust Implications*. New York: Free Press.

4

Players of the Game: Rationality, Choice, and Indeterminacy

Introduction: The Two Legs of the NIEH Body

In this chapter, I will examine the interaction between the behavioral (choice) foundations of North's NIEH theory and the role of ideology, cognition, social learning, and other foundations for informal institutions within it. Since in this domain in particular North's distancing from neoclassical economics is most rhetorically marked, and yet at the same time most incomplete, this requires in part a review of the well-established debate around rationality and rational choice approaches in social theory. Considerations of space and coherence do not allow me to engage here in a full discussion of all aspects of the rationality assumptions common in mainstream economic theory and their problems, nor to fully explore the vast literature on free riding and the prisoner's dilemma. Rather, I will try to focus on a few salient elements of the mental foundations of behavior as depicted in North's approach: (bounded) rationality, ideology, and cooperation.

North's critique of rational choice economics is perhaps the clearest and the most distinct area of methodology in which he explicitly differentiated himself from what he saw as neoclassical economics. As we have

M. Krul, *The New Institutionalist Economic History of Douglass C. North*,
Palgrave Studies in the History of Economic Thought,
https://doi.org/10.1007/978-3-319-94084-7_4

seen, North initially shared with many NIE theorists a kind of rational choice institutionalism: an approach in which institutions are seen as rational solutions by individuals to the problems of coordination, property rights enforcement, and information acquisition created by market failure and imperfect information. The view of the medieval manor as an efficient solution to a trade-off between safety and private property defended in North and Thomas (1971) is a good example. With the birth of the NIEH, North distanced himself from this approach, and the first monograph of the first stage of the NIEH (North 1981) definitively marks the end of the efficiency interpretation of institutions.

Such an interpretation disappeared, I think, for two reasons. Firstly, it came under repeated criticism from colleagues who argued that it was unrealistic and failed to take historical and political power dynamics seriously (Fenoaltea 1975; Field 1981). Secondly, North was never too keen on defending it himself, as even the original papers make clear. Once he had familiarized himself with the challenge of Karl Polanyi, it must have been evident that rational choice institutionalism was woefully underequipped to address the problems Polanyi set out. Hence, North's own rhetorical questions about how one would even begin to address the problem of nonmarket allocation as a dominant economic form, or to explain government in a realistic way, or to address the path dependence—as he would later define it—in the long term of institutional history, when "economic theory is confined to the analysis of markets" (North 1977: 706). But he remained committed to the general idea that NIE theory, in turn based on the microfoundations of economic choice theory, would, or should, be able to address these issues. The question therefore became what kind of NIE theory could do so. This can be seen as the central research question of the NIEH in response to Polanyi's challenge and the huge temporal and conceptual domain of research North set for himself.

After abandoning the rational institutionalism of his pre-NIEH work, North attempted to refashion the NIE framework to incorporate a wider scope for different types of agency. This can be seen as a natural outcome of the search for a new model of agency after abandoning rational choice, but it is also the result of North's increasing interest in the *origin* of institutions, above and beyond their application in contexts of market failure.

If institutions cannot simply be assumed to be efficient responses to market failure, and their function in a model of economic behavior therefore simply deduced from some form of incomplete property rights or transaction costs, the question has to arise what does determine what shape institutions take and where they come from. This led North to a deeper investigation, roughly from the late 1980s onward, into the origins of institutions in different belief systems and in constraints on rationality. Beliefs, even worldviews and mental models of the world, play an increasingly important role in the NIEH, and with them the room for traditional forms of rational choice shrinks.

In the second stage of the NIEH, North then expanded this interest in bounded rationality and belief systems to an even more fundamental level, the processes of cultural learning and inherited cognitive capacities, especially at the socially collective level. In his final model, beliefs are acquired through processes of collective learning (culture) in the face of changing and uncertain environments, and they persist because there is a considerable degree of leeway between the content of beliefs and the outside environment, such that it takes a great deal of disjunction between them for beliefs to seriously shift. Since institutions, especially the informal kind of norms and conventions, derive in some way from belief systems, their nature and trajectory can be explained by reference to the inheritance of culture and the different worldviews of different agents in a given society and time period (North 2005). Path dependence further constrains the possibilities of change along any of these dimensions, and the way beliefs form in response to particular cues is not really known at any fundamental level, so that the whole structure is one of very considerable degrees of freedom in the collective (societal) evolution of institutions. This provides North's NIEH with an account of institutionalized agency that is fundamentally historicist, sociocultural, collectivist, and indeterminate.

Various commentators have praised North's approach for its willingness to adopt a more sociohistorical and institutionalized perspective, and therein see convergence with Polanyi or the German Historical School (Didry and Vincensini 2011; Peukert 2001). But North's NIEH rests on two legs. One may be the level of path dependence, institutionalization, and the endogenization of sociocultural variables as part of the explanatory model or framework. The other, however, is the explicit purpose of the NIEH to be *complementary* to the neoclassical approach, and to be based in some way on the fundamentals of choice theory as familiar from the (postwar) orthodoxy in the discipline of economics—in other words, to be based on traditional microfoundations (in the sense of Weintraub 1979). The importance of the microfoundationalism in North's NIEH has been mentioned before, but is worth restating, as it will be the central focus of the present chapter. North's repeated statements to this effect should not be ignored. While North uses various terms at different points to indicate what he takes for granted, there is a clear continuity throughout his work in this regard. Already in his Polanyi paper North emphasizes the importance of "economic analysis" as "changes at the margin" (North 1977: 706, 715). He opens *Structure and Change* by arguing that "defining institutions as the constraints that human beings impose on themselves makes the definition complementary to the choice theoretic approach of neoclassical economic theory. Building a theory of institutions *on the foundation of individual choices* is a step toward reconciling differences between economics and the other social sciences" (North 1990: 5, emphasis added).

The same language pervades *UPEC*, where "structure of human interaction determines who are the entrepreneurs whose choices matter and how such choices get implemented by the decision rules of that structure" and where North assures us that "economics is a theory of choice – so far so good. But the discipline neglects to explore the context within which choice occurs" (North 2005: 6, 11). It should be emphatically clear then that for North the endogenization of the sociocultural world of beliefs and norms in no way diminishes the importance of microfoundations. So how are these two legs supposed to carry the same body of theory? North's solution is to reinterpret the vast cognitive, cultural, political, and socionormative structure that he has incorporated into his version of the NIE in such a way that all these diverse elements of social life become not variables creating degrees of freedom in the model but *constraints* on the fundamental choice theoretical structure that is invariant.

The very definition of an institution has to be consistent with this purpose. As North explains in *UPEC*, "the human agent in the face of [the gap between the agent's competence and the difficulty of the decision problem] will construct rules to restrict the flexibility of choices in such situations. We know these rules as institutions" (North 2005: 14). The indeterminacy at the heart of the historicist and institutionalized approach is resolved within the choice theoretical framework itself. The world is uncertain and full of many complex things that are difficult to know and interpret, North argues, and for that reason people create institutions, beliefs, and culture *so as to limit their choice set*: "By channeling choices into a smaller set of actions, institutions can improve the ability of the agent to control the environment … the deep underlying source of institutions has been and continues to be the effort by humans to structure the environment to make it more predictable" (North 2005: 14–15).

As is clear from this formulation, the ultimate purpose of such activity is to increase an individual's control over outcomes of choice behavior by rendering the choice-to-payoff structure less opaque, something which also improves the ability to coordinate agents' behavior. North is careful not to assume that such constraints will necessarily achieve their aim in any way; to do so would be falling back onto the efficiency approach to institutions. But on first sight, this 'leg' of the NIEH model appears as a (very complex) version of the rational ignorance approach, where individuals faced with limited information will seek to acquire only such knowledge as actually maximizes their returns on it. Recall that North's pessimism regarding 'political markets' discussed in the previous chapter also rests for a large part on such considerations: in such 'markets', individuals simply do not have the right incentives to acquire the necessary information as would make the political system have good overall outcomes (North 2005: 54).

In this fashion, bounded rationality is taken to an extreme: virtually, the entire social environment of any given economic behavior is a bound of one or another kind of the rationality of the agent in that choice. But the question then arises as to how much of the choice theoretical approach is actually preserved, if the constraints on choice are so extensive. So much so that the NIEH's peculiar way of endogenizing the socio-institutional world into the model could perhaps be called the method of extended constrained rationality. To answer the question as to how successful this approach is, however, we must first understand why North gave it this shape in the first place. We know from the discussion in the previous chapters that the importance for North of appearing to preserve traditional microfoundations rests on two things. One is the (perceived) complementarity of his NIEH with neoclassical economics. The other is the idea that choice theory could serve as a unifying element between his NIEH approach, economics in general, and other social sciences (North 1990, 1992). But what kind of choice theory, and why he settled on this, requires a more detailed investigation.

North's Critique of Rational Choice

The two-legged nature of his theory in terms of agency and rationality gives the strong impression, to put it bluntly, of the typical Northian habit of wanting to have his cake and eat it too. He is keen on preserving the legitimacy of economics as a discipline, which he sees as defined by choice theory, and its superior ability to provide economic explanations of virtually anything that could fall under institutional analysis. In fact, his "very substantial extension" of the NIE (North 2005: 10) in fact applies this dominion of economic theory to a much vaster scientific terrain than had ever been done before. This is the purpose of the NIEH, what I have described in terms of Polanyi's challenge. On the other hand, however, he is also a persistent critic of all economic practice that fails to take on board the whole apparatus of variables involved in cognition, belief systems, path dependence, institution formation, coordination problems, transaction costs, and so forth. His primary argument for this is that without this 'thick background' in terms of the mental and socio-institutional makeup of a particular (historical) society, economic theory will fail to be realistic and therefore fail to explain properly.

This view is made explicit in a 1993 article in *Public Choice*, where North excoriates the public choice tradition—which as we know he drew on extensively throughout his career—for too conveniently letting the rational choice assumption do the work for them. As he argues, "There are no institutions (or if they exist they play no independent role) in the world of the neo-classical economist because the instrumental rationality postulate renders institutions superfluous … In the world of instrumental rationality institutions are unnecessary; ideas, ideologies, myths, dogmas don't matter; and efficient markets, both political and economic characterize societies. But in the real world the actors have incomplete information and limited mental capacity by which to process that information. In consequence they develop regularized rules and norms to structure exchange" (North 1993: 159–160). Certainly, he continues, one might use rational choice analysis for those markets in which low transaction costs really prevail, and where choice is characterized by "simple problems, complete information, repetitive situations, and high motivation" (North 1993: 161). But, the implication runs, that is not often the case.

One might view this as a somewhat convenient argument, perhaps: the institutional economist argues against rational choice because with rational choice one does not need institutional explanation. But in the final stage of the NIEH the tone against rational choice becomes, if anything, more critical. In *UPEC*, North intones that "the uncritical acceptance of the rationality assumption is devastating for most of the major issues confronting social scientists and is a major stumbling block in the path of future progress. The rationality assumption is not wrong, but such an acceptance forecloses a deeper understanding of the decision-making process in confronting the uncertainties of the complex world we have created" (North 2005: 5). Similarly, in *VSO* the authors observe that "when economists claim that individuals are rational and act in what they perceive to be their self-interest, hackles rise in the rest of the social sciences. What is in the perceived best interest of individuals is a complicated amalgam of their preferences over different outcomes, the alternatives that they face, and their beliefs about how their actions will affect the world around them. People are intentional; they are trying to accomplish the best outcomes with their limited resources and choices, but how they behave depends critically on how they believe the world around them actually works" (North, Wallis, and Weingast 2009: 28).

We may therefore safely conclude that North's objection to rational choice (and with it, neoclassical) theory as unrealistic is not simply based in the economic historian's desire to extend the domain of explanation to more historical topics, but also in a real concern that such unrealistic assumptions will lead to unrealistic, or at least superficial, explanations of real phenomena. This dovetails with the shift in the final stage of the

NIEH, in particular in *UPEC*. The argument in that book is characterized above all by a strong emphasis on the need to understand the sources of decision-making in beliefs and cognition, rather than in informed, rational decisions pursuing private benefits. By the end of the book, the urgency of this task takes on almost apocalyptic tones: "To understand the human condition it is essential to focus on the intentionality of the players. Economists have the correct insight that economics is a theory of choice. But to improve the human prospect we must understand the sources of human decision making. That is a necessary condition for human survival" (North 2005: 170).

For North, if there is going to be unification of social scientific accounts of institutions, it will not be on the basis of rational choice. Instead, it will be on the basis of a form of choice theory that is much less clearly defined, but which seems to be captured by the term 'intentionality'. This concept corrects what North sees as the deficiencies of rational choice in two ways. One is the idea that the subjective mental perceptions and expectations regarding the environment in which choice behavior takes place need to be at the center of the model of agency involved. The other, building on this insight, is to accept a great deal of fallibility on the part of agents: because of cognitive limitations, because of a changing environment, and because of the strong effect of beliefs on the perceptions of that environment people are likely to have poor information about the real situation they are facing and therefore will misinterpret the payoff structure or fail to achieve the intended aim. Here the pessimistic anthropology of North is in evidence once again. His disputation with the rational choice economists is not just a matter of realism, but as the apocalyptic final note of *UPEC* indicates, it is also driven by his real concern that institutional change is much more difficult and policy prescriptions much more likely to fail than neoclassical economists are willing to see. Few societies have ever made it to the beneficent state of open access order, and even adaptive efficiency may have its limits (North 2005: 169).

Note, however, what North's critique of rational choice, and its replacement by the concept of 'intentionality', does *not* do. It does not reject rational choice analysis altogether, but relegates it to the status of a special case, just as North does with neoclassical economics in general. The complementarity has to be preserved, even as North's patience with the limitations of rational choice grows ever shorter. More importantly, it does not alter the fundamental conception of *homo economicus* at the heart of choice theory in economics, the view of the agent as motivated entirely by the self-interested pursuit of self-regarding preferences *given* the constraints. There are many more constraints than usual in North's model, not all of them clearly specified, but *within* those constraints the model is not much altered.

At least, not *consistently*. North's efforts to make beliefs and mental models really count run up against his equally frequent invocation of a different model, one based on bounded rationality but also on the pursuit of self-interest given a particular incentive structure: the model of the 'players of the game'. There's the rub, for it is not obvious that North can have both. If the view of agency as players of the game responding to incentives, which is so important to the meso-level of institutional analysis in his NIEH, fails to cohere with the view of agency as a heavily constrained 'intentionality' where strong beliefs are the most important, North's two legs fail to walk in the same direction. In order to examine this problem, we must look at this quasi-game theoretical concept, the players of the game, in more detail.

The Players of the Game

This model is, as I read it, an appeal to—or perhaps really more of a suggestion—a kind of implicit game theoretical structure. The agents are players and act in their own interests; the incentive structures (the payoffs) are given by the institutional order. It is undeniable that North uses virtually no formalized game theory. And yet the language of game theory, and the emphasis on how difficult it is to achieve cooperation through rational behavior, is omnipresent in his later stage work. This is already evident in 1990: "Institutional constraints include both what individuals are prohibited from doing and, sometimes, under what conditions some individuals are permitted to undertake certain activities … They are perfectly analogous to the rules of the game in a competitive team sport … the formal and informal rules and the type and effectiveness of enforcement shape the whole character of the game … The purpose of the rules is to define the way the game is played. But the objective of the team within that set of rules is to win the game – by a combination of skills, strategy, and coordination; by fair means and sometimes by foul means" (North 1990: 4–5). In *UPEC*, this is made even more explicit. The foundation of economic behavior, North here argues, is choice, which implies scarcity, which implies competition. The function of institutions in this analysis is to shape the game: "If our focus is narrowly on economics, then our concern is with scarcity and, hence, competition for resources. The structure of constraints we impose to order that competition shapes the way the game is played" (North 2005: 1).

While beliefs and culture are important, they do not fundamentally alter this structural representation of the nature of economic behavior in an institutional(ized) setting as analogous to a game in the sense of the theory of games. Rather, as before, the institutional order simply serves to buttress choice given the strong informational processing limitations imposed on it: "The richer the artifactual structure, the wider the range of routine decisions that can be made. In effect the game has been structured to relieve the individual of uncertainty in choice making" (North 2005: 36). In game theory terms, habits and conventions induced by cultural institutions serve to make the payoff structure of a game problem easier to identify, but they do not alter the logic of rationality that operates in the problem itself.

In order to understand why North would invoke this quasi-game theory, not ever quantitatively modeled but frequently referred to as an explanatory mechanism, it is essential to grasp some fundamentals of game theory itself and the context in which it arises in North's approach. I will consciously give a very simplified account here, shorn of jargon and complexity to the maximum extent possible. After all, the purpose is to elucidate a particular element of North's theory, not to review the literature on game theory in economics. That said: game theory is, simply put, the mathematical representation of strategic action by agents. That is to say, it models the *interaction* of multiple agents who are assumed to be to some degree rational and self-interested—they are defined as utility maximizers and the 'payoff', that is to say the outcome of the joint interaction of all of the agents, is defined in utility terms (usually with some set of numbers to represent the preference rankings of the agents over the possible outcomes).

There is a vast literature on game theory and its philosophical underpinnings and problems that I need not go into here.[1] Suffice to say, however, that it is in economics (and other social sciences) one of the most popular ways of examining the possibilities of coordination, cooperation, and conflict between agents, *given* a particular institutional arrangement (payoff structure). It shows a way of formalizing a social situation so that one can determine whether rational self-interested utility maximizers would, given the terms of that situation, end up interacting to mutual benefit or mutual disadvantage (or the advantage of the one over the other). The fundamental concept is that of the Nash equilibrium, the equilibrium outcome of the rational choices ('strategies') of each agent joined with the rational choices of all the other agents. Perhaps the most famous such game is the prisoner's dilemma, which demonstrates that given a particular payoff structure, the rational action of individuals to obtain their private maximum utility ends up having a Nash equilibrium that is suboptimal for all agents concerned. Instead of 'private vices, public benefits', the prisoner's dilemma shows that it is possible for rational agents to end up in the opposite situation. This illustrates the possibility of the failure of cooperation in practice despite the complete rationality and perfect information of all agents concerned. Game theory is also frequently used in the context of evolutionary analysis, about which I will say more in the next chapter.

At the heart of this type of game is the principle of *noncooperation*. In game theory parlance, one distinguishes cooperative games from noncooperative games, with the latter being the more popular (especially since cooperative games can be reduced to noncooperative ones). A 'noncooperative game' is not a term saying anything about the equilibrium outcome, but specifically means that individuals are not able to

[1] A full analysis of the implications of methodological problems in game theory for the kind of approach used by North, that is, as a means to provide a social contract analysis of the emergence of social institutions, would constitute an important contribution to the study of the NIE in general and North's approach in particular. Although I summarized it in my PhD thesis (Krul 2016), a proper treatment requires such length and complexity that it cannot be justified for full inclusion in this book. For some applications of game theory to the NIE and related economic theories, see Schotter (1981), Greif (1993, 1994, 1998), and Aoki (2001). For a valuable critical treatment of game theory from a philosophy of economics standpoint, see Hargreaves-Heap and Varoufakis (1995, 2004). A recent general treatment is Binmore (2007).

enforce agreements—attempts to coordinate—between them other than *within* the game, for example by signaling via particular moves. This is of particular interest because it can be used to analyze whether a particular explanation for the emergence of coordination between individuals, or for the emergence of an external enforcement mechanism (whether a third party, or an accepted retaliation mechanism), is a plausible one or not. The logic is that if individual agents acting rationally to maximize private benefit would not be able to reach an equilibrium state in which coordination is possible to mutual benefit, the explanation posited for the emergence of such coordination cannot be plausible. The same goes for the emergence of enforcement mechanisms to force parties to uphold their signals or promises.

Ultimately, the point of such analysis in backward explanation (so reverse engineering existing phenomena as opposed to forward-oriented market design) is the following strong implication: that if individual agents interacting simultaneously or sequentially, as the case may be, to maximize their own utility in a given situation cannot rationally end up with a particular institutional outcome as an (or *the*) equilibrium state, that institutional outcome cannot be explained as the result of that strategic interaction. Either then the model is misspecified—some important element of the payoff structure has been missed—or, and this is much the disfavored option, some other explanation for the institution has to be found that is not rooted in the strategic behavior of human individuals.[2]

While such analysis can be applied to many practical cases, from bargaining between different parties in an economic setting to the structure of auctions, it is not difficult to see that one could be tempted to extend it to a larger sociohistorical context. One could easily read the problem of the emergence of states, or for that matter power elites with a monopoly on violence, as enforcers of formal institutions as a coordination problem, and of course in *VSO* much of the material of the discussion is dedicated to just that. The social contract itself is a case study in coordination problems in a noncooperative game, and the different ways the problem was conceived between such thinkers as Thomas Hobbes, John Locke, Jean-

[2] Here, too, a full explanation would require a lengthy discussion of the different ways a game theoretical result can be interpreted, which I must forego on this occasion.

Jacques Rousseau, and even Adam Smith can be seen (perhaps crudely) as different specifications of the problem and its payoff structure.

It is my supposition that the reason North regularly invokes the language and structure of game theory—with his speaking of the 'players of the game' and the way he envisions strategic action to follow incentives within an institutionally given structure of rents or other returns—is to reinvigorate or reinsert this contractarian element within his larger NIEH approach. As we have seen in the discussion so far, for North the idea of institutional arrangements as a form of social contract came early in his intellectual career and quite naturally. He revised the assumptions and structure of this conctractarian view a number of times, most importantly by abandoning the efficiency assumption underlying the social contract model developed with Robert Paul Thomas (North and Thomas 1971, 1973).

North's de-emphasizing of the efficiency solution is probably the joint result of his abandoning of the efficient contracting interpretation of institutions and of realizing that such a model does not provide much room for the role of informal institutions. Traditionally, the weakness of such solutions to the dilemma is precisely in explaining how the state itself then comes to exist as a stable equilibrium outcome of a strategic interaction. In North's (and colleagues') later work, much more attention is paid to this problem, but the issue remains that states or elites, and their transaction cost-reducing powers, are explained as the result of a bargaining equilibrium (i.e. a cooperative equilibrium) between the resistance of the 'citizens' and the predation of elites. Ultimately, North et al. can only solve this problem with reference to the problem of beliefs and values: only with shared values and legitimacy can such third-party enforcement produce a credible mutually shared interest, that is, a Nash equilibrium outcome.[3]

After it had been put somewhat on the backburner, however, his turn toward Hayek described in the previous chapter revived North's interest in the idea of institutions as a historically evolved arrangement between the members of a society. But against Hayek, North always emphasizes

[3] Contrast North 2005 with, for example. North and Weingast 1989, where incentives do all the work and beliefs play virtually no role in the argument.

the 'intentional' rather than 'spontaneous' character of such arrangements (North 2005: 51). In *UPEC*, North portrays his analysis of intentionality as the basis of institutions as a middle way between Hayek's cultural spontaneity on the one hand and the application of Darwinian principles to cultural evolution on the other.[4] In *UPEC* and *VSO*, the state is not simply an efficient Hobbesian result, but he just as much takes inspiration from David Hume and John Locke: the emergence of the state is a solution where the consent of the governed, as an expression of legitimacy at the level of the belief system, and the agreement of all relevant parties to mutually desist from warfare when the benefits of doing so outweigh the costs is necessary for it to operate and become a more or less competent enforcer of formal institutions.[5]

One curious element of this 'as if' game theory, however, is that unlike in conventional game theoretical models, in North's approach it is a valid move within the game to alter the payoff structure. The 'players of the game' act to change the institutional framework itself. The possibility of error in decision-making, given a particular 'objective' payoff, which could represent the possibility of misidentifying the payoff structure, is not unusual to incorporate into game theoretical models (usually by means of an error term or probabilistic distribution).[6] However, North's approach is something rather different and fundamentally affects the logic of a game itself. North is nonetheless explicit about this. It results from the importance he attaches to incorporating power in some form into his analysis. Power in North's NIEH amounts to the ability to decide what the institutional order will be: "[the] economic market reflects the beliefs of those in a position to make the rules of the game, who enact rules that will produce the outcomes (that is, the sort of market) they desire, whether those desires are to create monopoly or to create a competitive market (always with the caveat that their beliefs may be incorrect

[4] The implications of this use of intentionality for his evolutionary argument are discussed in the next chapter.

[5] For North on the influence of Locke, see: Letter to David Nichols, May 23, 1991. For further discussion, see: Hough and Grier (2015: 50).

[6] This is the so-called trembling hand. The assumption that a 'trembling hand perfect equilibrium' must exist, put simply that a plausible strategic interpretation must be robust to the possibility of error, is an important qualification of the rational choice informational framework of game theory (Selten 1975).

and produce unanticipated consequences). When conflicting beliefs exist, the institutions will reflect the beliefs of those (past as well as present) in a position to effect their choices" (North 2005: 50).

The only way for this to be consistent is to assume that there is then a meta-level of strategic action in which agents act so as to determine what the game will be that the players will 'play'. Far from reducing the scope of instrumental rationality, this extends it. North's theory of political power is one explicitly based on rather traditional forms of rational action. In fact, in *VSO* this meta-level is explored at length in terms that sound very familiar from game theoretical analysis. When describing the natural state order, the nature of most societies in the present and all in premodern history, the authors write: "Elites – members of the dominant coalition – agree to respect each other's privileges, including property rights and access to resources and activities. By limiting access to these privileges to members of the dominant coalition, elites create credible incentives to cooperate rather than fight among themselves. Because elites know that violence will reduce their own rents, they have incentives not to fight. Furthermore, each elite understands that other elites face similar incentives. In this way, the political system of a natural state manipulates the economic system to produce rents that then secure political order" (North, Wallis, and Weingast 2009: 18). In other words: the power-holders, or elites, act as rational agents in their own right and know others to be so, and because they each want to maximize their own immediate returns (payoffs).

The emphasis on institutions as consciously created social phenomena allows North to depict them as the result of an (unequal) strategic bargain between different power-holders, mediated by their respective belief systems and fallible expectations about the outcome of instrumental action. In this way, North can embed the rational choice element and the social contract element in his theory into his wider cognitive-evolutionary account of institutional change. Clearly, the creation of initial formal institutions appears as a kind of prisoner's dilemma, as it does in Hobbes' account: something that can only be resolved by developing sufficient levels of trust and a belief in the legitimacy of both these institutions and the parties capable of creating them. Otherwise, they cannot emerge as equilibrium outcome of purely rational action, however much of a public good their existence is. Yet at the moment that some kind of elite formation occurs, in other words in the earliest prehistorical stages of class formation or the rise of persistent social differentiation, the logic of instrumental rationality already takes over (as per *VSO*).

A kind of 'as if' game theory, I conclude, exists in the background of North's NIEH in its later stages. Not a set of actual game theoretical models, but rather a reliance on the implications of strategic noncooperative interaction between individuals to bring about institutions as equilibrium results, and within these institutions bounded but instrumentally rational action can then operate. The repeated references to *incentives*, as well as the assumption that the 'players of the game' are likely in it to "line their pockets" or "improve their economic or political positions" rather than having other-regarding motivations (North 2005: 79, 2), and, finally, the importance North attaches to seeing economic performance as the unintended outcome of the strategic action of many individual agents, all points in the direction of a type of rational action operating in his NIEH. The invocation of game theory, I suspect, is intended to underpin the functioning of this rationality in his system, since the properties of game theory are well understood in economics and are probably the most sophisticated elaboration of choice theory. This also then dovetails with his larger contractarian approach to institutions, as just mentioned.

One may wonder, therefore, what role remains for belief systems in the account of state formation provided in *VSO* if all the explanatory weight is really carried by strategic interaction. Moreover, *within* an institutional structure, the rules of the game give a payoff structure for instrumental rational action to the players of the game. As North puts it, "The scaffolds humans erect not only define the economic and political game but also determine who will have access to the decision-making process. They further define the formal structure of incentives and disincentives that are a first approximation to the choice set" (North 2005: 52). Again, it is strategic interaction that dominates, as individual agents pursue maximum payoffs following valid strategies, both of which are determined by the given institutional order. Although belief systems and inherited cultural patterns are very important at the micro-level, to determine the constraints on individual choice that make institutions and history relevant to the explanatory framework, they somewhat awkwardly drop into the background at subsequent levels of analysis. At the macro-level, the evolutionary structure of institutions as carriers of adaptive efficiency takes over, as I will discuss in the next chapter. But what of the meso-level? Here, the interaction between agents and institutions is characterized primarily by strategic action, however much North attempts to qualify it. Strategic action operates within the game, as players act instrumentally on incentives, and strategic action operates to determine the rules of the game, as elites or other power-holders act strategically to create institutions that will maximize their returns as rents. It is by strategic action, not beliefs, that North attempts to close his system.

Methodological Individualism in North's NIEH

It is not difficult to see from the above analysis that there is a real tension in North's work between instrumental rationality and other forms of rationality, and between choice theory and the role of beliefs and culture. The micro-level and the meso-level are not effectively joined together. At the micro-level, North is clear that choice is determined by learning and culture, not by constrained rational action: "The key to the choices that individuals make is their perceptions … As noted in previous chapters, the mental constructs individuals form to explain and interpret the world around them are partly a result of their cultural heritage, partly a result of the 'local' everyday problems they confront and must solve, and partly a result of non-local learning" (North 2005: 61).

This is clearly a matter of the cognitive processes of the brain, in other words of neuropsychology, and on top of that exists a layer of representation that is the culturally transformed residue of past experience. Neither of these is clearly translated, or translatable, into even a constrained version of choice theory. While bounded rationality easily allows for limited information and even uncertainty, it is not so clear that it allows for the importing of the *content* of psychology and culture into the choice process. After all, the whole purpose of choice theory is to relegate psychological factors to unknowns, to be translated into probabilistic expressions of beliefs about states of the world.

This puts North's framework into a contradiction. The foundation of the NIEH project is to retain 'economic analysis'—which as we have seen amounts to choice theory plus the scarcity assumption—but to use it to develop institutional analysis, so that jointly they can answer Polanyi's challenge. The choice theoretical microfoundation, we know, is essential to North's aim of maintaining disciplinary cohesion, by integrating neoclassical economics into his research program rather than rejecting it altogether. All this is familiar by now. At the meta-level, regarding the NIEH research program itself, then, the analytical primacy is with choice theory. But this is not what ends up being the case for the actual structure of the theory itself. On the contrary, North develops his theory in such a way that the actual micro-level foundation is the opposite of this: in the final form of North's NIEH, the formation of institutions depends in analytical priority *first* on mental variables like cognitive psychology, cultural heritage, and what one might call strong beliefs, none of which are normally part of traditional 'economic analysis'.

Only once institutions, habits, and expectations are formed on the basis of that socio-psychological interaction with a changing and uncertain environment do we find that *within* a given institutional arrangement agents are modeled as acting instrumentally in response to (material) incentives. But since this concerns the same agents in both cases—individuals and the organizations they form, as well as the collectives of interests such as elites they make up—it is not clear how or why this division can be sustained. If subjective mental models and the inheritance of cultural patterns of habits, conventions, and expectations are strong enough determinants to account for the vast variation in social institutions visible in the long run of history, it is not clear why they should not also be strong enough to make agents' behavior in economic or political settings nonrational in the sense of instrumental rationality—precisely the point Polanyi argued applied to premodern societies, expressed in his concept of embeddedness. That North emphasizes constraints on rationality, in the form of limited information and limited competence, does not alter this fundamental contradiction. Bounded rationality is still instrumental rationality, unless the framework of utility maximization as conventionally used in economics is significantly altered or abandoned. There is no sign of that in North's work, and the references to incentives and motives of gain suggest the contrary.

In a trenchant critique, Ben Fine and Dimitris Milonakis (2003) have argued that the origin of such duality or ambiguity in North resides in what they call his 'methodological individualism'. They argue that North has adopted much of the information theoretical approach of contemporary economics in the form of the 'newer economic history', which is to say economic history that relies on the concepts of agents with limited information and bounded rationality (Fine 2000). As they describe this approach, "The rational, optimizing individuals of mainstream economics still prevail but they inhabit an informationally imperfect world that leads them to form and conform with institutions and customs" (Fine and Milonakis 2003: 548). However, as they point out, North goes beyond this. "The new and newer economic histories can in principle explain anything on the basis of rationality by pushing out the boundaries of the endogenous/rational, one by extending the scope of the as-if-perfect market, the other by appeal to market imperfections. By contrast, North has retained a continuing commitment to the role of ideology which occupies an uncomfortable position in straddling the rational/irrational divide" (Fine and Milonakis 2003: 553). In their view, ideology or beliefs fulfill two important analytical functions in North's framework. It explains everything that is not explained by instrumental rationality, although frequently expressed as a constraint on such rationality rather than an alternative to it. The other function is that it accounts for the possibility of group action (or action by organizations) to change institutions; it represents the glue that enables the overcoming of the collective action problems that fully rational actors would otherwise face in attempting such collective efforts.

They rightly cite North's observation that "it is belief systems that are the underlying determinant of path dependence, one of the most striking regularities of history" (North 1994: 385). But they argue that North's view of ideology is superficial. It fails to clearly distinguish structure from agency, or rather, dissolves structure into agency. They view as arbitrary North's insistence on ideology as the result of individual interactions with the environment, as opposed to being (co-)determined by structural factors, such as social position. This they attribute to his methodological individualism: "His approach might be best understood as a combination of rational choice theory with irrational choice theory, the latter comprising whatever is left aside by the former … Yet, if there is one thing to be learned from the literature on ideology, it is that, however widely cast, its origins, meanings and evolution cannot be found within the individual. Ideology, although individually held, is socially constructed" (Fine and Milonakis 2003: 567). The result is that the relationship between rational and irrational is arbitrary in his theory, with the latter filling the gaps of the former, and to this they attribute the absence of "genuine social theory" that can better address "collectivities, power, and conflict … capital and capitalism" (Fine and Milonakis 2003: 567).

To some extent, this critique suffers from the fact that although written after the beginning of North's 'cognitive turn', a factor the critics allude to, it was written before the full elaboration of the different levels of North's NIEH after this turn, in his 2005 and 2009 books. The result is that naturally North's comments on ideology seem more unsatisfying, based as they were on his first forays into a theory of ideology in the 1990s. In *UPEC*, what is meant by beliefs, learning, culture, and so forth is much more explicitly elaborated. What's more, it is elaborated on the basis of references to cognitive psychology and (vague) references to neuroscience, making much more explicit the (apparent) deviation even from a constrained utility maximization approach.

Another problem is that the concept of methodological individualism, although certainly relevant to philosophy of economics and the literature on 'economics imperialism', is notoriously lacking in a consensus definition (Hodgson 2007). In the critique of North's models of rationality and irrationality, Fine and Milonakis come closest to a definition when they attribute to North's NIEH the view that "the economy is made up of an aggregate of optimizing individuals who are burdened by imperfect and asymmetric information and corresponding transaction costs. Consequently, it is possible for economic and social structures to be explained, together with institutions, customs, and norms, as the individually rational but collectively reproduced response to such market imperfections" (Fine and Milonakis 2003: 551). In a different paper about North, they argue that "methodological individualism is North's most sacred analytical principle … despite the prominence of the structural framework in North's problematic, (individual) agency takes precedence over structural factors, and the latter are either treated as the result of individual action (in the form of rational choice) or else are taken as exogenously given, and as such are not explicable from within the model … institutions influence behavior by acting as constraints on individual action. Ideology, on the other hand, is an exogenously given factor that also acts on society by influencing and constraining individual action" (Milonakis and Fine 2007: 37). So, for the authors, North is essentially a methodological individualist, and this methodological individualism explains the disjunction between the different accounts of agency in his work. But equally, the implication is that this does not extend to the account of ideology itself: this is exogenous to the model of action within institutions.

To a good extent, this view squares with the analysis provided above. However, unlike Fine and Milonakis I do not—based especially on *UPEC*—view the level of ideology, supplemented by the importance of cultural heredity and of cognitive biases, as exogenous. Rather, as I have argued, I think it is best seen as the larger model, within which the account of instrumental action is a subsidiary model; to some extent, one can see this as analogous to North's own attempts to make neoclassical rational choice economics a subset of his own model of bounded rationality. Moreover, it is not clear whether one can really say that individual agency is paramount in North's account. Certainly, at the micro-level, the focus is in first instance on the human individual and their cognitive capacities. But as North emphasizes, learning is an important part of cognition and learning becomes a collective process when its results are shared and inherited via culture (Denzau and North 1994; North 2005: 27). Culture, in turn, is allowed to have a feedback effect on individual beliefs and mental models within North's approach, beyond individual agency alone (North 2005: 69). While North insists that "institutions must be explained in terms of the intentionality of humans" (North 2005: 42), in the larger context it is not obvious that this involves individuals taken abstractly in isolation. Rather, the effect of North's discussion of cognition, consciousness, and the origins of culture is to suggest a kind of dialectical feedback loop between individual experience and the collective inheritance of culture within a society. While this is certainly outside the realm of the bounded rationality approach as North uses it elsewhere, it is—especially in *UPEC*—not exogenous to the NIEH framework as a whole, but, on the contrary, provides a foundational mechanism within the overall model.

Aside from this, we also find that North is quite sanguine about the role of collective agents, perhaps surprisingly so for an author so steeped in the public choice literature on collective action problems. Organizations are important agents next to individuals, as noted. While, of course, organizations consist of human individuals, North spends virtually no time on explaining how they emerge from the rational or irrational interests of individuals-as-agents. We are simply told that "organizations consist of groups of individuals bound together by some common objectives … the entrepreneurs of organizations induce institutional change as they face the ubiquitous competition derived from an economic world of scarcity"(North 2005: 59–60). Here we are squarely in the meso-level of the model, where agents and institutions interact. But the classic collective action problems of how people can come to form organizations in the first place, or the principal-agent paradoxes involved, which form such a pervasive topic in the thoroughly rational individualist approach of public choice theory, are all absent. Organizations are fine as collective agents as long as they share interests or beliefs, and North does not seem to see a problem. That is not what one would expect from someone for whom every phenomenon has to be reducable to the logic of the interests of individuals, as in rational choice or indeed in the game theory framework North at other times alludes to.

The same goes for North's analysis of state formation in *VSO*. The structure, or order, of the natural state is distinguished not just from open access orders, but also from small-scale societies in which individuals will repeatedly interact face-to-face at a personal level.[7] The natural state order, unlike such small-scale societies, distinguishes the personality from the social persona, and thereby allows the latter to fulfill an impersonal, abstract role. While those social personas may be unique in each case, they are socially determined, not a matter of individual choice or attributes: "The development of impersonal relationships has to do with social persona. As long as social personas are unique across individuals, impersonal relationships are impossible. Impersonality arises as social personas become standardized. … The personality of an organization is

[7] This again brings to mind game theory: the significance of repeated games, in which choices can signal trust and in which strategies of retaliation are possible, thereby enabling mutually beneficial equilibria in certain cases where one-shot games do not permit them.

always a social persona, defined and supported by the larger society" (North, Wallis, and Weingast 2009: 33).

The emergence of organizations and also of individual power-holders acting as a social persona, rather than their social effect being dependent on their individual attributes, is therefore a process of regularization that operates at the societal level. Again, it is not reducible in a straightforward way to pure individual action. The game theoretical problem of strategic rationality involved—how in situations where repeated games between the same agents are unlikely, one can nonetheless establish organization- or institution-building equilibria—is simply bypassed at the same time as it is mentioned. Of course, North and colleagues also assert that in natural state orders some degree of individuality attaches still to the social persona, so that hierarchies and organizations are identified with individuals who lead them (North, Wallis, and Weingast 2009: 33–34). But this is a different problem than the necessity of explanation to be *reducible* to individual agency: how leadership or 'elite' formation emerges out of individual rationality, or lack thereof, is largely left implicit.

Admittedly, North does discuss patron-client networks and how elites define themselves by personal interaction at their level and interact with nonelites through patronage (North, Wallis, and Weingast 2009: 35–38). Even so, this is merely a consequence, not a cause, of elite organizational formation. The organizations, analytically, come first: "The intra-elite hierarchy roughly corresponds to the hierarchy of the organizations they represent. The most important source of rents binding the interests of the elites together is the rents that flow from their organizations" (North, Wallis, and Weingast 2009: 36). At the most fundamental level, this whole edifice rests in turn on institutions concerning organizational access, again at the societal level. "All this depends on identifying who gets the benefits: limited access identifies privileges, creates rents, and provides credibility to personal relationships throughout the society", as the authors write (North, Wallis, and Weingast 2009: 38). Since such institutions are fundamentally social rules, and emerge (presumably) through the diffuse collective culture-building process discussed previously in *UPEC*, the structure of *VSO* in this way does not touch ground from a strictly methodologically individualist perspective, if that is defined as the reducibility of each posited collective or social element to the choice theoretical strategies of individuals.

One can go on with this type of analysis, for example by pointing to the many places where, in North's late period works, 'society' in some form does the work of explanation. This goes particularly strongly for the macro-level, where societies as a whole are objects of cultural evolution, as we will see in the next chapter. Only on one occasion, in a footnote, do North and colleagues address the agency problem involved in this from the viewpoint of traditional choice theory and its methodological individualism. They hasten to reassure adherents of methodological individualism that they really mean 'society' as a shorthand for "the aggregate of individuals collectively dealing with a range of individual decisions in such a way to produce common and shared beliefs about choices, consequences, and outcomes"(North, Wallis, and Weingast 2009: 13n14). But this is simply begging the question: the entire purpose of choice theory, especially in the form of strategic analysis as expressed in game theory, is to understand *how* individual decisions can do so, or—in the 'reverse engineering' approach I mentioned above—how it is possible to explain observed social phenomena in terms of decision theory applied to individuals. Since North frequently invokes game theory and 'incentives' where it suits him, he ought to know that.

I would therefore reformulate Fine and Milonakis' objection. The contradiction in North's account of rationality and agency is not so much that he is a methodological individualist through and through, but that he is *inconsistently* so. He has his bounded-but-instrumental rationality and he has his strong beliefs and cultural causality also. Similarly, he has his strategic action expressed in the language of game theory, and he has his model of unequal power and ideological conflict. He has his microfoundations in choice theory, with the implication of reducibility to individual instrumental agency, and he has his collective agents as well. People are motivated by incentives and seek rents and to pursue interests, but people also can change the payoff structure of the game; *and* they have diverse sociohistorically determined beliefs and preferences that are the *result* of culture and (its) informal institutions. All of these are perhaps not inherently irreconcilable in a single model. A variety of approaches, from game theoretical models representing beliefs about the world probabilistically to social theories about the effects of social position on individual perception of interests, have sought to address all these in the social sciences. But North makes no effort to do so explicitly. At the level of rationality and methodology, he simply has his cake and eats it too.

Rationality and Indeterminacy

Given the above conclusions, we can see that in the final stage of his NIEH North did not succeed at formulating a consistent and coherent theory of action. Instead, he shifted back and forth between different concepts of rationality and decision-making depending on what was convenient for a given argument or on the level of his theory concerned. The remaining task then is to account for how this happened—why North would deploy this inconsistent methodology. There are various possibilities, depending on the degree of charity one wishes to apply in interpreting his work. In any case, it is my conviction that the cause is an underlying problem, one potentially common to all New Institutionalist approaches: indeterminacy.[8]

The problem is essentially this. The more North extended his model of rationality beyond the confines of strict rationality, the more realistic his approach became. This was, as we have seen, an important motive for his continuous reshaping of NIE theory itself. However, as Uskali Mäki has pointed out, realism can mean various things, not all of whom imply realisticness (see, for example, Mäki 2009). Leaving aside the philosophical meanings of realism for now, realism for North means realisticness. But even so, one must still distinguish realism of assumptions and realism of outcomes. When North discusses realism in the context of his critiques of rational choice theory, he effectively conflates both. His argument is based on the unrealism of outcomes—neoclassical economics is unable to account for social or historical phenomena or their change. But the next step in his theory is to change the realism of the assumptions, both in the form of an enormous set of institutional constraints on rational action

[8] See also the discussion of rationality and explanatory value in the NIE in Dequech (2006).

and in the form of the occasional appeal to determinants outside traditional choice theory.[9] The effect of this, however, is that the determinate predictions offered by strict forms of rational choice theory no longer apply. The broader the kind of inputs into a decision-making process that are permitted or assumed in the model, the greater the number of possible outcomes given a particular situation, and the less determinate conventional choice (or decision) theory will be. Put crudely, if anything can go into the model, anything can come out.[10]

The same problem operates at the level of institutions. The more North endogenizes social-institutional, historical, cultural, and even psychological elements into his theory, the less room there is for the mechanisms of choice theory to do anything in the explanatory framework. This is not what North intended, as his answer to Polanyi's challenge required that his theory be based on choice theoretical microfoundations—lest the special explanatory privileges of economics as a discipline be called into question. But the result is a fundamental ambiguity. Wherever he can, North hearkens back to well-understood mechanisms, such as the instrumental rationality of agents responding to incentives or the powerful analytical apparatus of game theory. Precisely because the properties of these analytical tools have been so extensively explored over the past decades, they provide the occasional solid ground for North to anchor his NIEH framework in. It also spares him the problem of having to specify the empirical basis for each further abstract mechanism posited in his analysis. But in the process, he overlooks or ignores that these very same tools are very narrowly circumscribed in terms of what kind of methodological assumptions and what kind of contexts they will tolerate. Rational choice analysis and game theory have been favored in certain branches of social

[9] This approach is very much in line with the earliest divide between neoclassical and New Institutionalist approaches. Mäki argues that Ronald Coase and Milton Friedman's early work can already be contrasted in this respect, in that Coase argued for realisticness of assumptions, whereas Friedman (not very coherently) argued against it (Mäki 1992, 1998). Of course, to what extent Friedman really was neoclassical can be disputed, but his famous essay on the methodology of economics is often seen as defining for the dominant postwar approach (Friedman 1953).

[10] As Langlois and Csontos (1993) make clear, much of the argument as to whether neoclassical rational choice approaches and 'behavioural' approaches based (in part) on psychological data are really in conflict depends on what demands are placed on assumptions in economic theory—that is, whether the assumptions themselves should be empirical or not. While they argue against this demand, it appears in any case North supported it.

science precisely *because* they are narrowly defined. This is what gives them their explanatory power, since the mechanism specifying how inputs (preference rankings or payoff structures) are translated into outcomes (choices or strategies) is absolutely transparent and the results therefore determinate—under ideal and idealized circumstances.

North seems, on my reading, to feel intuitively that the expansive scope of his theory, the huge number of moving parts at different levels of the framework, and his constant pushing for greater realism (realisticness) in assumptions jointly produce an approach that is as indeterminate as it is sophisticated. I suspect that his appeals to explanatory mechanisms defined by others outside his own theory, whether the work of cognitive psychologists or the work of game theorists, are an attempt to escape this predicament by, as it were, borrowing their explanatory power. But he does so without the due regard to in what contexts such mechanisms are actually applicable and do their work. In the next chapters I will explore this point regarding various proposed mechanisms in his NIEH, such as cultural evolution and adaptive efficiency. Here I will illustrate the point by returning to the case of his implicit references to game theory and its explanatory power.

The limitations of North's approach at the meso-level, and the way it is built on the foundations of constrained choice, are the limitations of his model of strategic action. In order to understand where this becomes a problem, we must delve a little further into the theoretical structure of game theory. (Again, I will consciously truncate and simplify the discussion so as to focus maximally on the main discussion, which concerns North, and not game theory itself.) In game theory, the common underlying model of rationality makes a number of assumptions, which allows the logic of strategic action to operate. One is that each agent knows the rules and, therefore, what the payoff structure is for each other agent. This means that each has, for the purposes of the game, perfect information about the preferences of the others.[11] Each agent knows that others have the same rationality as he does (common knowledge of rationality); and

[11] Strictly speaking, there can be uncertainty about this. One can have different types of agents all of whom have different preferences (and therefore different payoff distributions). But as long as the probabilities of encountering a given type of agent are known, this has the same effect as knowing the payoff distribution directly (Harsanyi 1967).

finally, common alignment of beliefs, which is to say that if each knows about the other being rational, they must each make the best response to the choice of the other and assume the other will do the same. In other words, they will know each other's beliefs about the state of the game because each has equal knowledge of the rules of the game and each knows the other to be instrumentally rational. Two instrumentally rational agents, the reasoning goes, will by definition not draw different inferences given the same information—purely rational agents cannot agree to disagree given the same knowledge.[12]

The function of this structure of game theory is the strictest possible separation between structure and agency and between beliefs and actions. Its purpose is to combat indeterminacy. But it can only do so at a considerable cost. Some major assumptions regarding the nature of beliefs, rationality, and the temporal nature of the game itself are required to generate a unique and sustainable Nash equilibrium that can account for the emergence of cooperation and thereby institutions. We can see how this works by tracing the way much of North's final NIEH argument actually traces the problems with game theory to their (often exogenous) solutions. This is the other significance of game theory for North's account: not just his references to players of the game, but also how his attempts to resolve the contradictions in his work, generated by the 'walking on two legs', (probably) unintentionally mimic the limitations of game theory itself. These limitations are the limitations of instrumentally rational action, strictly separating beliefs and preferences, as a mechanism to account for social institutions.

Recall that the point of game theory is to explain how the strategic—that is, instrumentally rational—action of individuals can bring about cooperation.[13] How cooperation is sustainably possible is also North's main research question in his NIEH work, at least in the second and third stages. Cooperation is simply an outcome in which both (all) agents in the game have a positive payoff in equilibrium. Institutions can be seen as a form of cooperation. They can only come about, whether as informal norms and conventions or as formal laws and rules, when they are the outcome of the interaction between individuals, and can only be sus-

[12] See Aumann (1976, 1987). This argument is not uncontroversial, however.

[13] The following account draws extensively on Hargreaves-Heap and Varoufakis (1995).

tained when there are plausible enforcement mechanisms or other coordinating elements that make the payoff structure robustly favorable to their persistence. Holding beliefs constant, game theory can account for how agents' preferences interact in such a way that a particular equilibrium result emerges. This can represent the emergence of an institution, but equally well model instrumentally rational behavior within institutions. It can determinately explain, again holding beliefs constant, whether a given payoff structure is a plausible explanation for actually observed forms of cooperation.

North's original models, social contract theories of institutions based on rational choice analysis, are not fundamentally different from such an analysis. The medieval manor could be modeled according to his work with Robert Paul Thomas as an equilibrium trade-off between rents and safety, such that both parties (peasantry and nobility) benefit. (Whether the outcome is actually strategically reachable in North and Thomas' original model is another question, but not germane here.) After Polanyi's challenge, North became increasingly obsessed with the origins of institutions. He realized they needed to be accounted for in terms of some kind of choice theoretical approach if that defining framework for the discipline (as he saw it) was to be saved. This meant that the instrumental rationality approach no longer applied directly, but the model was simply moved one level deeper: now strategic interaction of some sort had to be able to account for institutions, which in turn would set the payoff parameters for individual action within them.

It turns out, however, that this is not easy: the history of social contract theory demonstrates the difficulty of explaining public goods, enforcable and robust institutions, and other forms of cooperation in terms of instrumental rationality at that level. Even the strong assumptions of common knowledge of rationality and common alignment of beliefs will not do it if the structure of the game is akin to a prisoner's dilemma, as it often is. Only a particular payoff structure can render institutional development explicable as a Nash equilibrium, and the question is how that arises.[14] The only solution then is either to change the payoff structure, which is to

[14] For a thorough discussion beyond this off-hand comment, see Skyrms (1996, 2003) and some of the discussion in the following chapter.

say to reinterpret how institutions come about by bringing in exogenous valuation, or to follow one of the proven solutions in *repeated* games, in which the signaling of trust and the building of conventions are possible.

North's interests shifted precisely to these topics. The external valuations come from beliefs and ideologies, and *sometimes*, as we have seen, from assuming that at certain points in the model other than instrumental action is dominant. Repeated games are a problem, since in most societies the number of people is far too large and individuals too socially dispersed to see them as directly interacting agents at the societal level, hence North's (and colleagues') interest in personality and impersonality as well as power. Now one need only explain the emergence of elites as a result of strategic action (again shifting the explanatory burden one step). Next, the role of taking organizations and social personalities as the primary agents is that they *can* be said to interact repeatedly at the societal level, or at least more reasonably so, and in this fashion the outcome becomes strategically plausible. The beliefs and ideologies are in turn in *UPEC* accounted for in part as exogenous phenomena (cognition plus uncertainty), but also in part by a feedback loop between institutions and belief formation. So the payoff structure of an individual person depends on the payoff structure of others, which in turn depends on a shared system of ideological values and/or prior actions to change the payoff structure. Beliefs and preferences here interact.

Seen from this viewpoint, North's NIEH is an interlocking system of games in the game theoretical sense; but diachronically, the tendency in the framework is to shift the burden of explanation in terms of strategic action further and further away. More and more elements mediate the different levels at which a game is formulated, and those elements are themselves results of higher-order (lower-level) games but are not games. At some point, however, the game-like structures do have to actually do the work of carrying the explanatory burden of the theory. But here we run into serious problems, because game theory does not lend itself to the kind of interactive model between beliefs and preferences that the NIEH suggests. While such models exist in game theory, they precisely have the property of being completely indeterminate; no unique Nash equilibrium emerges (Geneakoplos, Pearce, and Stacchetti 1989). The point of instrumental rationality is to keep beliefs and preferences separate, or formulated differently, to separate the predictions about the world from the objectives in the world. When beliefs are not mere means of achieving preferences, but determinants of preferences, the instrumentally rational strategic approach breaks down. Not even conventions and habits can help by themselves, because the question has to be answered how these in turn become established. Appeals to evolutionary approaches, such as evolutionary game theory, are usually invoked at this point; we shall see more about whether this succeeds in the NIEH in the next chapter.

The point to take away is this. Much of the development of the explanatory structure of North's NIEH can be understood by grasping how each shift in that structure is a response to the problems posed by choice theory and its instrumental-strategic view of rationality. North leans on well-established frameworks of explanation in terms of instrumental rationality, such as game theory and bounded rationality, even as he rejects straightforward rational choice models. At the same time, however, as his theory becomes more and more 'institutionalized', the assumptions on which such well-established frameworks of explanation depend disappear from view. The core problem is that one can have explanations on the basis of instrumental reason in a narrowly circumscribed framework, such as rational choice, and sacrifice realism for determinacy. Or one can have complex systems of interaction between beliefs, preferences, and different kinds of rationality, in which the logic of agency is embedded in a Polanyian sense in the sociocultural context of the historical society. Then one has undoubtedly a greater degree of realism, but at the price of indeterminacy: it becomes impossible to know what the model predicts will happen given a particular set of beliefs, institutions, or political economic structures. North injects explanation in terms of strategic action at several points into his NIEH, both at the level of 'the players of the game' and their incentives and at the level of the contractarian account of institutional change (which persists even after the *rational choice* contractarianism of North and Thomas is given up). But these explanations fit awkwardly inside a larger shell based on psychology, culture, and various kinds of mental subjectivity that are not expressed in terms of instrumental rationality, and possibly cannot be. North wants to have his players of the game and he wants to have his sociocultural embeddedness too. But those two legs of his theory do not walk in alignment.

Conclusion

North is certainly not a simple thinker, and comprehending the complex role of rationality and the agency-structure relationship in his theory is not easy. I have tried to show that although it is true that North is a consistent critic of rational choice neoclassical economics, and that his theory is the furthest possible development of NIE theory in the direction of the full endogenization of social and cultural variables so far, this should not be taken to mean that his NIEH offers a consistent line of argument from those variables to ultimate economic outcomes. North retains a commitment to choice theory and its instrumental view of rationality at the same time as he argues against it in other contexts. Not, to be sure, the classic rationality with perfect information that he criticizes so many times in neoclassical economics. In these criticisms he returns time and again to the significance of belief systems and mental models, and the ahistoricity and asociality of rational choice. And yet when it comes to his usage of classic choice concepts like 'incentives', North does not make any real argument for incentives being different than the self-interested utility maximization familiar from orthodox microeconomics.

On the contrary: he relies on a traditional conception of incentives, and players seeking to maximize rents or other immediate economic returns, as assumptions to make the meso-level of his NIEH work. After all, the whole semi-historical contractarian account of the emergence of limitations on violence and enforceable property rights out of the bargaining between elites is only sustainable if those elites are assumed to maximize their rents. Similarly, the analysis of players' behavior within the game in terms of incentives makes the analysis of economic and political markets possible. Without it, beliefs, inherited cultural norms and habits, and other mental content would become the direct determinants of individual action. In that case, it is not clear what the outcomes or structure of economic or political markets would be, because their meaning would depend entirely on the cultural and mental specifics of the agents in the society in question—precisely the embeddedness of markets that Polanyi had argued for.

North only avoids that outcome by having *both* mental subjectivity operate as a revision of orthodox models of rationality *and* retaining a more instrumental view of rationality in certain parts of his NIEH where it suits him to do so. It is this latter injection of bounded rational choice that underpins nothing less than the role of institutions in his final NIEH framework. In North's final analysis, institutions have to be *constraints* on rational action, just as cognitive limits are *bounds* on rational action, but not *substitutes for* self-regarding instrumental rationality. But since the origins of institutions are not consistently explained, or indeed explicable, in terms of that same bounded rationality approach, each effort to dispel indeterminacy by reference to constraints on rationality simply makes it reappear at another level of the theory.

Ultimately, I suspect that these problems in North's NIEH are problems of the entire New Institutionalist approach. They are merely manifest most visibly in North's work because he is the most ambitious in scope and developed his theory most thoroughgoingly in the direction of the complete endogenization of the social. But for the whole New Institutionalist approach, the same difficulties apply. The more it seeks to incorporate social, cultural, and even psychological elements into the model as endogenous variables, the more this will cause problems of consistency with maintaining a purely instrumentally rational view of agency (whether rational choice in the classic sense or in the form of bounded rationality). These shortcomings are shortcomings of instrumental rationality in economics itself (Varoufakis 1991, 2014; see also chap. 6). And, if conversely the instrumental view of rationality is abandoned at any point, the specter of indeterminacy looms: without a severely constrained model of rational action, it is very difficult to determine which outcomes are predicted by a given set of inputs into the model. North simply ended up doing both. The consequence is that the two legs of North's NIEH end up walking in different directions.

For the NIE to succeed as a paradigm in social scientific research, it will have to make hard choices. Either it must accept the limitations of some form of rational choice but thereby retain the determinacy and tractability that has historically appealed to economists in that particular form of modeling or it can greatly expand its scope and seek unification with the other social sciences—history, sociology, anthropology—but at the cost of giving up on the choice theoretical microfoundations of economics, and to accept the high degree of indeterminacy and causal diffuseness that is common to explanation in those social sciences. One cannot, unfortunately, have both.

References

Aoki, Masahiko. 2001. *Towards a Comparative Institutional Analysis*. Cambridge, MA: MIT Press.

Aumann, Robert J. 1976. Agreeing to Disagree. *Annals of Statistics* 4 (6): 1236–1239.

———. 1987. Correlated Equilibrium as an Expression of Bayesian Rationality. *Econometrica* 55: 1–18.

Binmore, Ken. 2007. *Playing for Real: A Text on Game Theory*. Oxford: Oxford University Press.

Denzau, Arthur T., and Douglass C. North. 1994. Shared Mental Models: Ideologies and Institutions. *Kyklos* 47 (1): 3–31.

Dequech, David. 2006. The New Institutional Economics and the Theory of Behaviour under Uncertainty. *Journal of Economic Behavior & Organization* 59: 109–131.

Didry, Claude and Caroline Vincensini. 2011. *Beyond the Market-Institutions Dichotomy: The Institutionalism of Douglass C. North in Response to Karl Polanyi's challenge*. HALSHS-00601544.

Fenoaltea, Stefano. 1975. The Rise and Fall of a Theoretical Model: The Manorial System. *The Journal of Economic History* 35 (2): 386–409.

Field, Alexander. 1981. The Problem with Neoclassical Institutional Economics: A Critique with Special Reference to the North/Thomas Model of pre-1500 Europe. *Explorations in Economic History* 18 (2): 174–198.

Fine, Ben. 2000. *New and Improved: Economics' Contribution to Business History*, SOAS Working Papers in Economics 93.

Fine, Ben, and Dimitris Milonakis. 2003. From Principle of Pricing to Pricing of Principle: Rationality and Irrationality in the Economic History of Douglass North. *Comparative Studies in Society and History* 45 (3): 546–570.

Friedman, Milton. 1953. The Methodology of Positive Economics. In *Essays in Positive Economics*, ed. Milton Friedman, 3–43. Chicago, IL: University of Chicago Press.

Geneakoplos, John, David Pearce, and Ennio Stacchetti. 1989. Psychological Games and Sequential Rationality. *Games and Economic Behavior* 1 (1): 60–79.

Greif, Avner. 1993. Contract Enforceability and Economic Institutions in Early Trade: the Maghribi Traders' Coalition. *The American Economic Review* 83 (3): 525–548.

———. 1994. Cultural Beliefs and the Organization of Society: A Historical and Theoretical Reflection on Collectivist and Individualist Societies. *Journal of Political Economy* 102 (5): 912–950.

———. 1998. Historical and Comparative Institutional Analysis. *The American Economic Review* 88 (2): 80–84.

Hargreaves-Heap, Shaun P., and Yanis Varoufakis. 1995. *Game Theory: A Critical Introduction*. London: Routledge.

———. 2004. *Game Theory: A Critical Text*. London: Routledge.

Harsanyi, John C. 1967. Games with Incomplete Information Played by Bayesian Players. *Management Science* 14 (3): 159–182.

Hodgson, Geoffrey M. 2007. Meanings of Methodological Individualism. *Journal of Economic Methodology* 14 (2): 211–226.

Hough, Jerry, and Robin Grier. 2015. *The Long Process of Development: Building Markets and States in Pre-Industrial England, Spain, and their Colonies*. Cambridge: Cambridge University Press.

Krul, Matthijs. 2016. *Markets, Institutions and the Polanyian Challenge: A Theoretical Study of the New Institutionalist Economic History of Douglass C. North*. PhD diss., Brunel University.

Langlois, Richard M., and László Csontos. 1993. Optimization, Rule-Following, and the Method of Situational Analysis. In *Rationality, Institutions, and Economic Methodology*, ed. Uskali Mäki, Bo Gustafsson, and Christian Knudsen, 112–132. London: Routledge.

Mäki, Uskali. 1992. Friedman and Realism. *Research in the History of Economic Thought and Methodology* 10: 171–195.

———. 1998. Is Coase a Realist? *Philosophy of the Social Sciences* 28 (1): 5–31.

———. 2009. Realistic Realism about Unrealistic Models. In *Oxford Handbook of the Philosophy of Economics*, ed. Harold Kincaid and Don Ross, 68–98. Oxford: Oxford University Press.

Milonakis, Dimitris, and Ben Fine. 2007. Douglass North's Remaking of Economic History: A Critical Appraisal. *Review of Radical Political Economics* 39 (1): 27–57.

North, Douglass C. 1977. Markets and Other Allocation Systems in History: the Challenge of Karl Polanyi. *Journal of European Economic History* 6 (3): 703–716.

———. 1981. *Structure and Change in Economic History*. Cambridge: Cambridge University Press.

———. 1990. *Institutions, Institutional Change and Economic Performance*. Cambridge: Cambridge University Press.
———. 1992. Institutions and Economic Theory. *The American Economist* 36 (1): 3–6.
———. 1993. What Do We Mean By Rationality? *Public Choice* 77 (1): 159–162.
———. 1994. The Historical Evolution of Polities. *International Review of Law and Economics* 14 (4): 381–391.
———. 2005. *Understanding the Process of Economic Change*. Princeton: Princeton University Press.
North, Douglass C., and Robert Paul Thomas. 1971. The Rise and Fall of the Manorial System: A Theoretical Model. *The Journal of Economic History* 31 (4): 777–803.
———. 1973. *The Rise of the Western World: A New Economic History*. Cambridge: Cambridge University Press.
North, Douglass C., and Barry R. Weingast. 1989. Constitutions and Commitment: The Evolution of Institutions Governing Public Choice in Seventeenth-Century England. *The Journal of Economic History* 49 (4): 803–832.
North, Douglass C., John Joseph Wallis, and Barry R. Weingast. 2009. *Violence and Social Orders: A Conceptual Framework for Interpreting Recorded Human History*. Cambridge: Cambridge University Press.
Peukert, Helge. 2001. Bridging Old and New Institutional Economics: Gustav Schmoller and Douglass C. North, Seen With Old Institutionalists' Eyes. *European Journal of Law and Economics* 11 (2): 91–130.
Schotter, Andrew. 1981. *The Economic Theory of Social Institutions*. Cambridge: Cambridge University Press.
Selten, Reinhard. 1975. Re-examination of the Perfectless Concept for Equilibrium in Extensive Games. *International Journal of Game Theory* 4: 22–25.
Skyrms, Brian. 1996. *Evolution of the Social Contract*. Cambridge: Cambridge University Press.
———. 2003. *The Stag Hunt and the Evolution of Social Structure*. Cambridge: Cambridge University Press.
Varoufakis, Yanis. 1991. *Rational Conflict*. Oxford: Blackwell.
———. 2014. *Economic Indeterminacy*. Abingdon: Routledge.
Weintraub, E. Roy. 1979. *Microfoundations: The Compatibility of Microeconomics and Macroeconomics*. Cambridge: Cambridge University Press.

5

North's Theory of Cultural Evolution

Introduction

The last two chapters have presented a systematic treatment of North's NIEH as a perilous journey between Scylla and Charybdis. As I have interpreted his work, he set himself a double task: on the one hand, to make institutions and history 'matter', against the practice and methodology of both neoclassical economics and the rational choice NIE tradition, and on the other hand to defend the discipline of economics and its analytical tools as the only way of meaningfully doing so. The ship of theory by means of which he has undertaken this journey has a complex structure, whose seaworthiness I have sought to assess. Before moving on to the next aspect of its functioning, let me briefly review what we have learned of its properties so far.

One aspect of the theory is the argument that institutions arise out of market failures, including absent or incomplete markets, and transaction costs. This view, in which institutional structures can be explained along functionalist lines as responses to the market that would have been there if there had not been transaction costs to prevent it, suffers from serious and evident historiographical problems. It is not clear how transaction

M. Krul, *The New Institutionalist Economic History of Douglass C. North*,
Palgrave Studies in the History of Economic Thought,
https://doi.org/10.1007/978-3-319-94084-7_5

costs can be meaningfully measured other than through the same market price mechanisms that are supposed to be explained by them. It is by no means obvious why we should start the inquiry with the implied question why there are no well-ordered price-making markets in Polanyi's sense in the first place, and North's institutionalized account of the emergence of markets is unable to decide the question whether market structure is an outcome or a cause of institutional order. If they are mutually interacting, the problem is an infinite regress. Either one simply declares that in the beginning there were markets, as Oliver Williamson averred, in which case North assumes what he must prove. Or in the beginning were institutions, and then one cannot explain institutions as a response to structural properties of the market, since there were no such properties to act as causes.

By analyzing North's concept of the 'Smithian result', I have tried to show that underlying this circular reasoning is a classical liberal contractarian ideology, which sees the well-ordered market first and foremost as a normative *desideratum* and institution formation as a market-like ('as if') process. The market therefore, in this view, naturally creates itself because human interaction in society is a market-like process, namely in the form of an (implicit) social contract. However, North does nothing to establish or defend the plausibility of either this normative view of 'the market' or the contractarianism that persists even past the abandonment of the North-Thomas model. He appeals to the inspiration of Hayek and his theory of spontaneous order, although differing from him in that North emphasizes what he calls the intentionality of agents. In so doing, he does not really address Polanyi's point about the significance of the coexistence of markets and other allocation systems: that on Polanyi's view, this suggests—at least for premodern societies—the embedded (institutionalized) nature of particular concrete economic markets, as opposed to the imposition of a view of 'the market' as a singular, transhistorical social algorithm.

I then looked at North's critique of neoclassical economics as unrealistic and ahistorical, and how he built on this critique an account of the origins of institutions based on belief systems and the cognitive limitations of the human brain. As I have tried to show, while North's account of the emergence of rules, norms, and conventions out of the attempt to impose regularity on an uncertain and ever-changing world is reasonable by itself, it is difficult to reconcile this micro-level of the theory with the meso-level of markets and institutions discussed above. North veers uneasily back and forth, sometimes assuming forms of bounded rationality that deviate little from fairly common models of rational agents with limited information, sometimes giving an enormous role to mental subjectivity in a way not obviously reconcilable with his 'as if' market account of how agents interact with institutions and organizations. He avoids discussing the important problems of collective action involved in how public goods and collective organizations can come to exist in the first place, by referring to the role of beliefs and shared mental models. But these same beliefs and shared mental models must then in some fashion override self-regarding utility maximization, the very same choice theoretical paradigm he set out to defend and continues to use in other contexts.

This ambiguity arises, I think, from his decision to answer Polanyi's challenge by having his institutional explanation and his choice theory too. The result is that at any given point, one of the two must be a special case of the other, and North is indecisive about which it is to be. His eventual settling on the 'players of the game' approach does not help the problem, but merely serves to highlight its presence. North seems to intuit that game theory is a powerful tool precisely to explain institutions as the stable result of the strategic interaction of individuals, and that it can also be used to model the operation of market-like behavior in situations where the institutional setup is known and the payoffs for each agent understood. It therefore appears like choice theory, refined as the analysis of equilibrium in strategic action, can solve North's problems at multiple levels.

But whether explicitly quantitative models, or as in North's case, rather in the form of narrative allusion and underlying assumptions about agency and rationality, all such explanations in terms of strategic interaction require instrumentally rational individuals with relatively strong substantive rationality to operate. If such conditions do not obtain, the result becomes indeterminate, as no definite sustainable equilibrium arises in many games. If traditional choice theory is abandoned, and each of the vast number of socio-institutional variables North incorporates into his theory has independent explanatory power, indeterminacy is certain to arise; but as it turns out, arbitrarily incorporating a layer of instrumentally rational action within such a framework merely ends up moving the indeterminacy around in the theoretical structure. This is what ends up happening in North's NIEH. Following his abandonment of the efficiency assumption about institutions, North has expanded the scope of institutional explanation to an unprecedented degree while simultaneously seeking to banish the specter of indeterminacy. But in his 'players of the game' approach, his account of agency and his account of structure do not match, and the indeterminacy is not banished but simply forced from one place to the next.

However, there is one more important aspect of the explanatory structure that needs to be discussed before I can move on to discussing the wider implications of North's NIEH. This is the point where the Hayekian tradition and the game theoretical approach meet: North's theory of cultural evolution. In the last stage of his NIEH, in particular in *UPEC*, he developed a view of culture as a collective evolutionary learning process, and this process underpins in turn the imposed regularities of society that make up institutions. What's more, this evolutionary process is also claimed to operate at the macro-level, insofar as economies and entire 'artifactual frameworks' of societies are said to have evolutionary properties at the historical level. Both at the micro-level of beliefs and culture and at the macro-level of societal trajectories, therefore, the same cultural evolutionary principle is posited: they have descent with modification and varying degrees of adaptivity, and those that are unable to adjust to changing circumstances disappear. At the heart of this mechanism in North's theory is his concept of *adaptive efficiency*, and the discussion must therefore begin there.

Adaptive Efficiency

Fitting what I would call the contemporary 'turn to biology' (rather than physics) as source of inspiration for the social sciences, and with North's stated admiration for Hayek's theory of cultural evolution and its importance for economics, North sought to do with evolutionary arguments what his indeterminate choice theoretical approach cannot: explain the origins *and* function of institutions and beliefs in terms of their effect on differential survival. As North describes it, "Put simply the richer the artifactual structure, the more likely are we to confront novel problems successfully. That is what is meant by adaptive efficiency; creating the necessary artifactual structure is an essential goal of economic policy" (North 2005: 70).

We have to observe the peculiarities of the term 'adaptive efficiency'. We know that North abandoned the 'efficiency view', the approach which functionally explains institutions as efficient responses in a given environment, long ago. North's understanding of what makes for efficiency in the case of a whole artifactual framework would then need some explanation. More importantly, however, is the term 'adaptive'. This term is unmistakably a reference to such efficiency coming about as the result of an evolutionary process: adaptations and adaptive are terms of art in evolutionary biology to describe how the unit of selection adjusts to its environment such as to increase its 'fitness'. (This is not to preempt the debate on what precisely a unit of selection is, which I will return to below.) If the efficiency of institutional arrangements as a whole is part of an evolutionary process, as the term suggests, this would imply that societies as a whole are, for North, units of selection in a process of cultural evolution. He makes this clear at various points, like when he calls adaptive efficiency "the ability of some societies to flexibly adjust in the face of shocks and evolve institutions that effectively deal with an altered 'reality'" (North 2005: 6) or "the ability of the society to survive in the face of an ever-changing array of problems and difficulties" (North, Wallis, and Weingast 2009: 133). At the macro-level, then, society is an independent entity—at least for the purposes of an evolutionary explanatory mechanism. Finally, it is important to note that North considers adaptive efficiency to be "the kind of efficiency that has characterized the United States and western Europe" (North 2005: 78), a point to which I will return later.

This is as regards the macro-level. The cultural evolutionary implications of the term become more obvious when we look at its usage at the micro-level of the NIEH. Although North begins *UPEC* by explicitly disavowing an immediate analogy between 'Darwinian evolutionary theory' and the process of institutional change he sets out to describe, he attributes this difference not to the absence of a selection mechanism (say), but to the intentionality of agents in bringing about institutional arrangements. This intentionality makes the process of change one of unintended consequences and path dependences at macro-level, produced by the peculiar "blending" of beliefs and preferences North sees as the bedrock of choice at the micro-level (North 2005: viii). The micro-level operation of cultural evolution that creates institutions, particularly informal ones, in turn forms the basis for the possibility of adaptive efficiency; in fact, the latter depends entirely on the former. With North's warning that "adaptive efficiency evolves only after a relatively long period of evolving informal norms and we know of no shortcut to this process", the micro- and macro-levels of his NIEH are joined together into a single—but layered—cultural evolutionary theory (North 2005: 163).

At that level, evolution operates for North in two ways to produce that blend. Firstly, there is the genetic heritage of humans, a consequence of humans being subject to natural selection. This is, everyone will accept, a Darwinian process. And secondly, North identifies a process of cultural evolution, an allegedly non-Darwinian process that leads to the formation of institutions. Jointly, they help solve the problem of regress discussed above, the question how humans can cooperate in the first place sufficiently so that institutions can sustainably emerge. This question, the possibility of cooperation, is central to North's discussion of cultural evolution at the micro-level: "Part of the scaffolding humans erect is an evolutionary consequence of successful mutations and is therefore a part of the genetic architecture of humans, such as innate cooperation within small interacting groups; part is a consequence of cultural evolution such as the development of institutions to favor larger group cooperation" (North 2005: viii–ix). It is also, as we will see, not coincidentally a central problem of evolutionary game theory.

Non-Darwinian Evolution?

It is not obvious, however, why this intentionality should *ipso facto* prevent the operation of a process of Darwinian selection, if evolution is said to operate to begin with. North repeatedly asserts that his difference with a 'Darwinian' approach and with evolutionary economics rests on the importance of intentionality (likely especially beliefs, given their important role in North's theory) of individuals (North 2005: viii, 66). The point seems to be to distinguish whatever process of cultural evolution he identifies from the blind logic of natural selection, because the individuals subject to the process are in some fashion directly involved in shaping it. This does not immediately seem a clear distinction, given that the goal-oriented behavior of animals does not mean natural selection does not apply to them.

North, however, proffers two major distinctions between his approach and a Darwinian evolutionary approach to economic change, which he acknowledges is an evident possibility once the idea of social evolution is permitted (North 2005: 65).[1] The first is the argument about intentionality mentioned above, whereby one should keep in mind that 'intentionality' is used by North to describe his view of rational agency in other contexts (see chap. 4). The core point here is that North is concerned with a forward-looking ability of humans: intentionality involves "beliefs about the eventual consequences", something which invokes his arguments about beliefs as well as the importance of the payoff structure and the possibility of error (North 2005: 66). The other argument is the lack of analogy for a source of variation. As North puts it, in biology "variation occurs through mutation and sexual recombination along Mendelian lines. There is no close analogy in economic evolution" (North 2005: 66).

This is all the more striking because North's subsequent argument does not actually imply any such disjunction between his view of evolution and the Darwinian process, keeping in mind the rather radical implications of introducing evolutionary explanation into the framework to begin with. Far from seeing intentionality and its product, culture, as some form of irreducibly 'thick' social process that cannot be meaningfully explained in evolutionary terms, as some social scientists do, North

[1] Here the references are to the work of Ulrich Witt (1992) and Geoffrey Hodgson (1993), as well as Arthur Denzau, with whom North had collaborated on exploring ideology before (Denzau and North 1994). It is curious that the references are so far before the publication date of *UPEC* and ignore subsequent work by these influential evolutionary economists. One gets the impression that North decided fairly early on that the evolutionary economics paradigm did not work for him, and perhaps ignored the literature after that.

himself undertakes his discussion in *UPEC* by rather suggesting the contrary. Firstly, he observes that human culture, including knowledge, beliefs, and learned habits, are a cumulative residue of past experience of members of a society, one that is inherited. This heritage not only "constrains the players" (here we are back at instrumental rationality), but in fact straightforwardly "determines societal performance at a moment of time", elsewhere called the "performance characteristics of societies" (North 2005: viii, ix). North also rightly points out that the cultural-institutional frameworks that make up human societies are themselves possible due to human genetic evolution, as mentioned.

Moreover, the process of path dependence and other factors that tend to create continuity between generations of a culture despite ongoing change operate analogously to heritability even in North's own description. He describes long periods of incremental changes interspersed with brief periods of rapid change as a case of "punctuated equilibrium change", and the temporal factor of economic history is explicitly mentioned as a reason to take inspiration (be it with the above reservation) from evolutionary theory (North 2005: 2–3, 65–66). On the whole, then, the suggestion is that evolutionary mechanisms do apply throughout the cultural-institutional layer. Finally, the first six chapters of *UPEC*, roughly half the book, are dedicated to explaining adaptive efficiency, and of that, at least three chapters (3, 4 and 6), and arguably chapter 7 too, are specifically about evolutionary processes in the most literal sense.

North allows, of course, for institutions, technology, and other factors to have causal power in their own right, but they are based on an evolutionary foundation: "Over time it is the variety of responses of humans to different environments expressed in terms of languages, customs, technologies, and organization that stands out. The differential hospitality of the physical environment to human development explains much of the historical difference in human well-being. But increasingly, as scientific knowledge has modified the differences in the physical environment, the complex interplay between demography, the stock of knowledge, and the institutions of societies shapes performance" (North 2005: 94). Intentionality, then, is the product of a Darwinian process, and therefore so are institutions. Why should not they also be part of an overarching Darwinian model of cultural evolution then, just as the cultural behavior of animals—dam-building by beavers, cooperation in ants, squirrels burying nuts in the winter—must be and can be explained in Darwinian terms? North's terse statement is not sufficiently convincing on its own. This leaves us with the problem of variation. But here North in a sense refutes himself. At the macro-level, adaptive efficiency operates on "the immense variation in the performance characteristics of societies" (North 2005: 6), and at the micro-level institutional variation appears as a result of the naturally (genetically) different responses of the cognition of human individuals to different naturally given environments. Variation, then, is given by North's own framework. It may be so that there is no gene analogy on which variation operates. But as long the relevant properties of institutions for the purposes of cultural evolution, whatever they may be, can vary naturally—that is, exogenously—this is not essential.

Of course, there have often been suggestions that evolutionary theories do apply to the process of culture and institutional change, but not a Darwinian one, for example in the appeals to the theory of Jean-Baptiste Lamarck, where acquired characteristics can be inherited so as to improve fitness over time. There is something of a tradition of such appeals in the history of evolutionary approaches to institutions, including authors that North took inspiration from: as in the work of Friedrich Hayek (1952, 1983) and of Richard Nelson and Sidney Winter, pioneers of evolutionary approaches to institutional economics (Nelson and Winter 1982), as discussed below. But as has been understood in evolutionary biology for a considerable time, no Lamarckian inheritance mechanism can exist independently of the Darwinian: even if there is a Lamarckian form of inheritance at the cultural level, "the Lamarckian theory can explain adaptive improvement in evolution only by, as it were, riding on the back of the Darwinian theory" (Dawkins 1986: 300).

There can be no doubt then that whatever North's reservations about what he calls Darwinism and intentionality or his hesitations to wade into this minefield, a full discussion of North's work requires investigating his account as a theory of cultural evolution that at least should meet criteria comparable to the Darwinian framework. Of course, this leaves open the question whether it is a consistent and complete evolutionary framework by such criteria, which is what I will now discuss. But it is worth noting that for a theory of cultural evolution to conform to Darwinian criteria, it need not be a *complete* Darwinian theory. In fact, no Darwinian evolutionary approach is complete on its own: it provides mechanisms, but these always need application in specific empirical contexts and using auxiliary theories for the specific case. It does however, at least in its modern form, define these mechanisms and the criteria for their operation with some degree of precision.

In order to define what these are, we have to divide the discussion according to the two aspects of cultural evolution identified by North: the evolution of institutions as a problem of their *origins*, which operates at the micro-level of North's theory, and the evolution of institutions as a problem of their dynamics over time and economic effects, that is of their *persistence*, which operates at the macro-level. Put differently, the first question is how and why an 'artifactual framework' comes into being in the first place, and the second question is how it works and changes once it is there, and what this means for its adaptive efficiency over time. North's approach gives us sufficient means to discuss both aspects as part of an integrated process of cultural evolution that, if it is to succeed at all, must succeed in Darwinian terms, despite his own reservations. It is generally agreed that for a Darwinian-type process of evolution by means of natural (or artificial) selection to take place, all that is required is high-accuracy heritability or reproduction, variability, and differential fitness (competition) (Hodgson and Knudsen 2010). North's approach gives us these: we have cultural inheritance and path dependence (heritability), we have differential fitness (adaptive efficiency), and we have variation, as discussed above. In principle, then, we have both the necessary elements for a theory of cultural evolution in North that is really worthy of the term 'evolution', in the sense that it can use the well-established explanatory power of evolutionary theory within its own framework. This usage of theoretical inputs from outside the NIEH framework itself, inputs known to have great explanatory power, is not unique to evolution in North's work. Recall that the same phenomenon was observable in North's occasional reliance on a (quasi-) game theory.

North's Theory of Cultural Evolution in Context and Detail

The point of establishing the applicability of Darwinian criteria to North's theory of cultural evolution, despite his disavowal of Darwinism, is this. The term 'evolution' has many different uses in social science. These can vary from mere metaphor, as in cases where 'evolution' is virtually identical with 'development' or even with 'progress', to cases where a direct applicability of the biological criteria of evolution is intended, as, for example, in the theory of memetics (Cloak 1975; Dawkins 1976; Blackmore 2000).[2] There is no inherent reason to nitpick any particular usage of the term, therefore, since this wide range of application has been with the concept from the beginning. But for analytical purposes, it does matter what kind of usage is intended. When evolution is merely change or development, there is no harm but also no explanation. It is merely a descriptive term. When some entity is said to evolve and the intention is to convey the relevance of Darwinian selection theory, however, it is a different story. Precisely because the explanatory framework of Darwinian selection theory is so well established and its explanatory power familiar to many, it is tempting for any theory to invoke it, whether or not the criteria for applicability are actually satisfied. If a theorist makes reference to evolution as a mechanism in the context of explaining some social phenomenon, and does so with the explicit or implicit purpose of strengthening the theory by relying on the established explanatory power of Darwinian selection as a mechanism, that theory must demonstrate that this mechanism actually operates in the social phenomenon in question. Otherwise, the reference fails to carry the explanatory burden placed on it, and the theory is flawed.

It is for this reason that when theories of evolution are invoked in social science, including theories of cultural evolution, it is important to

[2] It is an irony of language that the concept of the meme has since then become more commonly used in a context where it is explicitly metaphor, as demonstrated on the internet today. And yet the widespread distribution of this particular metaphor could, at a meta-level, be taken as an example of the applicability of memetic theory. See Burman (2012) for a discussion.

establish whether the necessary elements of a real evolutionary mechanism are identified (the three described above), *and* whether these identifications are actually valid. In other words: such a theory must be assessed on the basis of whether it can plausibly argue that there is high-accuracy inheritance, random variation, and selection for fitness in the social phenomenon in question, and that the elements of the social phenomenon that are said to correspond to each of these submechanisms of Darwinian selection really *do* have those traits. This is why North's rejection of the applicability of Darwinian selection does not help his case. Not only because his arguments why it does not apply to his theory are unconvincing, but also because if they were convincing they would merely demonstrate that his theory of cultural evolution is not evolutionary at all, except in some vague metaphorical sense. In that case, it would fail to explain anything in its own terms from the get-go. But because his arguments for a special status for his 'intentional' evolutionary theory fail, the possibility that it is in fact a legitimate theory of cultural evolution—and therefore can carry the explanatory burden North places on it in his wider NIEH framework—remains. In a sense, I am doing his theory a favor by rejecting his special pleading.

Of course, the precise carriers of these selection processes will be very different in the context of human society and culture than in the case of evolutionary biology. But the generalization of Darwinian theory simply follows from the nature of Darwinism itself: it is a process that applies if and only if the criteria of variation, selection (through competition), and heredity apply, although its application to the social sphere requires identification of evolutionary units beyond the genetic, 'cultural' units such as habits or institutions. Howard Aldrich and colleagues, defending what they call a 'generalized Darwinism' in economics, observe that although "cultural selection processes are different from biological selection processes", it is nonetheless the case that where these criteria can be identified, "the *expression* of the underlying core Darwinian principles of variation, inheritance and selection differ in important ways, yet the overarching general principles remain… Darwin's principles of evolution do not themselves provide a complete explanation. Darwinism does not provide a complete theory of everything, from cells to human society. Instead, these principles are a kind of 'meta-theory', or an over-arching theoretical framework wherein theorists place particular explanations. Crucially, explanations additional to natural selection are always required to explain any evolved phenomenon... Selection is a general principle, but it operates in different ways in different contexts. Likewise, the general Darwinian principle of variation applies, but it does not itself explain *how* variation occurs" (Aldrich et al. 2008: 580, 585, emphases added). One need not accept the entire framework of 'generalized Darwinism' as formulated by these authors to see the validity of this point. Darwinian selection is a *general* theory, describing the nature and operation in abstract terms of a particular algorithmic process. For this reason, it is not limited to the description of the operation of particular biological mechanisms alone, but applies generally wherever the algorithmic process operates on relevant entities (Dennett 1995). Of course, the question where and when it does operate remains a very big one, and full of intricacies, and the field of evolutionary approaches to social science remains a new and open one.

Such an application is not new to institutional economics, either. The application of evolutionary arguments to the analysis of the modern economy, in particular that of the capitalist firm, goes back to at least the work of Thorstein Veblen (Veblen 1898). In more recent times, the work of Richard Nelson and Sidney Winter did much to put the identification of evolutionary dynamics in the economics of the firm, and by extension microeconomics in general, back on the agenda (Nelson and Winter 1982). In their work, Nelson and Winter applied the theory of selection to the interaction between firms in an economy over a longer period of time, emphasizing the effects of competition on the differential economic survival of such firms. While the idea of economic competition as akin to the 'survival of the fittest' was nothing new (already a favorite metaphor of Spencerian liberalism in the Victorian age), more significant was Nelson and Winter's identification of the units of replication and selection. Emphasizing that firms were not necessarily fully profit maximizing, nor the market necessarily in a state of equilibrium, they concentrated on the internal organization of the firm as the heritable equivalent to the genotype. The firm itself being the phenotypical expression of routines and habits of organizational behavior within it, such routines were, for Nelson and Winter, replicators that had both the necessary stability and heritability and the necessary potential for random or nonrandom variation required for a process of selection. These are then the units of selection.

In this way, Nelson and Winter could identify within the domain of industrial organization and modern market competition an evolutionary process by observing how it fulfilled the necessary criteria: the existence of sufficiently stable, but mutable, units of their heritability and of a process of differential survival. For the moment, the point is not whether Nelson and Winter were right to identify routines as units of selection in this manner, but simply to realize the significance of this argument. In Nelson and Winter's account, the interaction between the organization of firms and the competition between firms is identified as an *actual* process of natural selection, not merely a politically convenient *metaphor* or analogy as in the Spencerian tradition. Indeed, as Marcus Becker notes, the analysis of routines became very influential in reviving the promise of an evolutionary economics precisely because "the great promise that the concept of routines holds for evolutionary economics is that it might enable the application of an evolutionary explanation in economics", that is to say, it would be "a cornerstone of an evolutionary theory of economic change". With the identification of a gene equivalent, suddenly the prospect of actual Darwinian selection, not just metaphorical Darwinism, became possible in the economic sphere (Becker 2004: 2, 29).

The affinity of such approaches with institutional economics is easy enough to see. Evolutionary explanations serve to explain change, and rather than the static equilibrium approaches of perfect competition neoclassical economics, they are easily combined with imperfect markets and imperfect information assumptions. The behavior of economic agents under uncertainty is an important area of study of institutional economics, as we know, and therefore the two go together very easily. One early example is Armen Alchian's evolutionary analysis of competition under uncertainty, an inspiration for Nelson and Winter's work. In Alchian's model, the main theoretical innovation was to substitute survival (fitness) for profit maximization per se in the model of firm interaction and market change (Alchian 1950). Alchian's subsequent work with Harold Demsetz and William R. Allen would also be a significant contribution to the literature on transaction costs, costly information, and the market as a discovery process in the Hayekian vein, all themes that had their influence on North directly (Alchian and Demsetz 1972; Alchian and Allen 1983).[3]

In this context, North's NIEH is interesting precisely as an exemplar of the joining of certain strands in (new) institutional economics and in evolutionary economics, even if he attempts to distance himself somewhat from the latter. More than this, North also brings in behavioral (including experimental) economics and even gene-culture coevolution theory at certain points in the discussion. The result is therefore a framework for cultural evolution that is rich with potential. A closer examination is necessary to see how these elements are, or are not, integrated and to what extent the result, a two-layered theory of cultural evolution, fulfills the necessary criteria of applicability and plausibility described above.

North presents his account of the evolution of cognition as a necessary complement to standard accounts because of the inadequacy of rational choice equilibrium reasoning, that is, neoclassical economics. Here we are on familiar ground. Because beliefs matter, as North rightly insists, the acquisition of beliefs from the environment matters too. He surveys briefly theories of pattern recognition and the limited cognitive reasoning abilities of human minds. Then he observes how this contextualizes rational choice in a larger institutional framework, without doing away with it. This larger institutional framework is itself the process of evolutionary competition as a whole, and emerges from imperfect feedback on imperfect information and limited cognitive abilities. As he puts it: "The implication… for social science theorizing is that much of what passes for rational choice is not so much individual cogitation as the embeddedness of the thought process in the larger social and institutional context" (North 2005: 24). This shows how far removed this micro-level analysis is from rational choice, constrained optimization, or bounded rationality. Indeed, a fundamentally socio-institutional embeddedness (note the

[3] Unfortunately, there is no space in this book for a lengthier discussion of the intellectual influences on North beyond those discussed briefly in the respective thematic chapters. An intellectual biography of North should certainly note the importance of Alchian and Demsetz for North's ideas about the interaction between uncertainty, path dependence, and the transaction cost economics paradigm.

Polanyian term) of thinking is a way of approaching cognition that seems substantially different from any economics-based utility maximization model.

But of course our own cognition is the result of biological evolution, and this raises the sociobiological problem of what this means for human sociality and culture. It is I think a striking fact that North treats this in only a summary way, and mainly with the aim of emphasizing the importance of producing culture for human behavior. The main antagonist here is the sociobiological school of 'evolutionary psychology', represented by John Tooby, Lana Cosmides, and others, who have long asserted that the adaptive landscape of the Pleistocene has shaped a strongly modular human brain in such a way as to render much of our behavior only explicable as adaptations to a prehistoric context long gone (Tooby and Cosmides 1992). North accepts that such 'universals' may operate still, as maladaptations from a bygone era in the period of human civilization, but questions how far this can take social science given the vast variation in cultural traits displayed by human societies in history. Culture matters in an evolutionary picture, he rightly emphasizes, and it is not obvious how this school of evolutionary psychology can account for that in terms of institutional variation. As he insists, "The immense variation, however, in the performance characteristics of political/economic units over time makes clear that the Lamarckian characteristics of culture must also be central to the understanding of the process" (North 2005: 30). Here we see the Lamarckian gambit in operation. Its primary aim however is not to dismiss the applicability of evolutionary theory altogether, but only the 'evo psych' version of it.

Returning then to how culture emerges from "the link between the mind and the environment", Hayek again looms large for North. Most important is Hayek's observation from *The Sensory Order* that "the apparatus by means of which we learn about the external world is itself the product of a kind of experience. It is shaped by the conditions prevailing in the environment in which we live, and it represents a kind of generic reproduction of the relations between the elements of this environment which we have experienced in the past" (North 2005: 32–33; Hayek 1952: 165). This is another cue for North to insist on the holistic nature of learning, its dependence on the experience of the world as mediated by the human environment (the society) as much as by the natural. Rather strikingly, he cites Edwin Hutchins to the effect that "we cannot adequately understand cognition without accounting for the fact that culture, context, and history ... are fundamental aspects of human cognition and cannot be comfortably integrated into a perspective that privileges abstract properties of isolated individual minds" (North 2005: 33–34). So much for North the methodological individualist. At this point, North's evolutionary model of cognition and the emergence of culture is a thoroughly socialized affair, quite distinct from his much more boundedly rational analysis of individuals as constrained by institutions, as at the meso-level of the NIEH.

The bridge concept between this socialized view of cognition and the macro-level of evolution in the form of adaptive efficiency is *learning*. For North, learning is a collective process leading to a residue in the form of culture. This then hardens over time, as it were, into an institutional 'artifactual framework'. As he puts it: "Human learning is more than the accumulation of the experiences of an individual over a lifetime. It is also the cumulative experiences of past generations. The cumulative learning of a society embodied in language, human memory, and symbol storage systems includes beliefs, myths, ways of doing things that make up the culture of a society. Culture not only determines societal performance at a moment of time but, through the way in which its scaffolding constrains the players, contributes to the process of change through time. The focus of our attention, therefore, must be on human learning—on what is learned and how it is shared among the members of a society and on the incremental process by which the beliefs and preferences change, and on the way in which they shape the performance of economies through time" (North 2005: viii).

With this bridge concept, we have the evolutionary elements in North's theory. There is the genetic evolution of our cognitive predisposition as humans, which includes our fundamental sociality in small groups and our way of forming beliefs in the face of uncertainty. Then there is the cultural evolution of institutions out of that cognitive predisposition, the result of a collective learning process that creates culture and the normative content of culture. Some process of selection presumably operates here to determine which possible response to uncertainty survives in the form of culture or institutions in the longer run. This cultural evolutionary process also supports, in some fashion, the ability of humans to cooperate in larger groups where we do not consistently interact with the same people face-to-face. These institutions and cultures in turn integrate into artifactual frameworks, whose property is a greater or lesser degree of adaptive efficiency; selection also operates at this level, among such frameworks as a whole.

The upshot of this is to see, with Hutchins and Hayek, learning as "adaptive reorganization in a complex system", and institutions as cognitive instruments forming adaptations to present (or past, in the case of path dependence) environments (North 2005: 35–36). These institutional frameworks and their greater or lesser ability to generate adaptive efficiency are then the subjects of selection. In other words, learning operates at group level as much as at individual level, because of the importance of social context to individual learning processes. Because of widespread uncertainty and continuous change, human learning and retention of knowledge is an essential evolutionary development toward culture. Institutions allow individual learning to proceed from an inheritance of culturally stored knowledge. These learning processes cause this larger whole, the institutionalized society or group, to act as the unit of selection of cultural evolution. These societies as a whole act so as to maximize their fitness (i.e. they adapt intentionally). He cites approvingly the work of Andy Clark, who writes that "when the external scaffolding of policies, infrastructure and customs is strong and (importantly) is a result of competitive selection, the individual members are, in effect, interchangeable cogs in a larger machine. The larger machine extends way outside the individual, incorporating large-scale social, physical, and even geopolitical structures. And it is the diffused reasoning and behavior of this larger machine that traditional economic theory often succeeds in modeling" (North 2005: 24–25; Clark 1997: 182).

North makes this connection between the evolutionary origin of institutions in individual and collective learning and the macro-level evolutionary process explicit in a paragraph that forms the basis of the argument in *UPEC*. It is worth quoting in full: "When we move from Hutchins's dynamic social group … to the larger implications for the structure, functioning, and process of change for a whole society we can see that the cultural heritage provides the artifactual structure—beliefs, institutions, tools, instruments, technology—which not only plays an essential role in shaping the immediate choices of players in a society but also provides us with clues to the dynamic success or failure of societies through time. In essence, the richer the artifactual structure, the greater the reduction of uncertainty in making choices at a moment of time. Over time, the richer the cultural context in terms of providing multiple experimentation and creative competition, the more likely the successful survival of the society. These generalizations require careful elaboration and qualification, but they are a foundation of this study" (North 2005: 36).

At the macro-level, North moves from this cognitive framework to the unfolding of competitive, impersonal exchange as a mechanism making large-scale cooperation possible. This historical process is not predetermined to succeed. Indeed, on North's account, none other than the Western world have achieved it. The means of achieving such cooperation is a change in the payoffs in the game theoretical matrix such that cooperation becomes a dominant strategy. But because in North's theory the choice set of institutional arrangements depends on beliefs and previous institutional arrangements, in other words because path dependence matters, this is not something that can be arbitrarily willed into being: "The shift from personal to impersonal exchange has produced just such a stumbling block both historically and in the contemporary world. Personal exchange relies on reciprocity, repeat dealings, and the kind of informal norms that tend to evolve from strong reciprocity relationships. Impersonal exchange requires the development of economic and political institutions that alter the pay-offs in exchange to reward cooperative behavior. The creation of the necessary institutions requires a fundamental alteration in the structure of the economy and the polity which frequently is not in the feasible set given the historically derived beliefs and institutions of the players" (North 2005: 117–118). Nonetheless, North is explicit that the gains from trade, the competitive market benchmark discussed in chap. 2, is the sine qua non of evolutionary success: "Successful evolution has entailed radical alteration in economic institutions in order to make such long distance and impersonal trade viable" (North 2005: 118).

The developmental recipe North proposes then has 'evolutionary' flexibility, in that it concentrates on ability to adapt rather than simply 'getting the prices right'. But the recipe is itself not so different from classical liberal political economy, albeit with a renewed emphasis on cultural and ideological factors: strong property rights, stable and well-supported market exchange (in 'political and economic markets'), a limited government that is credibly committed to following its own rules and constraints, and, as the additional sociocultural element, a sufficient degree of conformity of values and beliefs and enforcement of these to glue the whole together, as it were (North 2005: 158). An important element here is the emphasis on the need to regularly shake up the institutional order. While "the creation of a set of property rights that will lead to an effective price system is a necessary step" (North 2005: 158), so that the market can do its beneficent work, it is also important that the institutional support structure for the market is flexible enough that it can change when needed. As the environment changes, so must the structure adapt: this is the evolutionary content of adaptive efficiency.

What must be preserved is the ability of the 'Smithian result' to obtain, in other words to let limited and competitive government, secure property, and widespread competitive markets lead to capturing the gains from trade. As North and colleagues put it, "Understanding social change in actual historical events requires separating institutions, organizations, and beliefs, as well as violence, in order to track their interrelated development over time… the transition [to open access orders] provides citizens with new tools, fewer restrictions, and greater scope for impersonal relations, all of which dramatically increase the gains from specialization and exchange while reducing the risk of expropriation" (North, Wallis, and Weingast 2009: 259, 261).

Here it is again incentives that are the main criterion. North seems unsure whether such incentives depend precisely on the Western classical liberal recipe. The open access order model suggests so, and so does the institutional package suggested above. On the other hand, he wavers: "It should be emphasized that the institutions that have emerged in the Western world, such as property rights and judicial systems, do not have to be faithfully copied in developing countries. The key is the incentive structure that is created, not the slavish imitation of western institutions… the Chinese developed an incentive structure which managed to produce rapid economic development without any of the standard recipes of the West. However, down the road the Chinese must embed the incentive system in the political/economic structure if they are to continue their rapid development and that will probably require institutions that come much closer to having the adaptively efficient features of western societies" (North 2005: 159).

Besides the reapparance of 'embeddedness', this tells us very little of substance. The Chinese can have success their own way, but, also, to have success one must follow liberal incentives, and that requires liberal politics and economics. I will leave a discussion of North's policy recommendations for the next chapter. For now, more important is North's general attitude that institutional change cannot be simply willed into existence, and that path dependence is generally a cause for pessimism about the possibility of achieving the open access order with its adaptive efficiency. Even seemingly successful societies may fail over time because adaptive efficiency is so hard to achieve, as the Soviet case demonstrates for North (North 2005: ch. 11). This fits the general pessimistic outcome of North's anthropology, as I have suggested before. In North's evolutionary theory, as in all his theoretical work in its most developed form, a consistent theme is the sheer difficulty of making institutions lead to good outcomes. So many variables in the model means so many variables that need to be aligned with each other to make the whole work. (Work, of course, within the meta-norms North retains.) The concept of adaptive efficiency seems designed to get that point across once more.

Evaluating North's Theory of Cultural Evolution: The Macro-Level

Returning to cultural evolution, let us restate the problem again. The point of contestation should not be whether Darwinian selection can in principle be generalized, but rather where in human sociocultural life it can fruitfully be applied and to what units of selection. This also entails, however, recognizing the warning of the evolutionary economists that

Darwinian theory, precisely because of its generality, is incomplete. It is all too easy to apply the language of selection to any given sociocultural process; it is quite another thing to demonstrate its real (rather than metaphorical) applicability. North's ideas are certainly defensible in principle when he proposes a theory of cultural evolution, but the use of evolutionary language is not sufficient on its own to constitute an appropriate explanation. We must keep this in mind when evaluating North's particular version of cultural evolution. Moreover, the precise operation of natural selection in a sociobiological context is also controversial, even if the *applicability in principle* need not be.

The interesting properties of Darwinian selection, well explored in evolutionary biology since the postwar period, lend themselves to the 'elective affinity' with institutional economics as discussed above. A discussion of this affinity must be undertaken with some care. As we have seen, the NIE is divided into more neoclassical-oriented and more radical strands, and they have different approaches to the origin and function of institutions (Eggertsson 1990). Moreover, as Jack Vromen has pointed out, there is an important difference between those evolutionary approaches concentrating on the evolution of market competition in capitalist economies, as exemplified by Nelson and Winter's work (but arguably also that of Veblen and Commons), and those approaches interested in the more sociobiological question of cultural evolution as a whole, within which economic evolution is a (central) special case, as exemplified by Hayek and North (Vromen 1995). Much of the 'neoinstitutional' tradition, as exemplified by the work of Oliver Williamson, Ronald Coase, and others, still hews closely to the neoclassical model of the agent as rational contractor. It allows only for change and learning in a static, probabilistic way. Although markets are imperfect and transaction costs persist in such models, they do not allow for the qualitatively distinct role of uncertainty, nor for understanding learning and innovation as ongoing processes of finding local efficiencies. This, in turn, means that they lack a natural affinity with the blindly searching algorithmic selection process that Darwinian natural selection represents (Hodgson 1998).

Keeping this in mind, the affinities between the generalized Darwinian approach and at least some institutionalisms are worth restating. Darwinian selection is blind, thereby not inherently requiring any particularly sophisticated rationality nor informational acquisition on the part of its 'phenotypes' and none at all on the part of its 'genotypes'. Even where no obvious equivalent to genotypes and phenotypes exists, it can still operate just fine without requiring any intentionality on the part of the replicators, *pace* North, as long as the criteria of generalized Darwinism apply. This lends itself well to its use in contexts where less than perfect rationality is assumed, and where uncertainty prevails and information is scarce. Moreover, Darwinian selection searches only for *local* 'efficiency', and defines such efficiency purely in terms of differentiated survival—contrary to popular belief, no actual implications of improvement, progress, or 'optimality' are implied by natural selection. This makes for a natural fit with approaches to economics that emphasize the contingency and limits of efficiency in markets (or other economic modes of organization), such as institutional economics. Finally, the core of modern evolutionary theory is the interaction between a population subject to selection pressures and its environment, and in an economic analysis this readily evokes the relation between economic agents and a social-institutional context. Moreover, the Darwinian structure of (mostly) incremental change on the basis of constraints on the possible set of viable mutations, determined by the inheritance of previous evolution, is closely analogous to the role of path dependence in institutional history as conceived of by North.

North's most recent works illustrate, as we have seen, all of these elective affinities. For this reason the evaluation of his work must have implications for assessing the utility of approaches in the general theory cluster one might call 'institutional-evolutionary economics' (involving both the Veblen-Alchian-Nelson/Winter school studying the evolution of the firm and the Hayek-North school studying the evolution of institutions), of which his NIEH is an important part. Even so, the differences between these two approaches are important for evaluating North's particular version. This becomes clear when we examine what the unit of selection is supposed to be in either case. Such an analysis usually rests on David Hull's influential division between 'replicators' (those entities that are stable and preserved in the hereditary process) and 'interactors' (the relevant units of the population subject to selection pressure)—the generalized theory of which the genotype-phenotype distinction is the biological special case (Hull 1980). Identifying these elements in a given evolutionary mechanism is an ongoing debate within philosophy of biology, and involves a number of different problems in a given case: What is the unit of selection, what it is that is doing the adapting, what it is that is subject to variable survival (i.e. what the replicator is), and what is the ultimate agent that 'benefits' from 'success' in the process of natural selection (Sober and Wilson 1994; Lloyd 2012)? The approach of Nelson and Winter and followers has to some extent converged on identifying routines and/or habits as replicators and units of selection (Becker 2004).

For my purposes, what matters is that in the specific case of the evolution of the firm, the advantage of the identification of routines and habits as the unit of selection and the subsequent literature theorizing its evolutionary mechanisms is that this literature can to some extent successfully answer these questions from philosophy of biology in a precise way. Moreover, the answers can be linked directly to empirically observable phenomena in the economic entities and behaviors in question. While this does not guarantee that the theory is the best or most fruitful description of competition and change between and within firms in a modern market economy, it does give the evolutionary approach sufficient grounding to be more plausible than a mere 'just-so' story. But unlike the tradition of Nelson and Winter, Alchian, and others, North is not primarily interested in an evolutionary explanation of market processes and organizational change themselves. In fact, if my argument in the previous chapters is right, he is so to speak consistently inconsistent in whether to take a more orthodox approach to this domain—focusing on rational pursuit of maximum payoffs when confronted with transaction costs—or to adjust, in some indefinite manner, the model to account for a different form of rationality.

North's evolutionary mechanism is not in fact located at the meso-level of the short- to medium-term operation of markets, hierarchies, and organizational and institutional structures within a given historical society's economic formation. It is located at the micro-level, in the importance of cognition and other human genetic heritage as products of evolution; and more importantly, it is located at the macro-level, in the evolution and adaptation of whole institutional orders, indeed whole societies and cultures, over the long run. As he himself has indicated, it is the tradition of Hayek, not of Veblen or Nelson and Winter, that is the most important for North's account (Hough and Grier 2015: 50–51; North 2005: 5, 31, 52). This presents two daunting challenges, since both levels must be assessed for validity and plausibility. If we accept the replicator-interactor distinction conventional in evolutionary economics as useful, at each level the relevance and plausibility of the evolutionary account then has to be justified in terms of the four questions posed above: What is the unit of selection, what it is that is doing the adapting, what is the replicator, and what is the ultimate agent that 'benefits' from 'success' in the process of natural selection? Since these are more closely connected, despite their different scopes and levels of abstraction, they require an integrated evaluation. I will begin this by concentrating on the macro-level role of evolution in his account, since it is arguably the most controversial, but this soon brings us to problems in North's micro-level evolutionary account as well.

A helpful start is to show the points of contrast between North's approach and that of Hayek. There are two major differences between Hayek's evolutionary account of spontaneous order and North's account of adaptive efficiency. The first is that, for Hayek, the rationality and intentionality of individuals was given and not in need of explanation. Culture in Hayek's view was strictly reducible to the cumulative outcome of the choices of individuals, and the nature of these choices as such was not in question (Hodgson 1994: 411–412). In North, however, the problem of the formation of beliefs and their interactive dialectic with the human (institutional) environment is a central area of concern. Unlike the Austrian tradition of Hayek, North has no difficulties per se with admitting psychology into the model of individual behavior. This leads to the second major difference, which is that for Hayek, the "selective evolution" of rules "by imitative learning" that he identified was undertaken according to the requirement of the fitness of a particular individual or group adopting the rule (Hayek 1967: 67–68). Since evolutionary accounts are always functionalist, this means one can have an efficiency view such as this, where each element in the system is assumed to contribute to the efficiency of the system and to be explained thereby, or a nonefficiency view, in which the phenomenon in question is still explained by its function within a larger system but without the assumption of this function contributing to the fitness of that system. (Instead, it may be an emergent property or an inherited neutral or even negative byproduct of some other fitness enhancing element.) The rational choice tradition and Hayek adopt the former view. North, at least in the later stages of his work (where evolution makes its appearance), seems to adopt the latter, given his overall rejection of efficiency explanations of institutions and his emphasis on beliefs and irrational elements of human intentionality.[4]

By adopting this distinct approach from the Hayekian model, North seems to have attempted to avoid the contradictions in Hayek's approach identified by Geoffrey Hodgson: namely, between Hayek's functionalist and fitness-maximization-based explanation of institutions as products of conscious choice and his equally evolutionary appeal to the unconscious operation, via routines and habit, of inherited cultural norms and traditions. These need not inherently be contradictory, but require a consistent explanation connecting the two. Hayek's refusal to specify how the psychology of the individual relates to a group, and how the relevant psychology or rationality of either is defined when 'choosing' institutions or when following habitual norms and routines, makes him—as Hodgson points out—incapable of explaining either the formation of institutions or the evolutionary process that supposedly generates spontaneous order (Hodgson 1994: 423–424).

Yet North's attempt at escaping these contradictions ends up generating analogous ones. Firstly, as I have argued in the previous chapter, North is inconsistent in his explanation of how individuals relate to institutions. Explanations in terms of self-interest clash with explanations in terms of potentially irrational belief systems, and, simultaneously, game theoretical models relying on fairly strict criteria of common rationality and beliefs are joined with explanations in terms of indeterminate and undefined constraints on individual choice sets. In light of Hodgson's critique of Hayek's evolutionary theory, North's inconsistency in models of rationality can now also be better understood. Tellingly, in North the problem of efficiency in functionalist explanation also recurs. While

[4] The excessive efficiency assumptions in Hayek's functionalism are criticized by Vanberg (1986), a work that influenced North's own distancing from Hayek on this point (North 2005: 51).

North has argued for a long time against the neoinstitutional assumption he once shared, that institutions are necessarily economically efficient, he nonetheless identifies an ideal type of society (the open access order) which has maximally adaptive properties, and so is both economically and evolutionarily 'efficient' in that sense (North, Wallis, and Weingast 2009: 133–136). It is this idea, that adaptive efficiency is a property of a particular set of institutions, that carries North's argument at the macro-level about the selective survival of artifactual frameworks as a whole. It requires serious scrutiny.

Hayek (rightly) denies on the basis of the blind nature of cultural evolution that one could determine one society to be 'good' as opposed to another, but simultaneously argues that the ideal-type classical liberal society (which Hodgson, after Hayek, dubs the 'Great Society' vision) is the yardstick of evolutionary progress (Hodgson 1994: 436). North engages in a similar double denial. While rejecting simplistic 'free market' arguments as insufficiently mindful of the suboptimality of most institutions and beliefs and the difficulty of moving away from such low-level equilibrium traps, he *does* maintain that the ideal-type classical liberal society—not a Great Society but an open access order—is objectively a society with the highest level of evolutionary fitness: it is most *adaptively* efficient. But by what criterion could North decide this? He asserts this, but can only justify it on the basis of the claim that market competition (in the economic and political sphere) equates to evolutionary competition. It is the 'Schumpeterian' properties of open access orders that give it "resiliency to crises". As proof, North asserts that natural state orders are more frequently subject to "political turmoil, macroeconomic instability, civil wars and ethnic conflict", although he simultaneously asserts that these also happen in open access orders but that the latter are better able to adjust their institutions to cope with new circumstances (North, Wallis, and Weingast 2009: 136). The argument seems to simply assume that if there is political-institutional change in a natural state order, this is a sign of its instability, but if there is such change in an open access order, this is proof of its resilience. This is, to say, the least, not very convincing.

A fundamental problem is the way North's account answers the four questions of any evolutionary mechanism described above. The unit of selection at the macro-level, if we follow North's account, is the 'society' or artifactual framework. It is this that is subject to change—being able to adapt to changing circumstances by changing its institutions—and it is this that differentially survives, as North's discussion of the rise and fall of the Soviet Union makes clear (North 2005: 154). In Hull's terms, the interactors in North's model are societies as a whole. But what are the replicators? What is actually inherited? This is far less clear. Institutions act in this model as 'traits' of societies, and their change is the means by which differential survival happens. But they are not clearly inherited from one 'generation' to the next, because North cannot consistently indicate what counts as a unit and as a generation for this purpose. The United States appears to count, despite its wars, crises, and institutional transformations, as the same entity that existed in the eighteenth century, and so does Britain despite its current institutional order being very different compared to even the pre–Second World War one. But the Soviet Union disappeared as an entity and failed to survive, because its name and institutions have disappeared. The latter seems fair enough, but the former seems dubious.

In evolution it is clear how individuals of a species relate to that species as a whole: the individuals reproduce and die, and through this process of differential survival it is the *population* (species) that evolves. In the evolution of the firm, this analogy also works somewhat clearly: one can see the bankruptcy or acquisition of a firm as its 'death', and the population can be the economic structure of a nation, evolving in a particular way (this is not free of similar problems, but is relatively straightforward). In North's account, natural state orders are presumed to have less survability because they are less adaptively efficient, and yet nowhere is it clear what would count as a natural state order actually 'dying'. Without dying, there is no differential survival at the level of individual organisms (here societies/artifactual frameworks), and therefore no evolution of the population. It is not clear at all in fact what the population itself is—all the societies on earth? But North is concerned with the success of individual societies, not the world-historical course of human culture in some Hegelian fashion.

In short, North can answer the question what the interactor is, the unit of selection. But he cannot answer who the beneficiary is of 'fitness' or indeed in most cases what the measure of fitness is, what the population is, or how adaptation actually leads to differential survival (and vice versa). That 'mutation' (institutional change) is nonrandom ('intentional') and not inherently a problem, but it becomes a problem for the model if the mutation of traits in an individual organism cannot be distinguished from the survival or death of the organism itself. It is rather as if we are concerned with mostly immortal organisms that bioengineer themselves to respond to exogenous environmental change, and where death only occurs insofar as the bioengineering happens to such an extent that the organism ends up looking unrecognizably different from before. This is an exciting concept from a science fiction point of view, but it is a poor basis for an evolutionary theory: because such creatures never really die nor reproduce, they do not differentially survive, and therefore natural selection would not operate on them.

If this all sounds a little silly, it is merely to point out the inadequacy of the evolutionary mechanism North proposes at the macro-level, and the undeveloped nature of his concept of adaptive efficiency despite a great amount of hinting at some evolutionary structure. In a way, the macro-level account of evolution is not so interesting within North's larger framework, however. It is my suspicion that he attempted to reformulate Hayek's cultural evolutionary theory at this level in an ad hoc fashion, primarily with the purpose of defending the superiority of the 'open access order' and its classical liberal properties. This superiority, I think, came analytically first, and the explanation in quasi-evolutionary terms was tacked on subsequently.

This also matches Hayek's own approach to his own theory. North differs strongly from Hayek in not believing that the price system itself is a sufficient mechanism to achieve the idealized adaptivity of the 'Great Society'; as he frequently avers, he differs with Hayek in that North sees 'social engineering' as necessary and therefore changes in institutions, political structures, and even belief systems as necessary for making societies more adaptively efficient (something Hayek denied was either possible or desirable). But this difference, despite initial appearances and North's own rhetoric, turns out to be mostly a difference of attitudes to policy interventions. The problems and inconsistencies in their respective theories of cultural evolution are fundamentally similar. Compare this to Hodgson's description of Hayek: "While Hayek rejects the suggestion that evolution automatically leads to progress, he also has a clear criterion by which advance may be judged: to the extent that rules consistent with the Great Society emerge, function, and overcome the assumed atavistic and collectivist instincts of humankind, then progress is deemed to be made" (Hodgson 1994: 436). As I will explore in more detail in the next chapter, I suspect that North's argument is similarly constructed so as to lead necessarily to his preferred policy conclusions at the level of development economics, and that it is really an (rather poorly executed) intervention in debates about the possibility of implementing institutional changes so as to promote desirable economic outcomes. From that viewpoint, the macro-level evolutionary account is merely a means to an end for North's NIEH, and is in principle dispensable. One cannot judge his overall framework by the success or the failure of that argument.

Instead, we should turn to the more interesting evolutionary argument at the micro-level. There is, naturally, a bridge between them, and nothing other than the market. For in the 'open access order', it is—as we know—the efficient market properties of the economy and the political structure that defines that order. And it is these properties that produce the "dynamic stability" identified with adaptive efficiency (North, Wallis, and Weingast 2009: 133–136, 145–147, 252). This by itself causes conceptual issues. Unlike in Hayek's view, where the spontaneous order of the market is the *vehicle* of cultural evolution, for Hodgson, if we want to take the evolutionary account of the emergence and change of allocation systems seriously, we must see 'the market' itself (in all its varieties) as one of the possible *outcomes* of the process of selection, and not the only one (Hodgson 1994). There may be no appeal to original creation: the story must be Darwinian all the way through. North seems to realize this insofar as he tries to derive institutional orders from beliefs that generate them, and equally market processes from institutional orders. In this argument, whole institutional orders/artifactual frameworks are interactors, in some senses analogous to phenotypes, whereas North appears to suggest that their success or failure depends on the "evolution of beliefs", which would make the latter the replicators (North 2005: 146).

We would therefore expect North to argue that the process of cultural evolution he describes is ultimately about the variable frequency of particular belief systems among the larger 'population' of societies or economic systems. But for North, the point of the Soviet illustration is to show that the Soviet Union was too internally rigid to adjust to the 'environment' when it changed, because it did not have the market-like properties of the open access order: "Adaptive efficiency entails an institutional structure that in the face of the ubiquitous uncertainties of a non-ergodic world will flexibly try various alternatives to deal with novel problems that continue to emerge over time. In turn this institutional structure entails *a belief structure that will encourage and permit experimentation and equally will wipe out failures.* The Soviet Union represented the very antithesis of such an approach" (North 2005: 154).

This does not suggest that the differentiating frequency of belief lineages throughout human history serves as the measure of evolution, that is, that surviving belief lineages are the ultimate beneficiaries of evolution—as would be implied by his discussion of the 'evolution of beliefs' and how the survival of whole societies depend on it. Rather, this suggests that in addition there is a different selection process going on where *internal* "failures" are "wiped out", supported by a belief system that allows such selection to take place: here belief systems are not subject to selection, but they determine *whether selection takes place.* This implies (although does not explicitly state) that we return rather to the Hayekian view of market competition *itself* as a process of selection, as is also suggested by North and colleagues' discussion of the advantages of open access orders. It also sits uneasily with the presentation of the Soviet case as an example of an organism that failed to survive due to its traits, if really the differential survival is a matter of competition *between* the traits. (In biology, of course, both of these can happen simultaneously, insofar as, for example, the bacteria in our body that are symbiotic with us have evolved to be so through a process of natural selection within their population and ours. But North does not make such a symbiotic mechanism explicit.)

Of course, the wiping out of internal failures could be exclusively at the level of institutions themselves, as different forms of cooperation. Such a reading is possible, and should therefore be explored. If the market is to be an outcome of a process of selection and not simply equated with it, as most—but not all—of North's larger argument suggests, we must also be able to account for the origins of such a system in terms of its evolutionary ancestors and explain how those ancestral forms could and did lead to those particular outcomes. Such reasoning is the bread and butter of much ethology today and is equally important in applications of evolutionary theory to social life. This means we must be able to trace North's evolutionary subjects or agents at the macro- and meso-level—crudely put, societies and markets, respectively—to their own origins in a consistent way.

Evaluating North's Theory of Cultural Evolution: The Micro-Level

We have seen that North's evolutionary theory is a dual one: it operates at the level of societies (or possibly markets?), and the other operates at the level of, as I put it above, "adaptive reorganization in a complex system", and institutions as cognitive instruments forming adaptations to inherited and changing environments (North 2005: 35–36). I think, at this level, North's account has the merit of rightly identifying one of the central problems in the sociobiological literature on the evolution of cooperation among humans, namely how such cooperation is possible and sustainable in larger groups where most will not be kin or even regularly interact, given limited information. North rightly seems to suspect, although this remains rather implicit, that this problem requires a solution in a better understanding of the conditions for the evolution of altruism and other-regarding behaviors and attitudes among humans. He also is keen, for example in his discussions of the evolution of cognition, to take human individuals seriously as evolved organisms and to examine the implications of this for the nature of human cooperation.

However, North does not develop this point particularly far. He does not pay sufficient attention to the implications this debate has, or rather should have, for his view of individual rationality and for his contractarian account of institutions. In the contractarian tradition he remains pessimistic about the ability of cooperation to emerge through instrumental reason, let alone through other means, at least in larger groups. He views cooperation in a Hobbesian framework as dependent on power and institutions that will restrain violence and self-interest even within given societies or groups, and such institutions only emerge because of the self-interest of those elites to which the Hobbesian problem gives rise. As we have seen in my discussion of his alternative models of rationality in the previous chapter, while his sophisticated approach to beliefs is laudable, his approach to preferences is more conventional. I suggest that those parts of North's account that still assume individual rationality to be fundamentally self-regarding, nonaltruistic, and only instrumentally cooperative be jettisoned in favor of those incipient tendencies in his work that take altruism and cooperation to be more fundamental. However, in order not to explain away the problem of cooperation, one must then place an explanation of such cooperative tendencies on a strong evolutionary and empirical footing.

Additionally, North's inadequate macro-level evolutionary theories prevent the necessary joining of such a macro-level theory of cultural evolution to the sociobiological foundations I believe the recent literature on sociocultural evolution makes possible. I can here only point in the direction of an alternative approach to the problem of cooperation to the one North uses, partially complementary to *some* (but not all) of his statements on the subject. In a larger sense this would require the integration or application of two literatures. One is the empirical literature on cooperation and altruism from behavioral economics, often based on experiments in testing the predictions of conventional choice theory in the form of experimental games.[5] The other is the sociobiological literature, often reliant on *evolutionary* game theory, on the origins and nature of altruism and cooperation in the human species.[6] As in the previous discussions, I intend no general overview of sociobiology nor of experimental economics, and the literatures in both areas have, in the three or four decades of their existence, already grown much too large to do even a cursory justice. All I can do here for now is sketch a (highly compressed

[5] Although I cannot represent it fully here, for my thought on this subject I have drawn upon a wide literature, including Camerer and Thaler (1995), Fehr and Gächter (2000, 2002), Fischbacher, Gächter, and Fehr (2001), Henrich et al. (2004), Gintis et al. (2005), Bowles and Gintis (2011).

[6] This literature is vast and goes back to Darwin himself. Some works I have drawn on for the present discussion include: Lumsden and Wilson (1981), Sober and Wilson (1998), Boyd and Richerson (1985, 2005), Richerson and Boyd (2005), Field (2001), Hodgson (2013), Sterelny et al. (2013).

and simplified) discussion, prompted by North's own comments on the origins of cooperation and its implications for his work.

North's theory of the evolution of cooperation can be summarized fairly effectively without too much loss of relevant detail as follows. For North, as pointed out before, the results of experimental economics demonstrate that in small groups cooperation is relatively easily achieved because of the adjustment to conventional self-interested rational action in such settings. However, in large groups or under private information, such cooperation is not the game theoretically plausible outcome (North 2005: 28–29; Hoffman, McCabe, and Smith 1998). This and the reference to evolutionary psychology following the discussion of Elizabeth Hoffman, Kevin McCabe and Vernon Smith suggest that North's explanation of individuals' "modification of their strict self-interest behavior" is based on an evolutionary argument: humans as evolved to cooperate in such (and only such) small-group settings. His repeated references to this innate small-group cooperation make it clear that this innate cooperativeness, however, is only relevant to such cases (North 2005: viii–ix, 46). In larger settings, North seems to suggest that institutions, beliefs, and incentives, that is, more conventional (nonevolutionary) models of rationality plus the normative power of culture, must do the job (North 2005: ix, 30). As an illustration of the latter kind of argument, we need but observe the claim in *Violence and Social Orders* that, in the absence of third-party enforcement, "cooperation by an adherent organization's members must be, at every point in time, incentive-compatible for all members" (North, Wallis, and Weingast 2009: 16). But whether this is true is disputable, as I will argue below.

In any case there is more trouble. North makes a single but important observation about the implications of experimental economics in testing the rationality assumptions formalized in game theory, a little after his discussion of Hoffman and colleagues' findings. Here he twice cites verbatim the results of the work of Joseph Henrich and his colleagues, who undertook experiments across a wide range of small-scale societies with very different cultures to measure empirically the degree of correspondence to predicted utility maximizing behavior in game theoretical settings. I will not cite these in their entirety here, but the upshot is as follows: "The canonical model of the self-interested material payoff-maximizing actor is systematically violated. In all societies studied, [ultimatum game] offers are strictly positive and often substantially in excess of the expected income-maximizing offer, as are contributions in the public-goods game, while rejections of positive offers in some societies occur at a considerable rate. Second, preferences over economic choices are not exogenous as the canonical model would have it, but rather are shaped by the economic and social interactions of everyday life" (North 2005: 46–47; Henrich et al. 2003: 40).

There is much to agree with in North's account of cultural evolution at the micro-level, at least insofar as it provides useful and interesting resources for building a larger theory. But such empirical violations of canonical rationality in a systematic way suggest the need for a revision of the specification of rational action involved in such choice behavior; if not in terms of some form of reconsideration of utility maximization, then at least its realignment to allow for more other-regarding preferences and utility beyond maximizing money returns (or indeed any returns) than is normally allowed. This should also change the way incentives and interests are represented in more general models of (economic) cooperation, something suggested by Henrich and colleagues themselves. But North does none of this. Expanding the discussion about alternative rationality models of chap. 3 to our present concern with North's explanations of cooperative behavior, we must note that they also have consequences—as a corollary of the above—for the contractarian perspective of how cooperation can (and cannot) be achieved through conventional incentive models. It is therefore all the more striking that these conclusions do not seem to warrant any further discussion on North's part; he simply concludes that they illustrate his point about the importance of learning and beliefs, and leaves it at that. That one cannot accept these findings and also deploy arguments based on rational behavior in social settings as a simple response to expected payoffs does not occur to him.

The central question raised by North's theory of cultural evolution is then as follows: Based on the discussions in *UPEC* and *VSO*, is North right to take as premise for his evolutionary account that humans have evolved to adjust their self-regarding rationality to allow small-group cooperation, but that in larger groups the free rider problem combined with the pervasiveness of violence will make cooperation (or 'order') possible only by means of a mixed Hobbesian-Lockean social contract, that is, by means of the formation of elites with control over violence who distribute rents to create incentives for obedience? I submit that he is not, and for two reasons. The first is that based on recent literature in evolutionary game theory, there are strong reasons to suspect that no evolution of human sociality would have been possible at all—even in realistic small-group settings—under 'contractarian' premises, that is to say, on the basis of evolutionary incentives to maximize fitness evolving only self-regarding behavior. Therefore, the only possible evolutionary explanation for the observed reality of human cooperation and sociality in small and large groups is that at least to a significant extent humans have evolved as being from our earliest behaviorally modern beginnings as, in the words of Herbert Gintis and Samuel Bowles, 'a cooperative species' (Bowles and Gintis 2011; Hodgson 2013). This implies that the contractarian perspective, in which human cooperation is explained on the basis of the interests of self-regarding actors to cooperate given correct incentives, is in all its forms at least radically incomplete.

Secondly, the results of game theoretical experiments demonstrate, as North himself briefly acknowledged, that the behavioral predictions of self-regarding utility maximization are not borne out in reality. Unlike North, however, I believe that these results significantly affect the plausibility of a (primarily) incentives-based account of the origins of institutions. While North also modifies this account substantially by ascribing a major role to the formation of beliefs, he gives no consistent evolutionary account of how such beliefs interact with Darwinian evolutionary pressures or with the operation of 'rational' behavior. Here, I will argue that such models can be more readily integrated into an evolutionary account of long-term change that *takes culture seriously* than North's own reliance on incentives and transaction costs. Put briefly, I think gene-culture coevolution and group rationality is more promising as an account of institutions and their sociobiological role than North's reliance on exogenously given beliefs and New Institutional models of bounded rationality, and will do the job that North wanted evolutionary theory to do better than his own approach does.[7]

[7] Interestingly, North himself indicates that his account is partially inspired by Boyd and Richerson's work on gene-culture coevolution (North 2005: 66n3). But his own explanatory framework does not seem to rest much on their arguments in practice.

I do not wish to suggest that they are wholly mutually exclusive, for many of North's theoretical tools remain useful: this is no argument against his definition of institutions, his claim that they matter for economic history, or his use of evolutionary concepts or path dependence, say. For a Northian evolutionary account to succeed, however, they need complementing by a gene-culture coevolution approach and a much closer attention to the functional role of 'culture' (in the broad sense of institutions, self-identifications, and cultural markers) in an evolutionary process of inheritance as well as in intentional behavior. Jointly, these two claims suggest that we need to greatly expand rationality to include other-regarding forms of utility maximization as well as the role of emotions, identities, and other non-maximizing aspects of choice behavior, and that we must go beyond contractarian accounts of the origins of social institutions to a more rounded perspective of humans as 'always already' cooperative. Finally, cooperation—even altruistic—is not itself sufficient. The *content* of culture, including the role of commitment and its moral and emotional component, also matters, and this can perhaps lend a new perspective to North's intuitions about the role of beliefs. I will now expand on each of these arguments in order.

As Alexander Field has pointed out in various critiques of New Institutionalism and similar approaches, any explanation of the emergence of institutions in terms of conventional models of rationality runs into serious problems of infinite regress. One can either explain institutions in terms of previous institutions, in which case these need explaining in turn. Or one can turn, as in the contractarian tradition, to a 'state of nature' in which the interaction between individuals will cause, spontaneously, the emergence of a particular original institutional order (Field 1979, 1981). The latter is how I have interpreted the approach of North to the origins of institutions. In *Violence and Social Orders*, any society grown beyond the 'small-scale' hunter-forager society will likely turn into a natural order. From the 'foraging order' where each individual knows all others, and to which presumably Hoffman and colleagues' findings apply, to the natural order is 'a long process of development'. Based on the work of Allan Johnson and Timothy Earle, North and colleagues argue that the transition from foraging orders to natural state orders takes place by a sort of Hobbesian process where 'chieftains' start controlling violence, a solution based on "the threat of coercion" and "by mutual interests" (North, Wallis, and Weingast 2009: 52–53; Earle 1997; Johnson and Earle 2000). The combination of coercion and incentives is what I mean by his contractarian theory, and it is expressed, as I have argued in chap. 3, by North's reliance on game theoretical language (though not its formalization) to suggest the operation of this kind of incentive structure in the formation of institutions.

Yet crucially, conventional game theory and state of nature contractarianism also fall afoul of Field's objections. As I have argued, one cannot have any conventional game theoretical presentation of the operation of individual interaction without already knowing the rules and payoffs applicable to that game. And these must therefore be given in advance. As Field points out, what this amounts to is that contractarian approaches to institutions, popular in economic theory, effectively smuggle the very institutions they seek to explain in through the back door, often implicitly (Field 1981). The infinite regress remains in operation. For this reason, New Institutionalist approaches must depart, as some of its theorists have recognized, from a given combination of institutions and individuals; it cannot explain the origins of human sociality per se (Aoki 2001). Indeed, no social theory can do so except by appeal to evolutionary models of the emergence of culture in behaviorally modern *homo sapiens*; and therefore any model of the path-dependent inheritance of such institutions (and all 'culture' more broadly) must begin with well-formulated evolutionary premises rather than contractarian assumptions about the emergence of institutions from incentives, including incentives to reduce violence. Humans must *first* be a cooperative species.

Recent literature on the evolution of human cooperation has demonstrated just that, by studying the emergence of altruism in evolutionary game theoretical models. I will not review the methodology of evolutionary game theory here, but it is important to note the distinction between conventional game theory and evolutionary game theory in one respect. While the formal aspects are much the same, the difference is that where conventional game theory assumes *payoff maximization* on the part of individuals, and is therefore subject to critiques of the plausibility of this assumption based on Field's arguments as well as the testing of this assumption (described below), evolutionary game theory is based on *fitness maximization* assumptions in natural selection. Evolutionary game theoretical models therefore have the distinct advantage that their maximization assumptions give a solid explanatory grounding of a kind that conventional game theory, reliant as it is on rational choice analysis, does not (Gintis 2009). After all, Darwinian selection is blind and instrumental, and has no intentionality that could provide for anything but (local) optimization.

Space does not, unfortunately, permit the lengthy discussion of the evolutionary game theoretical arguments underlying the logic of cooperation in humans. I will therefore have to be content with summarizing the results.[8] We must begin with the central problem for cooperation: the possibility of altruism.[9] Altruism is here defined as behavior by an individual of a species enhancing the fitness of another individual at a fitness cost to the first individual (Sober and Wilson 1998: 7). The importance of altruism and prosocial dispositions in explaining human cooperative sociality is enormous, because (as the prisoner's dilemma would demonstrate) under normal circumstances a strong selection mechanism like natural selection would be expected to select against behavior that favors others at the expense of oneself. If helping others at the expense of oneself by definition diminishes fitness, it will diminish ceteris paribus the likelihood of procreation, and therefore genes favoring such behavior should not survive. Over evolutionary time, prosocial behavior should not occur, and therewith neither cooperation nor the emergence of institutions in large-scale societies should be possible. For this reason, E.O. Wilson has called altruism "the central theoretical problem of sociobiology" (Wilson 1975: 3).

In sociobiology, for a considerable time the most common explanation of the emergence of cooperation was twofold: 'inclusive fitness', also called kin altruism, and reciprocal altruism. Kin altruism as a concept was developed by William Hamilton to explain the altruistic behavior of many organisms observed in nature. Hamilton pointed to the fact that

[8] A longer treatment of the same argument is found in Krul (2016).

[9] Sober and Wilson (1998: 53–54) even argue that the emphasis on using 'cooperation' rather than 'altruism' as the term for the relevant *explanandum* of human sociality appears in the literature because the former sounds more contractarian, more a matter of self-interest, and therefore better fits preconceived ideas about the nature of sociality and institution-building.

maximization of genetic fitness would favor altruistic behavior by individuals toward kin, that is, other individuals who carry substantially similar genes. Even if the individual with altruistic genes is selected against, the fitness benefits accruing to the kin may outweigh this and in this manner selection may permit the emergence of altruistic behavior within kin groups as an evolutionarily stable strategy (Hamilton 1964). Reciprocal altruism, in turn, is based on the so-called tit-for-tat strategy in repeated games: namely that in indefinitely repeated games cooperation rather than defection can be a winning move, as long as cooperation can be expected from the other player. To simplify somewhat, if the probability of reciprocation is high enough, selection will favor genetic makeup that behaviorally expresses itself as altruistic, since cooperating individuals in a species will then be cooperated with down the line, and so outcompete the selfish defectors who cannot expect assistance at a later point (Trivers 1971; Axelrod 1984).

Neither of these, however, has proven to be sufficiently evolutionarily stable explanations. This has led to the revival of multilevel selection (sometimes group selection) as an explanatory approach. Owing its origins to George Price's equations describing the interaction of selection pressures at different levels of populations, multilevel selection describes the insight that selection does not just take place between genes in an individual (meiosis aside) and between individuals in a population, but also between groups (subpopulations) in a global population. This higher-order selection among groups affects selection within groups and vice versa, and their relative strengths depend on the relevant specifications of the model. A group is simply defined as "a set of individuals that influence each other's fitness with respect to a certain trait but not the fitness of those outside the group" (Sober and Wilson 1998: 92). The significance of this insight rests in the observation that selection pressures between groups can outweigh selection pressures within groups under particular circumstances. This means, in turn, that as long as groups are relatively stable (vis-à-vis migration, for example), certain traits—such as altruistic ones— can be evolutionarily successful in particular groups by their effects on that group's fitness relative to other groups. This provides an obvious way to think about the advantages of for example, altruistic sacrifice by individuals of a group for the benefit of that group's competitiveness with other groups in the (relevant) global population of a species. This behavior is observable, and therefore in need of explanation, in a wide range of species from ants to humans.

But reciprocal altruism has serious difficulties of its own: there is little evidence of its operation among any other species than humans.[10] This would point to the need for additional hypotheses in the human case. Moreover, in larger-scale human societies, or if information is private and imperfect, or if migration levels are high, it is unlikely that reciprocal altruism can be evolutionarily stable as an explanation of cooperation, as the likelihood of repeat encounters with the same player would be low, fitness costs would be high relative to benefits, and it is sensitive to error rates. So a community of reciprocal altruists would be vulnerable to 'invasion' by rare individuals with genes 'coded for' defection (Bowles and Gintis 2011: 63–70). It is therefore by no means clear that reciprocal altruism suffices as an explanation for observed behavior, even if it is a likely component. One solution to this problem has been a focus on indirect altruism, where reputation-building plays the main role. In such cases, long-term cooperative benefits may result from 'reciprocal' altruism even when individuals do not interact repeatedly with the same other individuals (as is likely in large groups), because altruistic behavior signals a prosocial attitude.

The work of Bowles and Gintis, on which I here rely, is a fruitful investigation of these possibilities. In group selection models, *as opposed to* reciprocal 'altruism' models, altruists benefit from interactions with other altruists because of the positive assortment of altruists into groups and nonaltruists into others. Such explanatory models are called models of inclusive fitness, and Bowles and Gintis helpfully distinguish them from 'mutualist' models such as reciprocal and kin altruism. Such positive assortment is particularly likely in human communities because of the assortative aspects of cultural markers and of communication through language, something I will discuss further below under gene-culture coevolution (Eshel and Cavalli-Sforza 1982). For now it is worth noting that positive assortment can take place genetically, but also culturally, by the intentional adoption through learning of favored behavioral traits.

[10] Hammerstein (2003). See, however, Carter and Wilkinson (2013).

What Bowles and Gintis have demonstrated is that applying more realistic, but therefore also more restrictive, constraints on the standard evolutionary game theoretical arguments for 'mutualist' reciprocity, they find that such models cannot account for the evolution of human cooperation. As Bowles and Gintis show, when groups are very large, error terms large, information private or very imperfect, or no common alignment of beliefs exists (i.e. the choices of other players are not known in advance), cooperation cannot be explained on this basis (Bowles and Gintis 2011). Indeed, this finding is simply an implication of the observation, discussed in chap. 4, that except for the simplest types of games, no Nash equilibrium is likely to be found absent the criteria of common knowledge of rationality and common alignment of beliefs.

A more relevant and generally accepted solution is the correlated equilibrium, a suitable substitute for a Nash equilibrium in evolutionary models. What this essentially means is that some external and commonly known 'agent' interacts with the actual players of the game so as to coordinate their actions, by sending signals in such a manner that if all players accept the signal, no player can improve their payoff by switching strategies. The interesting thing for our purposes is that for human players, the most obvious form of the correlating device in concrete terms is the social norm, that is, an *institution*. As Bowles and Gintis explain, a "cooperative equilibrium supported by social norms is one in which not only is the equilibrium evolutionarily stable, but also the social norms are themselves an evolutionary adaptation, stable against invasion by competing norms" (Bowles and Gintis 2011: 90). This is necessary because otherwise the contractarian's infinite regress would operate again: a norm may not be evolutionarily assumed without explaining away the problem. This means that individuals in a group that shares a norm must learn what the norm is (what behavior it demands), learning that most in the group know the norm and follow it, and learning that the norm is common knowledge among those (i.e. they all know this about each other as well).

For Bowles and Gintis, this role of social norms must be analytically prior to any explanations in terms of self-regarding individuals finding a cooperative solution, since absent such coordinating functions *no evolutionarily accessible and stable cooperative solution can be found under realistic conditions*. As they argue, this finding explicitly refutes the contractarian and 'invisible hand' approaches to the folk theorem, since such approaches are not robust to realistic restrictions on common alignment of beliefs and on the likelihood of error. Again, given the importance North rightly places on the role of varying beliefs and their independent explanatory role in behavior, it is justified to conclude that to pursue a realistic evolutionary account of the emergence of institutions, North cannot resort to any 'invisible hand' or contractarian-type explanations. Nor does the recognition of cognitive limits and bounded rationality suffice to compensate for that: the explanation must begin with seeing human individuals as *already prosocial* (Bowles and Gintis 2011: 91).

As they argue: "The failure of the models underlying both the folk theorem and the fundamental theorem [i.e. welfare economics, MK] is hardly surprising, for they sought to explain cooperation among large numbers of self-regarding strangers without recourse to pre-existing norms and cooperative institutions, something that most likely never occurred in the history or prehistory of our species… the economic models of cooperation that assume pre-existing solutions to these problems thus do not accomplish their goal, namely explaining cooperation among amoral and self-regarding individuals… Economic theory, favoring parsimony over realism, has sought to explain cooperation without reference to social preferences, and with a minimalist or fictive description of social institutions. This research trajectory … may have run its course" (Bowles and Gintis 2011: 91–92). This, then, requires a new microfoundation. Here we must finally and definitively cut orthodox choice theory, North's preferred anchor of social theory, loose. A plausible account of cultural evolution at the micro-level simply cannot be sustained on the basis of instrumentally rational agents, and the social contract paradigm is not sufficient to explain the origin of institutions *at any level*. Even in evolutionary game theory, multilevel selection does what simple reciprocal altruism—the rough equivalent of social contract theory at that level—cannot.

But what kind of prosociality? And how is this to be integrated into a cultural evolutionary account such as North's? Bowles and Gintis, building on Boyd and Richerson's theory of gene-culture coevolution (which I will turn to shortly), therefore applied simulations based on parameters deduced from both sources of evidence and varied these within that range, so as to obtain realistic and robust, if not guaranteed, results. On this basis, they have proposed a theory for the origins of what they call 'strong reciprocity', which consists of two components: a predisposition to cooperate, that is, a form of innate altruism, *and* a willingness to punish noncooperators (Bowles and Gintis 2011).

Where North sees the problem of violence as central and its reduction as the natural aim, the 'constructive' importance of violence in the form of punishment—physical, social, or emotional in nature—to the evolution of cooperation and institutions is equally paramount. Punishment is the key means by which the costs to free riders can be reduced, as North himself observes in the context of the problem of enforcement. Even wholly self-interested individuals may cooperate when punishment for not doing so is sufficiently likely and severe. But enforcement is not without costs, as North also observes; and this applies to evolutionary contexts also. In simple evolutionary models, the fitness costs of punishing to the punishers and the possibility of error selects against the likelihood of its evolution, just as with altruistic cooperation. But there is one core difference: the cost of punishment declines as more individuals engage in it, because the frequency of punishment will reduce cases of defection and thereby reduce the frequency with which the costs of punishment actually have to be incurred (Boyd et al. 2003). Because of group selection, more cooperative groups are likely to outcompete others; if punishment is therefore evolutionarily stable and 'accessible' over a wide range of parameter values, sustained by group selection, as Boyd et al. argue, this is one foundation stone for the evolution of institutions. Moreover, empirical evidence supports the observation that punishment can solve the free rider problem also due to its 'quorum' quality: individuals often punish as a group, only undertaking it if sufficient are disposed to punishment, and so solve the internal free rider problem among the punishers (Tuck 2008; Boehm 2012). Finally, a major role is played by the punishment of nonpunishment. Once punishment can become stable and common, second-order punishment also becomes possible. As we shall see in the discussion of gene-culture coevolution, this is important, because second-order punishment, once common, can stabilize *any* norm (Boyd and Richerson 2005: 91).

The upshot of all these arguments is to demonstrate that the most likely evolutionary explanation for the evolution of institutions and the emergence and persistence of cooperation is, to a considerable degree, strong reciprocity or "genuine altruism: a willingness to sacrifice one's own interest to help others, including those who are not family members, and not simply in return for anticipated reciprocation in the future" (Boyd and Richerson 2005: 199). The experimental evidence, so quickly dismissed by North, gives substantial support to this view. Such experiments across a wide range of societies and cultures show that responses to various standard games, such as the ultimatum game and the dictator game, fluctuate wildly and (most importantly) in strong correlation with the institutional and political economic structure of the societies in question. In no case whatsoever was the postulate of maximization of expected returns actually observed (Henrich et al. 2004). There is considerable evidence to suggest that humans are strongly inclined to participate in collective projects and to punish free riders even at their own cost. Collective action problems are solvable (and solved) by the operation of group enforcement mechanisms that are not in the individual interest of any members but that depend on strong reciprocity and prosocial forms of rational action, that is, forms of group rationality and identification that are stronger than individual utility maximization (at least of the conventional kind); and such mechanisms go beyond the markets or hierarchies dichotomy of the NIE tradition (Gintis et al. 2005: ch. 13).

Arguably there is a natural affinity between multilevel selection theory and gene-culture coevolution, in that the latter builds on the methodological developments of the former and in turn has aided the evolutionary game theoretical advances represented by the work of Bowles and Gintis. Although the idea that selection pressures at phenotypical level and cultural dynamics interact via the mechanism of group selection goes back to Charles Darwin himself, contemporary gene-culture coevolution theory originates in the 1970s–1980s with the revolution in sociobiology. This revolution revived the evolutionary study of social life and culture and placed it on a more scientifically secure footing than the speculative or metaphorical evolutionary approaches of the Victorian age. The core insight of gene-culture coevolution is that, as Boyd and Richerson put it, "cultural evolution is a population phenomenon" (Richerson and Boyd

2005: 241). Relying on multilevel selection theory, gene-culture coevolution allows the examination of the interaction between population-level phenomena and individual-level phenomena, just as we have seen in Bowles and Gintis' arguments regarding the origins of human cooperation (which are consciously compatible accounts). The difference is that Boyd and Richerson concentrate on the effects of one particular evolved tool particular to humans, the ability to intentionally develop culture and to acquire existing cultural traits through social learning. The effects of such traits on the formation of groups and thereby on group selection, as well as on the fitness of individuals acquiring (or rejecting) a particular cultural trait, and the modeling of the evolutionary interaction of these phenomena at genetic and cultural level is the domain of gene-culture coevolution. This, too, is an extension of generalized Darwinian thinking (Richerson and Boyd 2005: 247).

From the viewpoint of gene-culture coevolution, North is decidedly right to concentrate on the role of learning in accounting for the role of institutions. However, North's discussion of learning processes emphasizes the cognitive limitations of rationality in a rational choice context, and the importance of uncertainty for the acquisition of (potentially 'irrational' or wrong) beliefs. Gene-culture coevolution, by contrast, makes learning a central bridge between the genetic explanation for the origins of human sociality on the one hand and the function of institutions and cultural markers, once they exist, on the other hand. For Boyd and Richerson, culture (at least as far as this theory is concerned) is "information capable of affecting individuals' behaviour that they acquire from other members of their species through teaching, imitation, and other forms of social transmission" (Richerson and Boyd 2005: 5). Culture is an evolved ability of humans as a species, and it performs powerful functions in this way indirectly shaping our evolved behavior—functions we require social cooperative skills to perform. Culture is adaptive because the behavior of other humans can be acquired by learning, and it provides valuable information about the environment that need then not be independently rediscovered, over and over again, by individual reason. This is the major advantage culture (in particular via language) provides humans over every other species (Richerson and Boyd 2005: 12).

Culture is therefore, as North rightly emphasizes, an important proximate explanation of human behavior, but a thoroughgoing Darwinism requires that its ultimate explanation always remain evolutionary in nature—and so does a consistent theory of cultural evolution. But culture is not reducible to genes. Nor is culture simply part of 'the environment' with which our genes interact via our 'extended phenotype'. Knowledge, traits, and beliefs are not part of the environment, and are not acquired from it in one go; moreover, in very similar environments there can be vast differences in cultural traits, beliefs, and technologies (Richerson and Boyd 2005: 26–29).

What gene-culture coevolution can do for histories of the evolution of culture/institutions (economic in focus or otherwise) can be clarified by looking at the various forces that operate on its transmission. Drawing on Richerson and Boyd's analysis, we can usefully divide these into two types: forces of random variation and forces of nonrandom (guided) variation and inheritance. The former consist of cultural mutation and cultural drift, which respectively refer to any unintentional changes to cultural traits (they use the example of misremembering) and effects caused by the emergence or dying out of rare (new) traits in a small population. More important are the forces of guided variation: changes made in the process of learning and innovation. Learning, in turn, can be subdivided into different functional types of 'biased transmission', concentrating on by what mechanism the trait is acquired by an individual—intentionally or unconsciously, as in the case of evolved learning processes in small children. These are threefold. The first is content-based bias, which depends as the name suggests on the content of the trait, and is acquired either through cost-benefit analysis of a boundedly rational type (this one best corresponds to North's model)or because of the attributes of the trait that allow it to be better remembered or learned. The second is frequency-based bias, and refers to learning based on how common the trait is; this is also called conformist learning. Finally, there is model-based bias, in which a particular figure is treated as a 'model' for learning based on attributes that make them likely to be a good source of acquired information. A common form of such biased transmission is doing whatever the most successful or highest prestige figures do, or imitating those with traits marking them as similar to oneself (Richerson and Boyd 2005: 69).

So much for inheritance. But if such traits are to be subject to a process of natural selection, they must also have differential survival. This means the traits must, in a sense, be in competition with one another. Boyd and Richerson suggest this happens in two ways: through the opportunity costs of time spent learning (and the limits on what one can learn) and through control of behavior. If one must act, one act or another will be chosen, and one can only obey the imperative of one cultural trait at a time: one can know how to speak multiple languages, but one speaks only one on a given occasion, even if one can switch in mid-sentence. Given this, how does natural selection operate on culture? The usual requirements can now be straightforwardly applied. People vary because they have acquired different beliefs, values, or habits through social learning. Their trait variation affects the probability that others will, through social learning, adopt their trait. And finally, many cultural variants compete with each other to some sufficient extent. In such cases, natural selection will operate at the level of these traits, even if it is difficult to identify precisely what they are in discrete terms (Richerson and Boyd 2005: 76). Here we see an account of cultural differentiation and institution formation that, unlike in North's case, does not immediately jump from cognitive predispositions (themselves not explained) to learning and from learning to culture; these steps are basically right, but need to be grounded in the same methodology if they are to be consistent and if we are to avoid the gaps in the 'joints' that North's framework displays.

The important implication of these forms of biased transmission and random change is that culture need not be adaptive in fitness terms, even though it is subject—as humans always are—to the processes of natural selection at genetic level. Unlike in the genetic case, but much like the case of rational choice, the process of descent with modification of cultural traits is therefore not inherently fitness maximizing (Boyd and Richerson 1985: ch. 5). How does this then translate into a more macro-level theory? The final dynamic to understand is the effect of the interaction of these forces with group formation. Groups form among humans by cultural markers (which need not be behavioral in nature) and particular traits (which are). As long as guided variation is error-prone and biased transmission plays a considerable role, and in particular as long as there is sufficient conformist bias and enforcement of norms through punishment, the amount of variation within groups will decline over time and the amount of variation between groups will increase. This, in turn, will strengthen the effect of group selection insofar as human groups compete with each other (Richerson and Boyd 2005: 162–163).

While the degree and dimensions of competition between groups is controversial, there is little reason to doubt that human groups historically have often competed, in particular if one defines groups as designated by the existing variants of the relevant cultural traits (language X vs. Y, or Protestant vs. Catholic, or whatever). Where this is relevant, the competition between groups will be competition between sets of cultural traits and markers, and the extinction of particular marker groups (physically, or by absorption into the winning group) means an increase in the frequency of the traits and markers of the more adaptive group. In this sense, there is a certain adaptive efficiency of culture, to put it in North's terms—a classic example being the Nuer organizational structure favoring its competitiveness vis-à-vis the Dinka (Kelly 1985: 65). There is some evidence that competition between groups, leading to 'cultural extinction', is common among small-scale societies at least, although it is not conclusive (Soltis, Boyd, and Richerson 1995). Even so, we must be careful—North never specifies what competitive process allows for differential variation in 'efficiency' or 'performance' to make one society more adaptive than another, and this greatly weakens the claim to an actual selection process in his account. More than competition, diffusion from one group to another of group functional traits is a fast and plausible process through which differential variation of traits can operate on global populations (that is to say, supra-societal ones, not necessarily literally across the whole world). A salient example is the success of evangelizing religions in competition with nonevangelizing ones (Richerson and Boyd 2005: 210–211). Competition should not be simply presumed, and where implied, its mechanism of operation should be clearly identified.

This account as a whole will probably not satisfy most readers as a substitute theory of cultural evolution to the Northian one. That is because it is not. It provides an explanation of why and how contractarian and (nonevolutionary) game theoretical accounts of institutions will fail to explain their emergence, and why any theory of cultural evolution must in all likelihood be based on some form of multilevel selection, and apply it consistently from micro- to macro-level. Gene-culture coevolution theory as developed by Robert Boyd and Peter Richerson provides some tools for that kind of analysis, but, of course, with any such explanations the risk of multiplying speculative just-so stories is considerable. However this may be, what is more useful is to consider this discussion as identifying analytical premises and tools that are *necessary but not sufficient* for a cultural evolutionary argument of the type developed by North to succeed. Integrating strong reciprocity and its role in the origin of institutions with the persistence, change, and inheritance of institutions via gene-culture coevolution gives us a powerful conceptual apparatus that is both flexible and methodologically well founded in the most robust functionalist theory that the social sciences have available, Darwinian natural selection.

The evolution of human complex societies and the ongoing significance of traits and beliefs need then not be explained (solely) in terms of social contracts, boundedly rational choice, or market(–like) competition. Culture—institutions, beliefs, and markers—and the evolution of strong reciprocity and prosocial instincts like first- and second-order punishment go hand in hand as tools to explain both origin and change of human societies. As Boyd and Richerson argue, "In the short run, cultural evolution, partly driven by ancient and tribal social instincts and partly by selection among culturally variable groups, gave rise to the institutions we observe. In the longer run, cultural evolutionary processes created an environment that led to the evolution of uniquely human social instincts" (Richerson and Boyd 2005: 235). This in turn provides the basis for a theory of embedded economic behavior that integrates economic phenomena into institutional explanation without assuming humans are instrumentally rational actors and without disjunction between the account of the origin of institutions and the account of the *effect* of institutions.

Conclusion

An evolutionary account is both helpful and inevitable to overcome the infinite regress problem in joining instrumental reason and institutional structure in explaining social phenomena. Equally, an evolutionary account at the macro-level could provide North's historical narrative with a powerful functionalist type of explanation, buttressed by the well-understood 'trinity' of Darwinian natural selection. North's theory of cultural evolution can be read as attempting to take both these steps. I applaud North's turn toward evolutionary thinking beyond the evolution of organization and the firm: the best aspect of the Hayekian tradition is precisely this willingness to integrate micro- and macro-level evolutionary perspectives with the historical and theoretical dimensions of economics. However, there are serious problems with this tradition and with North's account as well, and these I have discussed at length in this chapter. I argue that North cannot avoid the infinite regress problem merely by appeal to learning and intentionality, for he misunderstands the role of intentionality in a Darwinian account. He mistakenly believes that the importance of cultural variation and intentional action makes sociobiological theory less applicable to a theory of cultural evolution.

Secondly, North's account of natural selection operating on societies via the adaptive properties of market competition is both implausible and incomplete, failing to rigorously describe the necessary prerequisites of a Darwinian process. Thirdly, North still fails to account in a systematic evolutionary manner how the human sociality that gives rise to our particular institutionalized and complex forms of socio-ethical reason comes about. As Boyd and Richerson rightly emphasize, decision-making forces (as they call them) are *derived* mechanisms: they must in evolutionary terms have their origin in other forces of selection. Which account of such origins makes sense, therefore, matters a great deal for what account of rationality is most plausible (Boyd and Richerson 2005: 290). Because he simply assumes away this central question in sociobiology, he also does not realize the significance the experimental economic evidence testing the relation between culture and utility maximization has for his work, nor the full import of models of the evolution of his 'foraging orders', which he leaves to the controversial work of Allen Johnson and Timothy Earle. He neglects the implications of findings in behavioral economics for how rationality can and—especially—cannot explain institutionalized economic behavior.

North himself could not find an internally consistent answer, because of his unwillingness to abandon classical game theory and Simonian bounded rationality with their reliance on conventional forms of utility maximization. But the gene-culture coevolution approach coheres very well with taking seriously other-regarding and group rationalities as well as the role of the emotions. As evolved behaviors, these both give rise to and interact with the necessary *forms* of social life, which are historically path dependent, arbitrary, and also dependent on the *content* of the institutions and beliefs in question. Here, functionalism and contingency can quite comfortably fit together in a historical and evolutionary account. But there is a price to pay: major Northian themes, such as the adaptive 'efficiency' of market competition, the use of indeterminate forms of bounded rationality in games as a contractarian explanation of the origins of institutions, and the neglect of sociobiology and anthropology must be given up. The result, however, would be a less implausible and more consistently evolutionary economic history, and without sacrificing the centrality of institutions and beliefs.

All this is of course not sufficient on its own, just as appeals to contracts or transaction costs are not sufficient on their own: specification by means of individual case studies is always needed. Moreover, the evolutionary perspective does not avoid the problem of nonergodicity North rightly draws our attention to: the role of norms, arbitrary conventions, and group markers in cultural evolution and the considerable room in institutional 'design space', to put it in Daniel Dennett's terms, give rise to historical path dependencies and 'runaway dynamics' that cannot be predicted in advance. Nor can an explanation of such historical dynamics be reduced to the maximization of either utility or fitness. In all evolutionary writing on the origins and function of certain sociocultural phenomena, it is a question of competing plausibility arguments: no account can be proven with any degree of certainty; the purpose of sociobiological modeling is to establish which accounts are the least implausible. In such arguments, it does not suffice to simply argue that a particular account is incomplete or overly simple, since one is always abstracting from certain things and much of the work is still in the stage of establishing basic parameters. Rather, it is necessary to point to specific mechanisms identified in the model as inadequate, and/or to point to missing dynamics that would matter for the account (Boyd and Richerson 2005: 303–306; 410–414).

But the larger-scale, long-term view is aided by this perspective, one that is to my mind better grounded and more empirically plausible than the medley of social contract theory and evolutionary psychology offered by North. Finally, the sociobiologically integrated perspective has one additional interesting property: in emphasizing how second-order punishment can evolve and be sustained, and how it can stabilize *any* norm, the substance of norms becomes *sui generis* of importance and an explanatory cause in their own right. In observing the importance of norms for the cultural evolution of societies, the gene-culture coevolution perspective paves the way for a more explicitly 'embedded', even anthropological, treatment of institutions in economic thought.

References

Alchian, Armen A. 1950. Uncertainty, Evolution, and Economic Theory. *The Journal of Political Economy* 58 (3): 211–221.

Alchian, Armen A., and William R. Allen. 1983. *Exchange & Production: Competition, Coordination and Control*. Belmont: Wadsworth.

Alchian, Armen A., and Harold Demsetz. 1972. Production, Information Costs, and Economic Organization. *The American Economic Review* 62 (5): 777–795.

Aldrich, Howard E., et al. 2008. In Defence of Generalized Darwinism. *Journal of Evolutionary Economics* 18 (5): 577–596.

Aoki, Masahiko. 2001. *Towards a Comparative Institutional Analysis*. Cambridge, MA: MIT Press.

Axelrod, Robert. 1984. *The Evolution of Cooperation*. New York: Basic Books.

Becker, Marcus C. 2004. Organizational Routines: A Review of the Literature. *Industrial and Corporate Change* 13 (4): 643–677.

Blackmore, Susan. 2000. *The Meme Machine*. Oxford: Oxford University Press.

Boehm, Christopher. 2012. Costs and Benefits in Hunter-Gatherer Punishment. *Behavioral and Brain Sciences* 35 (1): 19–20.

Bowles, Samuel, and Herbert Gintis. 2011. *A Cooperative Species: Human Reciprocity and Its Evolution*. Princeton: Princeton University Press.

Boyd, Robert, and Peter J. Richerson. 1985. *Culture and the Evolutionary Process*. Chicago: University of Chicago Press.

———. 2005. *The Origin and Evolution of Cultures*. Oxford: Oxford University Press.

Boyd, Robert, et al. 2003. The Evolution of Altruistic Punishment. *Proceedings of the National Academy of Sciences* 100 (6): 3531–3535.
Burman, Jeremy Trevelyan. 2012. The Misunderstanding of Memes: Biography of an Unscientific Object 1976–1999. *Perspectives on Science* 20 (1): 75–104.
Camerer, Colin, and Richard H. Thaler. 1995. Anomalies: Ultimatums, Dictators and Manners. *Journal of Economic Perspectives* 9 (2): 209–219.
Carter, Gerald G., and Gerald S. Wilkinson. 2013. Food Sharing in Vampire Bats: Reciprocal Help Predicts Donations More Than Relatedness or Harassment. *Proceedings of the Biological Sciences* 280 (1753): 20122573.
Clark, Andy. 1997. *Being There: Putting Brain, Body, and World Together Again*. Cambridge, MA: MIT Press.
Cloak, F.T. 1975. Is a Cultural Ethology Possible? *Human Ecology* 3 (3): 161–182.
Dawkins, Richard. 1976. *The Selfish Gene*. Oxford: Oxford University Press.
———. 1986. *The Blind Watchmaker*. Harlow: Longman.
Dennett, Daniel C. 1995. *Darwin's Dangerous Idea: Evolution and the Meanings of Life*. New York: Simon & Schuster.
Denzau, Arthur T., and Douglass C. North. 1994. Shared Mental Models: Ideologies and Institutions. *Kyklos* 47 (1): 3–31.
Earle, Timothy. 1997. *How Chiefs Come to Power*. Stanford: Stanford University Press.
Eggertsson, Thrainn. 1990. *Economic Behavior and Institutions*. Cambridge: Cambridge University Press.
Eshel, I., and L.L. Cavalli-Sforza. 1982. Assortment of Encounters and Evolution of Cooperativeness. *Proceedings of the National Academy of Sciences* 79 (4): 1331–1335.
Fehr, Ernst, and Simon Gächter. 2000. Fairness and Retaliation: The Economics of Reciprocity. *Journal of Economic Perspectives* 71 (1): 159–181.
———. 2002. Altruistic Punishment in Humans. *Nature* 415 (6868): 137–140.
Field, Alexander J. 1979. On the Explanation of Rules Using Rational Choice Models. *Journal of Economic Issues* 13 (1): 49–72.
———. 1981. The Problem with Neoclassical Institutional Economics: A Critique with Special Reference to the North/Thomas Model of Pre-1500 Europe. *Explorations in Economic History* 18 (2): 174–198.
———. 2001. *Altruistically Inclined? The Behavioral Sciences, Evolutionary Theory, and the Origins of Reciprocity*. Ann Arbor: University of Michigan Press.
Fischbacher, Urs, Simon Gächter, and Ernst Fehr. 2001. Are People Conditionally Cooperative? Evidence from a Public Goods Experiment. *Economics Letters* 71 (3): 397–404.

Gintis, Herbert. 2009. *The Bounds of Reason: Game Theory and the Unification of the Behavioral Sciences*. Princeton: Princeton University Press.
Gintis, Herbert, et al. 2005. *Moral Sentiments and Material Interests: On the Foundations of Cooperation in Economic Life*. Cambridge, MA: MIT Press.
Hamilton, William D. 1964. The Genetic Evolution of Social Behaviour. *Journal of Theoretical Biology* 7: 1–16.
Hammerstein, Peter. 2003. Why Is Reciprocity So Rare in Social Animals? A Protestant Appeal. In *Genetic and Cultural Evolution of Cooperation*, ed. Peter Hammerstein, 83–93. Cambridge, MA: MIT Press.
Hayek, F.A. 1952. *The Sensory Order*. Chicago: University of Chicago Press.
———. 1967. *Studies in Philosophy, Politics and Economics*. London: Routledge & Kegan Paul.
———. 1983. *Knowledge, Evolution, and Society*. London: Adam Smith Institute.
Henrich, Joseph, et al. 2003. In Search of Homo Economicus: Experiments in Fifteen Small-Scale Societies. *The American Economic Review* 91 (2): 73–79.
———. 2004. *Foundations of Human Sociality: Economic Experiments and Ethnographic Evidence from Fifteen Small-Scale Societies*. Oxford: Oxford University Press.
Hodgson, Geoffrey M. 1993. *Economics and Evolution*. Ann Arbor: University of Michigan Press.
———. 1994. Hayek, Evolution, and Spontaneous Order. In *Natural Images in Economic Thought: Markets Red in Tooth and Claw*, ed. Philip Mirowski, 408–447. Cambridge: Cambridge University Press.
———. 1998. The Approach of Institutional Economics. *Journal of Economic Literature* 36: 166–192.
———. 2013. *From Pleasure Machines to Moral Communities: An Evolutionary Economics Without Homo Economicus*. Chicago: University of Chicago Press.
Hodgson, Geoffrey M., and Thorbjørn Knudsen. 2010. *Darwin's Conjecture: The Search for General Principles of Social and Economic Evolution*. Chicago: University of Chicago Press.
Hoffman, Elizabeth, Kevin A. McCabe, and Vernon L. Smith. 1998. Behavioral Foundations of Reciprocity: Experimental Economics and Evolutionary Psychology. *Economic Inquiry* 36 (3): 335–352.
Hough, Jerry, and Robin Grier. 2015. *The Long Process of Development: Building Markets and States in Pre-Industrial England, Spain, and Their Colonies*. Cambridge: Cambridge University Press.
Hull, David L. 1980. Individuality and Selection. *Annual Review of Ecology and Systematics* 11: 311–332.

Johnson, Allen W., and Timothy Earle. 2000. *The Evolution of Human Societies*. 2nd ed. Stanford: Stanford University Press.

Kelly, Raymond Case. 1985. *The Nuer Conquest: The Structure and Development of an Expansionist System*. Ann Arbor: University of Michigan Press.

Krul, Matthijs. 2016. *Markets, Institutions and the Polanyian Challenge: A Theoretical Study of the New Institutionalist Economic History of Douglass C. North*. PhD Dissertation, Brunel University.

Lloyd, Elisabeth. 2012. Units and Levels of Selection. In *The Stanford Encyclopedia of Philosophy*, ed. Edward Zalta. Winter 2012 ed. http://plato.stanford.edu/archives/win2012/entries/selection-units/.

Lumsden, Charles J., and Edward O. Wilson. 1981. *Genes, Mind and Culture: The Coevolutionary Process*. Cambridge, MA: Harvard University Press.

Nelson, Richard R., and Sidney G. Winter. 1982. *An Evolutionary Theory of Economic Change*. Cambridge, MA: Harvard University Press.

North, Douglass C. 2005. *Understanding the Process of Economic Change*. Princeton: Princeton University Press.

North, Douglass C., John Joseph Wallis, and Barry R. Weingast. 2009. *Violence and Social Orders: A Conceptual Framework for Interpreting Recorded Human History*. Cambridge: Cambridge University Press.

Richerson, Peter J., and Robert Boyd. 2005. *Not by Genes Alone: How Culture Transformed Human Evolution*. Chicago: University of Chicago Press.

Sober, Elliott, and David Sloan Wilson. 1994. A Critical Review of Philosophical Work on the Units of Selection Problem. *Philosophy of Science* 61 (4): 534–555.

———. 1998. *Unto Others: The Evolution and Psychology of Unselfish Behavior*. Cambridge, MA: Harvard University Press.

Soltis, Joseph, Robert Boyd, and Peter J. Richerson. 1995. Can Group-Functional Behaviors Evolve by Group Selection? An Empirical Test. *Current Anthropology* 36 (3): 473–494.

Sterelny, Kim, et al., eds. 2013. *Cooperation and Its Evolution*. Cambridge, MA: MIT Press.

Tooby, John, and Leda Cosmides. 1992. The Psychological Foundations of Culture. In *The Adapted Mind: Evolutionary Psychology and the Generation of Culture*, ed. Jerome H. Barkow, Leda Cosmides, and John Tooby, 19–136. Oxford: Oxford University Press.

Trivers, Robert L. 1971. The Evolution of Reciprocal Altruism. *The Quarterly Review of Biology* 46 (1): 35–57.

Tuck, Richard. 2008. *Free Riding*. Cambridge, MA: Harvard University Press.

Vanberg, Viktor. 1986. Spontaneous Market Order and Social Rules. *Economics and Philosophy* 2 (1): 75–100.
Veblen, Thorstein. 1898. Why Is Economics Not an Evolutionary Science? *Quarterly Journal of Economics* 12 (4): 373–397.
Vromen, Jack J. 1995. *Economic Evolution: An Enquiry Into the Foundations of New Institutional Economics*. London: Routledge.
Wilson, Edward O. 1975. *Sociobiology: The New Synthesis*. Cambridge, MA: Harvard University Press.
Witt, Ulrich. 1992. *Explaining Process and Change: Approaches to Evolutionary Theory*. Ann Arbor: University of Michigan Press.

6

North's NIEH as Global History

Introduction

In the previous chapters, I have attempted to interpret various aspects of the structure of North's NIEH and have assessed the arguments North presents in terms of their coherence, validity, and plausibility. I have tried to do justice to the theory in its wide scope and ambition, to explain its intellectual trajectory, and to point to a number of serious difficulties with the theory and why the latest versions of the NIEH framework have, if anything, magnified them. Where the first chapters have provided a more chronological and trajectory-oriented analysis of what the NIEH is and where it has been going hitherto, up to the moment of North's passing, the subsequent chapters have been dedicated to a more philosophical-systematic assessment of its claims. In this chapter, I want to round off that systematic treatment by looking closer at the economic historical purpose of the theory.

So far, I have focused primarily on the challenge of Karl Polanyi: the defense of economics' ability to explain institutional embeddedness and change via an NIE-based transhistorical theory, as opposed to Polanyi's argument that only historically specific socioanthropological studies

M. Krul, *The New Institutionalist Economic History of Douglass C. North*,
Palgrave Studies in the History of Economic Thought,
https://doi.org/10.1007/978-3-319-94084-7_6

could do so. This challenge, I have argued, represents the purpose and guiding thread of the NIEH as an explanatory research program in economic thought and social science. Not because Polanyi himself remained an enduring reference point for North, but because of what Polanyi represented: the fear that (postwar) economics as a discipline and a way of framing problems might fail to cover the vast historical and institutional ground it would have to cover if it wanted to address the problems traditionally raised in anthropology, history, and sociology—the disciplines Polanyi himself relied on for his critique of the applicability of economics to these problems. North's gambit was, on my reading, to reassert the ability of economics to address these problems by combining traditional choice theory in innovative ways with bounded rationality, NIE theory, public choice theory, and elements of cognitive science and cultural evolution. In so doing, he enormously widened the scope of what (this kind of) economics seemed capable of, making this new medley a potent tool for expansion into the domain hitherto reserved (for the most part) to those other historical and social sciences.

In the next chapter, I will elaborate more on what I see as the context and implications of that move for the NIE and for economic thought in general. Here, however, I want to do justice also to a different aspect of the NIEH's purpose. After all, North's work was never just a contribution to economic and economic historical thought. Like most 'working economists', he also had a practical aim: namely, to contribute to offering policy advice on the basis of his theory and for his theory itself to constitute an intervention into debates about economics-based policy recommendations *as well as* serving as an explanatory theory. In fact, the one naturally depends on the other. The recommendations North's theory can give in terms of development economics and other policy advice depend on to what degree it constitutes a correct analysis of the historical trajectory involved in achieving virtuous institutional arrangements. In this chapter, I want to discuss the NIEH as a joint contribution to both those ends.

North made no secret of this aim. Recall his declaration in *UPEC*: "Successful economic development will occur when the belief system that has evolved has created a 'favorable' artifactual structure that can confront the novel experiences that the individual and society face and resolve positively the novel dilemmas. Failures will occur when the novel experiences are so far removed from the artifactual structure of the evolved belief system that individual and society do not have the 'building blocks' of the mind and artifactual structure to resolve the novel problems. If we are going to come to grips with an understanding of the differential performance of different parts of the world both over time and cross-sectionally in the modern world it is here that we must begin. Put simply the richer the artifactual structure the more likely are we to confront novel problems successfully. That is what is meant by adaptive efficiency; creating the necessary artifactual structure is an essential goal of economic policy" (North 2005: 70).

A similar policy-oriented formulation can be found in *VSO*, where the authors point out that "political scientists have never had an adequate definition of political development, let alone one that mirrors the consensus surrounding the economists' notions of economic development… Every society evolves in unique ways, so that a deep understanding of change must go beyond broad generalizations to a specific understanding of the cultural heritage of that particular society. The paths and policies that created open access in the Western world cannot be indiscriminately applied to foster the transition among today's limited access orders… Development policy has been based on the institutions, policies, organizations, and beliefs essential to the open access order's success. The logic of the natural state enables us to see why open access policies and institutions directly threaten the stability of the natural state. Economists typically conclude that natural states suffer from too much market intervention, laws fostering monopolies and other rent-creating privileges, inadequate property rights, ineffective public goods provision, and incomplete markets. All this is true. The economists' natural prescription is to suggest that a country introduce reform, that it should systematically adopt policies that mimic those in open access orders: easier entry by firms, less regulatory control, reduction of monopolies, more secure property rights, improved public goods provision such as education, and more complete markets. Until societies are at least on the doorstep of a transition to opening access, however, transplanting these institutions and policies cannot produce economic development in natural states" (North, Wallis, and Weingast 2009: 270–271, 264).

It is clear, then, that at least part of the purpose of the NIEH framework in its final stage is to help steer economists away from poor development policy interventions and toward+ a more historically and institutionally grounded reorientation. Such a reorientation should take into account the path dependent historical formation of the prevailing institutional order of a society, the way that this institutional order does or does not function as an efficient constraint on violence, and the possibilities *embedded in that order* for institutional or other policy interventions to have desired effects. As I have pointed out earlier, North's general attitude to such problems tends toward pessimism: his NIEH emphasizes the difficulty of successful policy interventions rather than giving clear prescriptions about what one could or should do. The importance of a more institutionally embedded view, as the NIEH provides, is to show that one-size-fits-all recommendations are unlikely to succeed. Incentive structures are determined by the institutional order and the institutional order in turn depends on a larger, historically given, sociocultural 'artifactual framework'. Good luck changing that, one can almost hear the author say. This one could take to be the primary lesson of *UPEC* for development economics.

VSO, however, does give some hints of a more positive prescriptive nature. More than that, it gives a certain normative coloring to the theory, where certain institutional arrangements are portrayed as inherently and enduringly better than other ones. Both of these aspects are captured by the concept of 'open access orders' in the *VSO* framework. Recall that open access orders have adaptive efficiency in a way that even very mature natural state orders do not. As North and colleagues argue, "Competition in open access orders to address major social problems fosters adaptive efficiency, the ability of the society to survive in the face of an ever-changing array of problems and difficulties. Schumpeterian competition provides political and economic entrepreneurs with incentives to devise better and more attractive solutions to their society's problems" (North, Wallis, and Weingast 2009: 133).

They give two reasons why open access orders, and *only* open access orders, should have this property. The first is that such orders provide greater room for experimentation, because more different parties are involved in the process. "Experimentation provides the best opportunity for open access orders to persist. In comparison to the absence of open access or competition in authoritarian natural states and the more hobbled version of electoral competition in many natural states, competition to solve problems in open access orders works reasonably well. The aggregation of information and ideas in the open access's free society gives these countries strong advantages over natural states in searching for solutions to problems" (North, Wallis, and Weingast 2009: 134). The second is the ability to make 'credible commitments', a recurring concept in *VSO*, which allow open access orders to resolve social and political conflict through inclusive resolutions: "Political conflicts arise in all societies, for example, between rich and poor, agriculture and industry, workers and firms, and among different regions. The ability to make credible commitments in open access orders combines with this order's ability to deliver impersonal benefits to widen the set of feasible solutions to conflicts. Open access orders therefore more readily address these conflicts without disorder" (North, Wallis, and Weingast 2009: 135).[1] Almost as an afterthought, the authors add to these two some liberal economic considerations as well. In open access orders, the free and competitive market can solve problems ("some problems faced by natural states never become problems for open access orders because markets emerge to solve or mitigate them") and they don't suffer from "macroeconomic imbalances" such as hyperinflation (North, Wallis, and Weingast 2009: 135).

Overall it is clear that competitiveness, given an evolutionary meaning as adaptive efficiency (see previous chapter), is the most important attribute of the open access order, via the market-like functioning of economics and politics. The more these social domains resemble a market with extensive competition and low barriers to entry, the better a society will function in dealing with problems. Viewed in more detail, however, the direction of recommendations comes out more clearly when the natural state order is contrasted with the open access one. Besides limits on political competition, in the more obvious case of the usually autocratic form of rule that has prevailed in most cases historically, in natural state orders the focus is on the ubiquitous failure to work with the market . We

[1] In this respect, North and colleagues are actually *less* pessimistic than some of their predecessors. They argue that Mancur Olson and other public choice theorists are wrong to see the channeling of private interests into organizations as a threat to the market order. Rather, they argue, in open access orders such organizations are important contributions to its functioning, because it is via organizations that political competition primarily takes place, a concept reminiscent of J.K. Galbraith's 'countervailing power' (North, Wallis, and Weingast 2009: 141–142; Galbraith 1956).

are told that their "limited ability to provide impersonal benefits means that natural states cannot sustain public goods and social insurance programs that share widely the benefits of the market economy in ways complementary to markets", that "social programs serve immediate political goals, such as reelection, rather than their intended purposes", and that "many natural states grant governmental employees, unions, and teachers privileged positions with above-market wages and with various rights to jobs that insulate them from market forces". They also "pursue populist policies that are far more detrimental to their economies than are the social insurance policies of open access orders" (North, Wallis, and Weingast 2009: 137–138).

These are rather familiar litanies of (neo)liberal development economics: the developing countries are too little concerned about letting the market work, getting the prices right, and so forth, and are too concerned with 'populist' programs that are actually popular in the countries in question. For all the disavowal of simple recipes, the Washington Consensus development view is not too far in the background here. Seen from this viewpoint, it appears North's strictures against the imposition of simple free market solutions is not because he thinks they are wrong, but that they will only work given 'doorstep conditions': they are right in principle but should not be imposed *too early*. In open access orders, the rising tide of the free market will ultimately lift all boats: "Another feature of open access markets reflects the idea that this order widely shares the gains of the market economy: when one sector of the economy experiences significant improvements and expansion, the dynamic aspects of the economy mean that the effects are felt throughout the economy. If the expanding sector employs a significant portion of the workforce that raises wages, for example, then factor price equalization raises wage rates in other parts of the economy, resulting in a greater sharing of the gains of economic growth… The same effect holds for productivity gains produced by open access markets. As labor productivity increases, so too do wages" (North, Wallis, and Weingast 2009: 130).[2]

Frankly, one may doubt whether many of these observations have empirical merit or even much coherence. Certainly American politics is famously

[2] Note that in these and other such discussions, no evidence from macroeconomics or development economics is offered to prove this point. It is merely asserted, as if self-evident.

riddled with limits on political competition through gerrymandering, voter suppression, the demands of campaign financing, ballot restrictions for third parties, and similar measures. Equally, it is full of 'pork barrel' projects that redirect public funds to favored constituencies to allow politicians to be reelected rather than acting in a general utilitarian fashion. Similar things can no doubt be said of other 'open access orders' (Japan for instance, or Italy). North and colleagues are sanguine about such things, just as they are sanguine about the idea that open access orders guarantee 'economic performance' despite the rather poor growth rates of these societies compared with North's Soviet counterexample, or contemporary China (also rather the opposite of an open access order). Similarly, they are sanguine about the way that institutional transformations, economic crises, and civil wars are counted *for* open access orders as proof of their ability to adapt to changing circumstances, while the very same phenomena are counted *against* natural state orders as proof of 'disorder' and 'violence' and failure to become adaptive.

But this is not the most interesting thing to say about the macro-level analysis of the NIEH. I have already detailed how it smuggles in various kinds of political ideas that are not supported within the theory, but are taken for granted, and which I have attempted to describe with the label of classical liberalism. I have also set out why I think the other macro-level dynamic in the theory, the theory of adaptive efficiency as a form of evolutionary selection between societies, does not function as an explanatory device. That said, we are not left with nothing, however. For shorn of its more dubious Hayekian flavoring, the NIEH's substantive theoretical contributions do offer us some building blocks for comparative global history.

The NIEH as a Contribution to Global History: Path Dependence

Global history as a field, or subdiscipline, of history has been defined above all by the quest to explain the 'great divergence' (Pomeranz 2000): the emergence of Europe as a technologically, economically, and militarily dominant subcontinent, capable of subjugating virtually the entire globe and of building a new global institutional order on top of it. While there have been, and are, ongoing disputes about when precisely this happened and to what extent it happened, there is little doubt that the turn toward answering such questions has had the effect of forcing economic and social historians to recontextualize the familiar terrain of national or cultural narratives into a global context. More than anything else, global history is about reexamining what is known by asking what role given historical events or phenomena played in the larger context of world history as an integrated, interconnected whole (Conrad 2016). The quest to explain European (or sometimes Western) hegemony, for however long it has lasted or might last, has had the curious impetus of 'provincializing Europe' (Chakrabarty 2000) and making comparative studies across the globe a more favored means of historical examination.

While much of what I have written about North's NIEH so far has been about its role as a contribution to economic thought, I do not want to neglect the historical dimension of its scientific potential. For the NIEH is quite clearly concerned with explaining the divergence between 'the West' and 'the rest'. It originated in North's dispute with the Cliometricians and the neoclassical economists about the ability of economics to provide a properly long-term *historical* account of institutional change. Polanyi's challenge, too, revolves around whether some form of economics as recognizable from the postwar development of the discipline is capable of explaining the different forms the embeddedness of economic institutions has taken in history. For North as well as for Polanyi, this required an approach to the problem that would be both comparative and historical in method. *UPEC* begins with 'the rise of the Western world' as the first case to be explained. Moreover, together with (cognitive) uncertainty, nonergodicity—the nonreversible nature of historical time—is one of its core concepts (North 2005: 1, 13). North's account is therefore thoroughly historical in intent, even if much of his (mature) work is focused on theoretical topics. To assess it, we have to separate his theoretical concepts—his historiographical tools—and his actual historical narrative. I begin with the former, starting with the concept of nonergodicity, or path dependence.

The concept of nonergodicity simply means the nonequilibrium, nonreversible state of a set of phenomena. As North explains, in neoclassical economics the assumption of ergodicity is crucial, because the assumption that future events will return to the mean of the results of the past—effectively that time makes no independent difference to the account—allows one to model the whole as the equilibrium outcome of a set of causal factors. North cites none other than Robert Solow and Paul Samuelson to this effect (North 2005: 19). As North points out, however, this methodological principle of ergodicity is incompatible with a historical account focused on the reality of change through time. As North hints, it is really borrowed from analogy with the role of equilibrium in the natural sciences and serves to make behavioral microfoundations more tractable; it does not serve the purpose of providing greater 'realisticness' in explanatory results.[3] In reality, North argues, the future is often not like the past, and the ability of anyone to predict the longer-term outcomes of behavior in the present is very limited beyond a narrow time horizon. The result is that people try to adapt institutions, beliefs, and circumstances to changing conditions, and they will do so in differing ways. These changes in the 'human environment', as he calls it, in turn cause further unpredictable cascading effects, and the result is a highly unstable, unpredictable, and nonergodic historical dynamic of social change. There is a kind of butterfly effect: even small shifts in beliefs, cultural inheritance, institutions, or simply exogenous shocks can lead to responses that in turn accumulate further reactions over time in an unpredictable way. Small changes can lead to great divergences of outcomes.

The core concept here is path dependence: the way the possibilities for future change, and their relative costs, are defined by the existing artifactual structure as it has been inherited from past change. As North defines it, path dependence is simply "the way by which institutions and beliefs derived in the past influence present choices" (North 2005: 21), but perhaps it's more precisely seen as the way that the results of past 'choices' (in the behavioral sense) appear as environmental parameters for the present. The classic discussion in economics, invoked by North on various occasions, is the QWERTY keyboard. As described by the economist Paul David, who first drew the attention of economic historians to this phenomenon, this keyboard is the standard layout for personal computers throughout the English-speaking world, but it is highly inefficient from

[3] See Mirowski (1989) for a longer discussion of this point.

the viewpoint of actual letter usage. It derives, however, from an arrangement of keys used in typewriters precisely because overly fast typing would lead to jamming of the mechanism. Since this was institutionally inherited, the costs of changing to a new layout (and having to learn to type with it) are considered higher than the costs of sticking with the inefficient system, a phenomenon David called 'lock-in' (David 1985).

For North, this 'lock-in' element is an indispensable part of the historiographical significance of path dependence. After all, that the present depends on the past may be a truism for all but neoclassical economists. But as North rightly points out, there is more at stake. After all, the meso-level of North's theory is devoted to the explanation of how institutions create their own incentive structures and collective agents devoted to pursuing those incentives. Given this fact, the institutional heritage of the past also creates its own local equilibrium, so to speak, because a given institutional setup will entrench certain interests, power structures, and reproduce certain belief systems through collective learning. As North puts it: "[Path dependence] could mean nothing more than that choices in the present are constrained by the heritage of institutions accumulated from the past. But if that were all there was to path dependence then we could undertake radical change when we observed that the institutions were performing badly. A step toward a more comprehensive understanding of the term is to recognize that the institutions that have accumulated give rise to organizations whose survival depends on the perpetuation of those institutions and which hence will devote resources to preventing any alteration that threatens their survival… Path dependence is not 'inertia,' rather it is the constraints on the choice set in the present that are derived from historical experiences of the past" (North 2005: 52).

One notices here, of course, the smuggling back in of the choice theoretical principles (constraints on, and within, rational choice) that he earlier dismissed as behaviorally insufficient in light of the importance of beliefs and cognitive science (North 2005: 19). But leaving this aside, this emphasis on path dependence combined with the essential distinction between institutions and agents in North's model provides him with a powerful tool for analyzing both the synchronic and the diachronic structure of societies for the purposes of comparative history. The micro-level cultural evolutionary model, flawed as it is in its current form, does much the same. It allows North to treat ideological or worldview differences as having both synchronic significance (as bounds on rationality) and diachronic significance, in how they contribute to collective social 'learning' as culture and how they are part of the continuous "testing [of] constructs (read theories) against evidence to see if they have explanatory value" (North 2005: 83). Finally, there is the meso-level, where individuals, organizations, and institutions are analytically distinguished, so that a clear division between structure and agency emerges. This is possible in the theory without necessarily prejudging the nature of that society's incentive structure or the kind of rationality involved, even if in practice North does not always hold himself to that. All of this gives North's NIEH a remarkable degree of flexibility in modeling historical differences between societies, without—as often in economics—leaving out dynamics of culture, power, or beliefs. And yet at the same time, it has sufficient precision and determinacy because the interaction between the different concepts is quite clearly defined, even if I have argued that the precise mechanisms and arguments North proffers for those theoretical 'hinges' are not always compelling.

Much of the development of comparative analysis in global history has been aimed at not just explaining the origins of the great divergence, but also in hoping that lessons for developmental purposes can be drawn from them.[4] North's historiographical contributions are no exception to this. The very purpose of *UPEC*, and with it of the NIEH in its most mature stage, is to intertwine the rethinking of economic historiography with grasping the implications of that rethinking for the possibility of institutional change in the present and future. North's pessimism in the face of the complexity of his many-tiered and many-variabled structure should not be seen as abandoning the idea that economic history can and should contribute to developmental study. As he summarizes the research program expressed in *UPEC*, "we must explore the way consciousness interacts with diverse experiences that produce diverse cultural—institutional—patterns. We must account for the origins of belief systems that either provide a favorable milieu for the creation of productive political and economic institutions or conversely thwart the creation of such insti-

[4] See, among others, Vries (2010) for a discussion of the developmental implications of the 'California school' of global historians and of the great divergence question in general.

tutions. Whether the institutional constructs create a favorable or an unfavorable milieu for improving economic performance, we have to understand the complex structure that has evolved… Transaction cost economics provides us with an opening to widen and deepen economic analysis to confront these issues. But very little work has been done to understand the complex interdependence of the evolving social structure the human mind has created. Without that understanding we are basically crippled in attempting to improve the economic performance of societies" (North 2005: 83–84).

Ultimately, then, the NIEH does both history and development policy: it innovates in the usage of NIE concepts for the study of economic history and historical change, and it in turn uses these historiographical reformulations to reconsider the way we think about economic development and the possibilities for institutional change in the present. To understand the great divergence, such a glaring fact of our present world, we need to understand historical economies. To do that, we need to understand institutions. To understand institutions, we need to grasp the nature of power, incentives, culture, and beliefs. And to understand these, we need to understand the roots of human cooperation. And all of these elements are independently capable of change and historical variation, and all of them show path-dependent properties. North does not shy away from the far-reaching implications of trying to combine a fully endogenizing institutional economics with a long-term historical theory to explain economic outcomes in the present. However flawed some of the major components and interlinking parts of this theory may be, the historiographical toolbox that remains impressively combines analytical clarity with flexibility of application. In that regard, it is in the best traditions of global history.

The NIEH as a Contribution to Global History: The Narrative Account

We should not, however, conflate the NIEH as a set of tools with the NIEH as North actually used it to make specific arguments or to provide a specific historical account. I have already dealt at some length now with the various arguments and interventions North makes about markets, rationality, cultural evolution, and so forth. I have also questioned his account of open access orders and natural state orders at various levels. This divide not coincidentally maps precisely onto the West/rest construct, and reflects at best only an American post–Cold War retrospective vernacular view of their own position in the world. I think in any case the tools provided by North's theory are more important and valuable than the specific account North gives of the divergence. Even so, it seems only fair to provide a short discussion of North's application of his own tools to the divergence question. The main materials for this are chapter 10 of *UPEC* and much of the historical content of *VSO*.[5]

In *UPEC*, North's account of the rise of the Western world (the chapter is so titled) hearkens back to his first NIE models of the medieval European manorial system. The rise of the West is explained virtually exclusively in intra-European terms as arising out of the transformation of the feudal system in late medieval Europe. A combination of factors led to the decline of the medieval world: feudalism decaying as a result of labor shortages after the plague, an attempt by centralizing courts to increase military revenues by distributing property rights, and the growth of long-distance commerce through urbanization and merchant networks. The core dynamic is the social contract view of the emergence of commercial society, elaborated on at much greater length in *VSO*: "The economic institutional structure was made possible by the evolution of polities that eventually provided a framework of law and its enforcement. Such a framework is an essential requirement for the impersonal exchange that is necessary for economic growth. The development was a long process of (some) polities gradually shifting from extortion to trading 'protection and justice' for revenue" (North 2005: 133).

In essence, this is for North sufficient to explain the longer-term course of events, with the early modern emergence of a more impersonal fiscal-military-bureaucratic state being merely a further outgrowth of the same core principle. As he sums up, "These contrasting stories of economic growth and decline have been, with appropriate but usually minor modification, repeated endlessly in history and in the modern world. Growth

[5] See also North (1995).

has been generated when the economy has provided institutional incentives to undertake productivity-raising activities such as the Dutch undertook. Decline has resulted from disincentives to engage in productive activity as a consequence of centralized political control of the economy and monopoly privileges. The failures vastly exceed the successes" (North 2005: 134).

However, North does not neglect the cultural/belief level of things entirely either, as such would be inconsistent with the spirit of *UPEC*. On the basis of the works of Max Weber and Lynn White, North provides the addendum that the Christian belief system of Europe was also particularly amenable to economic growth. "Christian belief gradually evolved the view that nature should serve mankind and that therefore the universe could and should be controlled for economic purposes. Such an attitude is an essential precondition for technological progress." However, this is an effect, not a cause, of institutional transformation. North emphasizes (in an uncharacteristically awkward formulation): "It was particularly the unique institutional conditions of parts of medieval/early modern Europe that provided the sort of experiences that served as the catalyst to precipitate such perceptions" (North 2005: 137). Here, the 'testing against experience' aspect of North's theory of beliefs comes to the foreground, although it remains very indeterminate and the explanation in question has more the character of a just-so story.

On the whole, this account is fairly conventional, rather old-fashioned, and not particularly informed by the larger global history literature since the Eurocentrism debates or by any of North's own theoretical innovations, for that matter. One could easily imagine a Robert Solow (say) endorsing roughly the same account, or indeed Weber doing so. In *VSO*, we do not find much more empirical historical narrative than in *UPEC*. There are many scattered references to historical cases, from the old Germanic laws to the Roman Republic and the medieval church, largely concentrating on European history. For the most part, these cases serve to illustrate particular theoretical points: examples of aspects of the natural state order, or analyzing historical political conflicts (e.g. the Investiture Crisis) as cases of strife within the 'dominant coalition'. Even the fairly lengthy discussion of English feudalism in the Norman period (chapter 3 of that book) serves primarily to illustrate what a natural state order looks like. As such, they serve their purpose. There is a larger historical narrative in *VSO* that contributes to the great divergence question and its developmental implications, however. North and colleagues define what they call the 'doorstep condition' for the transition to the open access order. They follow this up with an account of how those societies they describe as open access orders have actually historically reached that status.

Here, North and colleagues make the point that previous discussions of the 'rise of the West' have not properly distinguished the preconditions for transition to the open access order from the transition itself Both must be accounted for, and the one does not guarantee the other. Using the United States, Britain, and France in the nineteenth century as examples, the authors focus on particular transition events that contributed to the creation of an open access order. In the United States, they focus on general incorporation, taking the formation of corporate companies out of the hands of legislatures and making that form generally accessible to anyone. The role of state governments rather than the federal government is key for their account (North, Wallis, and Weingast 2009: 228–240). In Britain, the story is similar: the authors focus on the Great Reform Act of 1832, creating the first rudiments of general male suffrage, and the Registration Act of 1844 which generalized the corporate form. As in the United States, corporations and political parties became permanent features of the landscape as a result, and these—being permanently lived impersonal organizations – are core to the account of political competition that sustains the open access order's putative adaptive efficiency. In the French case, it is in the course of the struggles of the Third Republic that political competition is deemed to have become open, whereas with the corporate form during the reign of Napoleon III the same happened to economic competition (North, Wallis, and Weingast 2009: 217–229). In all these cases, the transition itself essentially consists of two things: the registered corporation and the creation of enduring political parties engaged in (mostly) peaceful competition for votes.[6]

[6] In the context of wider debates about the rise of 'modernity' in global history, or indeed about the rise of capitalism as distinct from mercantile society, it is interesting to note the periodization. Compared to many global historians, North and colleagues put the transition itself, the shift in fundamentals marking a qualitative difference in the logic of society, on the late end of the spectrum: in the 1840s–1850s for the United States, the 1830s–1840s for the United Kingdom, and the 1870s–1880s for France.

Almost seamlessly, this narrative then segues into the larger question why only Western societies should be open access orders in the first place. Here, North and colleagues make a number of important points. Firstly, that any such account of transition must be compatible with the interests of elites (what others might call the ruling class). Those in power in the societies in question before the advent of the open access order (what others might call modernity, or capitalism) did not intend to consciously drastically change their societies, and would have been horrified at the thought. It must therefore be explicable in terms that are compatible with their political and economic interests. Secondly, the preconditions can have taken any amount of time to emerge, certainly centuries, whereas the transition itself was the work of medium-term institutional reform, usually a process taking a few decades (as illustrated above). These are important historiographical arguments and make the distinction between the 'doorstep conditions' and the transition proper a useful way of thinking about the problem. It is my personal suspicion that much of the debate in global history has suffered from the desire to find the one locus, the single event, institution, or phenomenon that *ultimately* set in motion the causal chain toward European dominance and Europe-centric modernity. Often this has led to the procedure that comparative historical study has focused on identifying whatever single differences can be found between otherwise 'comparable' periods and places, and then to attribute to that difference the whole weight of the explanation. North and colleagues' point that the preconditions are one thing and the transition itself another, that both need explaining, and that accounting for the one is not accounting for the other is a salutary remedy against this tendency to temporal compression in the name of causality.[7]

To these observations the authors then add the great divergence question. As they formulate it: "If the transition involves a two-step process, then answering why the West went first divides into two components: first, how did the West come to meet the doorstep conditions and in the process come to dominate the world militarily; and second, why did the

[7] Some authors operating in the NIE tradition have also been guilty of this: the influential paper by Acemoglu, Johnson, and Robinson (2001) on colonial institutions and development trajectories can be read as a salient example of this phenomenon.

transition proper first occur in the West?" (North, Wallis, and Weingast 2009: 240). They answer this by emphasizing the European states' ability to come to control elite violence and to concentrate (or centralize) it in a unitary state, itself then ripe for opening up to competing interests. As they explain, "Where the military revolution thesis emphasizes war, our approach emphasizes organizations, institutions, and the internal dynamics of the dominant coalition in combination with war… Where models of the military revolution thesis begin with the assumption that the state has a monopoly on violence, we begin with the assumption of dispersed violence and argue that these states attain a monopoly on violence only at the end of the process of completing the doorstep conditions in the late eighteenth and early nineteenth centuries" (North, Wallis, and Weingast 2009: 241–242).

For North and colleagues, the doorstep conditions are summed up as "rule of law for elites, perpetual life for both organizations and the state, and consolidated control over the military" (North, Wallis, and Weingast 2009: 242). Often, they agree with the military thesis, these came about because of large-scale wars in Europe or beyond, forcing elites into agreements with one another to create separate bodies and to constrain themselves in order to promote greater fiscal and logistical efficiency for military purposes. But, as they stress, war is not always the sole or even primary engine for such institutional transformation. Equally important are political and social struggles within nations, forcing elites to attempt via reform or civil war to "solve the domestic political and constitutional problems" they were facing (North, Wallis, and Weingast 2009: 243; see also North and Weingast 1989).

Using his knowledge of naval history, North—for it must surely be his hand—ingeniously illustrates the formation of perpetually lived organizations such as the Victualling Board and the Admiralty in Great Britain during the Seven Years' War with France, in order to promote greater efficiency in the Royal Navy (North, Wallis, and Weingast 2009: 181–186). Similarly, the classic liberal account of the Glorious Revolution of 1688 sees this as establishing rule of law among the elites, insofar as even the monarch is explicitly bound by the legislative process from that point on and Parliament, as an impersonal body, acquires the main sovereignty. North and colleagues are actually somewhat skeptical of this account, but accept the importance of the Declaration of Rights and of the vesting of the public debt in Parliament rather than the Crown (North, Wallis, and Weingast 2009: 186–187).

At the heart of the historical analysis is the claim that although elites evidently did not intend to bring about a new form of society, they did intend to bring about changes that would enable them to include more members into the elite without upsetting the apple cart altogether. As North and colleagues tell it, the central element of the doorstep conditions that in turn enables the transition is the importance of *impersonality*: the institutionalization of the personal relations that characterize premodern states. In premodern states, personal attributes determine status, for example through dynastic position and kinship roles unique to the individual, and patron-client relationships dependent on the individual are often central to the maintenance of the elite and its ability to control where and when violence is dealt. It is the pressure that forces the elites to institutionalize these status and dependence relationships into impersonal bodies that is the core mechanic of the account in *VSO*.

The byproduct is then that such impersonal relationships become more open and porous and in turn create greater economic performance through capturing and distributing the gains from trade—whether or not that was the intent of the institutionalization reform itself in first instance. As the authors sum it up: "The three doorstep conditions illuminate the circumstances under which elites in natural states have incentives to create institutions that formalize their relationships, creating impersonal relationships between elites. The central insight is that when elites institutionalize their own impersonal intra-elite relationships, they lower the costs of expanding the size of the coalition covered by these institutions. Extending impersonality also holds the possibility of significantly expanding the size of gains from exchange" (North, Wallis, and Weingast 2009: 188).

Even so, the authors warn subsequently against any assumption that this involves simple and repeatable causal chains. For one, different countries reached the doorstep conditions, or will do so, via different routes, and this changes the problems of transition they (will) face. Another issue is a familiar one to global history: the fact of European ascendance in a particular period had strong effects on the rest of the world, including changes in technology, self-perception, and political organization, both as a result of colonialism and as a result of catch-up. As a consequence, we are again left with path dependence. The world after the European hegemony poses different developmental problems than the one before. The authors caution: "Historical developments that bring a particular society to the doorstep may not be sufficient to propel it to complete the transition, nor will the same historical developments necessarily bring another society to the doorstep. Differences in how societies get to the doorstep conditions are likely to be magnified in later transitions. After the first societies succeed in making a transition, beliefs about how the world works will change in other societies, therefore altering the process they will follow to the doorstep. These caveats apply *a fortiori* to the transition proper" (North, Wallis, and Weingast 2009: 243).

The authors in fact repeatedly reject what they call the 'Whig' or 'republican' history that focuses solely on the institution building of the Enlightenment era and even before, in which new constitutional orders emerged in the Anglo countries. Having a glorious generation of statesmen, or even several, is not sufficient, nor is military competition alone. These narratives underestimate the importance of nineteenth-century developments for actually making the transition itself happen (North, Wallis, and Weingast 2009: 78, 98, 245). The effects of the open access order are only felt from the 1850s onward, insofar as that is the period that, the authors claim, real wages started to rise systematically and modern economic growth took off, uninterrupted except for the Great Depression period (North, Wallis, and Weingast 2009: 247–248).

The result is that while there are clear lessons for how the transition itself became possible, and how it actually happened, for the case of the Western nations, it is much less clear how to reproduce this pattern. The developmental implications of this NIEH account do indeed suggest a pessimistic view of the possibility of imitation of the West. It is clear enough that, from the NIEH viewpoint, "in each of the two parts of the transition – the doorstep conditions and the transition proper – institutions develop that transform the ability of elites to form organizations inside and outside of the state. These new institutions and organizations supply the tools that allow elites to credibly commit to respect fundamental elite rights, which all elites share. The transformation of elite privileges into rights marks the steps in the transition from natural states to open access orders" (North, Wallis, and Weingast 2009: 249). But how to get the right combination of elite incentives, shared beliefs, institutional parameters, and freedom of action to make it happen? Here the authors can only point to the need for including some of their conceptual tools within a larger analysis of social cooperation and change, but they can give no recipes. As they admit, "Our recommendations for new research entail an in-depth understanding of violence, institutions, organizations, and beliefs in the natural state that we do not currently possess...The paths and policies that created open access in the Western world cannot be indiscriminately applied to foster the transition among today's limited access orders... We can do better if we are self-conscious about the limitations of human understanding and stand ready to maintain institutions that will encourage adaptive efficiency" (North, Wallis, and Weingast 2009: 271).

Conclusion: The NIEH as a Toolkit for Global History

If we take into account the objections I formulated above about why the unqualified identification of the West with openness and economic success is dubious at best, and the critique of the macro-level evolutionary notion underpinning the concept of adaptive efficiency, what are we left with that the NIEH might offer? In order to answer this question, we must again disentangle the two aspects of the theory as a historical framework, that is, the analytical utility for the purposes of comparative historical study and the policy utility for the purposes of development economics.

On the latter front, the moments where North is most pessimistic and skeptical are probably the most valuable. In the same vein as the skeptical institutionalism of Dani Rodrik (2007, 2011), one can read the pessimistic face of the NIEH as cautioning against the 'one size fits all' approach of Washington Consensus development economics, and as arguing that even those interventions that have provably worked in some institutional contexts cannot be assumed to do so in others. Policy proposals closely tailored to the particular histories, institutional orders, and incentive problems of particular societies are more likely to succeed than attempts to simply impose a Western-style economy by fiat.

One need not accept North's notion that institutional change has to be incremental, especially since that is a subjective concept. But the NIEH's Hayekian warning that social scientists and think tank paper writers will likely lack much of the relevant information to assess possible paths to progress in given countries should be heeded. It suggests that one would do well to pay more attention to issues of democratic legitimacy and popular demands about institutional reform from people who, through direct experience from the bottom-up, are intimately familiar with them, rather than overreliance on prescriptions based on deductions from economic theory. So too the importance he attaches to ideology, and its real power both in shaping possible institutional solutions and in directing the incentives that a given set of institutions provides, is an important step forward compared to purely 'economistic', rational, incentive-based accounts of economic rules and practices.

Of course, contrasting with this is the idealization of the open access order, a realm of prosperity, freedom, and efficiency so qualitatively distinct from every other society that it is scarcely believable. I do not think the open access/natural state order distinction is very viable, since it is too transparently based on a preconceived notion of the superiority—and superiority in permanence, at that—of the Western liberal institutional order. One may well have good reasons to think such a society the best kind, or the least bad, but the theory is custom-built and reverse-engineered to lead to that conclusion, and that is too strongly a case of motivated cognition to take entirely seriously. In any case it is not really true that Western societies are *evidently* less corrupt or conflict-ridden than other societies, although they may indeed be less violent on average. The experience of two world wars, however, suggests that they do not have innately superior abilities at resolving institutional conflicts without violence. Equally, it has not been the case that Western liberal societies have throughout had higher growth rates than the 'natural state orders'. The anti-Eurocentric school of global historians would probably also call into question the NIEH depiction of the trajectory toward openness and high living standards in the West as one purely achieved by internal reforms and on their own strength. From this viewpoint, it is all the more true as North and colleagues say that in all likelihood the path toward development for developing countries today does not run along the same course as that of France, Britain, or the United States (and indeed these countries may impede that path), nor is slavish imitation likely to serve them well.

For purely historiographical purposes in global history, the NIEH offers in my view a useful toolkit, more than any new insights into the process of the great divergence itself. The notion of path dependence may well seem obvious to many working historians, but the temporal dimension has often been treated highly abstractly or not at all in economics. From the viewpoint of the reconciliation of those two fields, North's specification of the topic is worthwhile. In this context, we should note the subtle differentiation involved in his treatment of path dependence. On the one hand, there is his explicit embrace of a nonequilibrium approach to historical dynamics in the longer run, and on the other there is the more equilibrium-oriented ('quasi-game theory') modeling of the short- to medium-term implications of particular institutional orders. I think much of this will likely come naturally to historians, but it is nonetheless from a methodological viewpoint important to distinguish those two levels (as it has been in macroeconomics). The coherence between the two levels will require further development, as I have tried to show in this book, since the NIEH's treatment is unsatisfactory.

But I think North's treatment here is in principle very viable: to support comparative study between societies by treating institutions as fixed in the short to medium run, and then examining the kind of political and economic incentive structures they produce and the belief systems, cultural patterns, and socioeconomic parameters that give rise to them; but in the longer run, to treat institutions as fully endogenous and to focus on the way they change over time.

Related to this is the essential distinction between institutions-as-rules and organizations-as-agents. This has rightly been identified as one of the strongest theoretical innovations of North's work (Didry and Vincensini 2011). It also distinguishes his approach from that of other NIE theorists who do not systematically separate the two. The advantage is that it gives a clear structure and agency distinction and allows one to hold constant either of the two elements for the purposes of an analytically more tractable and more transparent model of historical dynamics. The same can be said for the way North and colleagues in *VSO* do not treat the state as a unitary agent (such as the 'stationary bandit' along Olsonian lines: Olson 1993), but disassemble the concept into the component 'elite' coalitions and competition that, for the vast majority of human history as settled state societies, have in reality made up the institution-producing institution we call the 'state'. Again, here the analysis has precisely the advantages often attributed to the methods of economics: increased clarity and tractability, leading to more flexible and more transparent models (even when such models remain entirely narrative and qualitative in nature).

A third example, discussed at some length already, is the temporal and conceptual distinction between the prerequisites for a particular 'stage' such as 'modernity' and the actual transition itself. The analysis in this regard naturally remains within the realm of thinking in terms of successive qualitative stages or types, and although the theory does not prescribe per se how they are to be called or defined, this is certainly not an approach without its critics. Even so, in practice much of the discussion in global history has been concerned with tracing the causal conditions for some kind of major temporal and qualitative transition, whether to capitalism (Woods 1999), modernities as structural differentiation (Eisenstadt 2000; Knöbl 2007), hegemony (Abu-Lughod 1991), identity (Hobson 2004), or even just a particular swing of the East-West pendulum (Frank 1998). Within that context, the general framework of identifying ideological, institutional, and political preconditions and subsequently separately the elements of the transition itself, and doing so in a way that is compatible with the incentives of power-holders within the specified model and that disentangles the component parts of the transition (whichever one chooses to focus on), is a useful way of thinking. This does not require accepting the particular application of this framework followed in *VSO*, such as the natural state/open access order distinction.

Finally, as ever, the strength of the NIEH lies in the very ambition and purpose to endogenize, and integrate, all the levels of the theory into a single historical framework. Such a framework is always going to have problems at the joints, and is always going to be vulnerable to more detailed critiques of one or another individual component of the theory. This present work is an example of that. But the point is not to nitpick the theory, but on the contrary to point a way forward to follow this same ambition in a better way. The ambition itself, and the virtuoso intellectual performance of North in pursuing it, even to the point of rendering his often highly abstract discussions eminently readable and exciting, is worthy of praise instead of condemnation or dismissal. The most important lesson of the NIEH for comparative historical practice, in my view, is that *something like* the NIEH's attempt at economic and historical integration can be done; indeed must be done, if the disciplinary gaps between economics, history, and other social sciences are ever to be bridged. In the next chapter, I will provide some more general reflections on the ultimate inability of North's NIEH to achieve the aim he set for it, in answering Polanyi's challenge, and what this means for the wider NIE research program. But regardless of that observation, it is also important to emphasize that this does not mean the ambition itself was misplaced. Certain core elements of North's approach are, I think, fatal to his overall project, but the ambition itself remains. Global history has been concerned for several decades now with the debate about Eurocentrism and about the causes of the Industrial Revolution. A larger and consciously interdisciplinary approach, in the style of the NIEH, may form the necessary bridge between such focused comparative approaches and the ultra-wide perspective of 'big history' (Christian, Brown, and Benjamin 2013).

References

Abu-Lughod, Janet. 1991. *Before European Hegemony: The World-System AD 1250–1350*. Oxford: Oxford University Press.

Acemoglu, Daron, Simon Johnson, and James A. Robinson. 2001. The Colonial Origins of Comparative Development: An Empirical Investigation. *The American Economic Review* 91 (5): 1369–1401.

Chakrabarty, Dipesh. 2000. *Provincializing Europe: Postcolonial Thought and Historical Difference*. Princeton: Princeton University Press.

Christian, David, Cynthia Stokes Brown, and Craig Benjamin. 2013. *Big History: Between Nothing and Everything*. New York: McGraw-Hill.

Conrad, Sebastian. 2016. *What Is Global History?* Princeton: Princeton University Press.

David, Paul A. 1985. Clio and the Economics of QWERTY. *The American Economic Review* 75 (2): 332–337.

Didry, Claude, and Caroline Vincensini. 2011. *Beyond the Market-Institutions Dichotomy: The Institutionalism of Douglass C. North in Response to Karl Polanyi's Challenge*, halshs-00601544.

Eisenstadt, Shmuel N. 2000. Multiple Modernities. *Daedalus* 129 (1): 1–29.

Frank, Andre Gunder. 1998. *ReOrient: Global Economy in the Asian Age*. Berkeley: University of California Press.

Galbraith, John Kenneth. 1956. *American Capitalism*. New York: Houghton Mifflin.

Hobson, John A. 2004. *The Eastern Origins of Western Civilisation*. Cambridge: Cambridge University Press.

Knöbl, Wolfgang. 2007. *Die Kontingenz der Moderne*. Frankfurt: Campus.

Mirowski, Philip. 1989. *More Heat than Light: Economics as Social Physics, Physics as Nature's Economics*. Cambridge: Cambridge University Press.

North, Douglass C. 1995. The Paradox of the West. In *The Origins of Modern Freedom in the West*, ed. R.W. Davis, 7–34. Stanford: Stanford University Press.

———. 2005. *Understanding the Process of Economic Change*. Princeton: Princeton University Press.

North, Douglass C., and Barry R. Weingast. 1989. Constitutions and Commitment: The Evolution of Institutions Governing Public Choice in Seventeenth-Century England. *The Journal of Economic History* 49 (4): 803–832.

North, Douglass C., John Joseph Wallis, and Barry R. Weingast. 2009. *Violence and Social Orders: A Conceptual Framework for Interpreting Recorded Human History*. Cambridge: Cambridge University Press.

Olson, Mancur. 1993. Dictatorship, Democracy and Development. *The American Political Science Review* 87 (3): 567–576.

Pomeranz, Kenneth. 2000. *The Great Divergence: Europe, Asia, and the Making of the Modern World*. Princeton: Princeton University Press.

Rodrik, Dani. 2007. *One Economics, Many Recipes: Globalization, Institutions, and Economic Growth*. Princeton: Princeton University Press.

———. 2011. *The Globalization Paradox: Democracy and the Future of the World Economy*. New York: W.W. Norton.

Vries, Peer. 2010. The California School and Beyond: How to Study the Great Divergence? *History Compass* 8 (7): 730–751.

Woods, Ellen Meiksins. 1999. *The Origin of Capitalism: A Longer View*. London: Verso.

7

Revisiting Polanyi's Challenge: North and the Limits of the New Institutionalism

Introduction

In the course of this work, I have sought to examine the origins of Douglass North's NIEH and its development over time, concentrating on its historiographical and economic theoretical methods and their justifications. A guiding thread throughout my study of the various themes in North's conceptual apparatus—for example, markets, game theory, evolution, institutions, states, and social contracts—has been North's complex and often contradictory relationship to rival approaches. If my interpretation is plausible, North's NIEH has a peculiar character. On the one hand, in its increasing emphasis on the institutional, cultural, and even cognitive context of economic rationality and choice behavior within and without well-defined markets, it seeks to move the mainstream of economic theorizing about historical change into a direction much closer to that of the other social sciences. His extensive critiques of neoclassical economics and its straightforward rational choice analysis, his increasing emphasis on the importance of beliefs, and his rejection of efficiency interpretations of institutions make this clear.

M. Krul, *The New Institutionalist Economic History of Douglass C. North*,
Palgrave Studies in the History of Economic Thought,
https://doi.org/10.1007/978-3-319-94084-7_7

On the other hand, North is simultaneously unwilling to give up all of the analytical framework of the economic tradition from which he emerged. In particular, North's thinking about the function and effect of market competition acts as a force pulling him back to the other direction. He is keen to insist on the classic welfare economic implications of well-ordered markets, sees such markets as necessary (if not sufficient) prerequisites for economic growth, and therefore takes a good deal of neoclassical consumer and growth theory and its larger micro- and macroeconomic implications essentially for granted. In his framework, 'the market' can only function properly if complemented by transaction cost-reducing institutions and by sets of beliefs that make such institutions possible in turn. But that the full unfolding of 'the market' in its competitive structure with low barriers to entry is ultimately the *desideratum* of economic policy is not in dispute for North—to the extent that he ascribes to it not just growth-enhancing, but even evolutionarily adaptive properties.

However much North outwardly rejects rational choice theory and insists on a bounded and constrained form of choice, even at times allowing preferences and beliefs to be intelligible and derivable only from a given social matrix, he equally when it suits him presents it as a matter of the 'players' of a 'game'. North cannot decide when self-interest is a valid assumption for the understanding of economic behavior and when it is not. As keenly aware as he is of the limitations of such an approach when it comes to his micro-level analysis, he nonetheless resorts to such behavioral assumptions when to do otherwise would limit the relevance of 'the economics approach'. Indeed, this, if nothing else, remains of the 'economics approach' that North wished to defend against the Marxist and Polanyian rivals, as he outlined in the 1977 paper I took as starting point of my investigation. As Geoffrey Hodgson has argued, "The case for the conquest of other social sciences and biology by neoclassical economists rests on the presumed universality of such ideas as scarcity, competition, and rational self-interest" (Hodgson 1999: 104). North is clear about his rejection of neoclassical economics. However, it is much less clear whether for his own conquest of the social sciences by NIE theory he is any more able to do without such presumed universalities than the neoclassical economists are. This makes it dubious whether he can avoid being pulled back into the same 'economistic' reasoning that Polanyi decried, and which has made previous economists' forays into the broader social-historical sciences so difficult for their colleagues outside economics to accept.

This larger disciplinary context also contributes to my decision to focus on the importance of the challenge of Karl Polanyi for understanding North's NIEH. In part, this is because—as I pointed out in chap. 2—North's 1977 paper on this challenge remains the main occasion during which North set out, via his 'shadow' debate with Polanyi's posthumous publications, the actual questions and aims driving his NIEH as a research program. While the NIEH itself changed shape, topic, and emphasis many times since then, I have sought to show that the questions posed in that paper allow us to see a guiding thread throughout the whole.

However, that is not all. Polanyi's challenge also matters at another level. At the heart of his 'challenge' to economics was the notion that a comparative historical approach to economic behavior and its institutional forms could not proceed from (the mainstream of) economic theory as it then stood. The NIEH represents an attempt on North's part to demonstrate that economics *as a discipline* could provide such a comparative approach; but that doing so would require some substantial revisions of neoclassical orthodoxy in the direction of NIE, bounded rationality, and (later on) cognitive theory and cultural evolution. The anchor of this entire project, however, remained fixed in the ambition to show that it was *economics*, what he called 'the economics approach' or 'economic analysis' *tout court*, that could do this. This was and is an implicit rebuttal of the views of Polanyi, and thinkers like him, who have argued that approaches from anthropology and other social sciences would be better suited.

From that viewpoint, the NIEH is not just a research program to answer the questions posed in the 1977 paper: how to explain institutional variation, how to explain inefficiency throughout history, how to explain the emergence of effective states and well-functioning markets, and so forth. North's adaptation of NIE theory, and his enriching of it with a medley of elements from other fields, is also an intervention in an intra- and interdisciplinary contestation—perhaps even conflict. It is about proving that choice theory, the microfoundation of mainstream economics, can do all the things critics say it cannot. It is about proving that, suitably institutionalized, mainstream economics can supplant its heterodox critics. And it is about showing that this newly extended approach can absorb the domain traditionally part of other social sciences, and do a better job (at least from the viewpoint of the methodological norms prevailing in economics) of explaining the phenomena in that domain. In that sense it is explicitly a form of 'economics imperialism' (Milonakis and Fine 2007; Boldizzoni 2011). 'Polanyi' in this sense, as in 1977, stands for the idea that comparative institutional history needs an alternative to the mainstream of economics, and alternative explanatory norms than tend to prevail in the discipline of economics, to be successful.

With this in mind, the present chapter serves two purposes. One is to provide an assessment, on the basis of the discussions in the foregoing chapters, of how well North's NIEH really has fulfilled the aims it set for itself. Such an assessment has to be fair and holistic, of course, and not rely solely on criticisms of theoretical particulars. It must take into account the value inherent in the interdisciplinary ambition the NIEH has displayed itself, but also take heed of the fact at least some of that ambition was aimed, at least *de facto*, against the claims of those other disciplines to the domain of comparative institutional analysis in historical time.

The other purpose is to use this occasion to reflect on the implications of this study for the NIE as a whole. North's NIEH is a paradigmatic case study in the attempt to apply NIE methods and ideas to a broad range of historical and social science contexts. Many of the attributes of the NIEH discussed in this book are no doubt specific to North's work, but there are also aspects of my analysis that I believe carry over to the larger NIE research program—or family of research programs—in general. These are problems that relate to the very idea of using a combination of transaction cost and imperfect information economics joined with otherwise fairly standard choice theory to explain institutional dynamics across a wide range of space and time. While a lot could be said about this, here I will focus primarily on the key theme of indeterminacy. The problems confronted by revisions of rationality in the NIE paradigm are really part of this larger problem of indeterminacy, and so is the NIE struggle to define precisely what an institution is, and how it relates to conventional economic incentives. This is an especially pressing problem if the selling point of the NIE(H) is to be the incorporation of dynamics, such as culture, ideology, and power, that have traditionally been domains that economics had trouble incorporating and that the discipline has been criticized for not addressing sufficiently. Building on this, I will conclude with some reflections about the implications of the neoinstitutionalist turn for the idea of interdisciplinarity and unification in the social sciences. Here, the figure of Polanyi will return once more, now in his role as icon of the largest previous debate in economic and historical thinking about these topics: the arguments about formalism versus substantivism and primitivism versus modernism, which I see recurring with the advent of the neoinstitutionalist turn in the historical social sciences.

Did North Answer Polanyi's Challenge?

In the preceding chapters, I have outlined the *Werdegang* of North's NIEH from its origins in Cliometrics to its final form in *UPEC* and *VSO*. As just mentioned, a central role in this analysis has been allotted to the challenge of Karl Polanyi. Not because Polanyi himself continued to be an explicitly important reference point for North in later stages of his oeuvre, but because the challenge of Karl Polanyi represents the formulation of the aims and nature of the NIEH as a research program. I have for that reason subjected a number of the major themes and innovations of North's NIEH to a critical interpretation and assessment, with an eye to the way they have contributed to the direction of that research program and have represented North's idea about how economics as a discipline could answer such a challenge.

It will not have escaped the reader that in many respects my assessment has not been unambiguously positive. I have found significant flaws of plausibility, internal coherence, consistency, and even sometimes empirical proof in his theoretical framework. I have pointed out how North's overall tendency was to formulate theoretical innovations in a manner perhaps best described as 'two steps forward, one step back'. Each time he moved further away from conventional microeconomics, he threatened to cut loose from the disciplinary authority as the secure port he sought to defend, and to float adrift in the sea of social science. Fearing this result, he had a habit of reintroducing the very same behavioral assumptions whose foundations he had undercut in his criticisms of neoclassical economics, and to reiterate claims about the idealized workings of liberal market economics that he could not (and did not) defend on the basis of his own theory.

There is therefore from the beginning a strong and inescapable ideological element in North's approach, one that in fact impeded his own progress. While close reading his work, one seems to sense sometimes a kind of frustration with his own thinking. This is perhaps most visible on those occasions where he veers awkwardly between a pessimistic outlook about the possibility of institutional change and a hyperidealized view of Western liberal society as the one *desideratum* of all political economy. His consistent attitude of dismissiveness toward neoclassical economics, ahistorical institutionalism, and even his older inspirations in public choice theory, his insistence on the importance of culture, learning, cognition, beliefs, every possible source of social variation, all these point him away from anything that easily fits within the received notion of economics as a discipline. And yet he wants to belong and to defend that discipline and its (alleged) demonstration of the 'fundamental theorem of markets' and the successes associated with the 'Smithian result'. Make no mistake, however. This is not simply the workings of motivated cognition. It is precisely North's most admirable trait, his dogged and unflinching commitment to pursuing the methodological changes necessary to make economics fit for unification with the historical and social sciences it has so long excluded, that makes it so visible on close examination when his own ideological stances prevent him from achieving this goal.

North's theoretical innovations are real and not to be sneezed at. He remains with Robert Fogel the only winner of the Nobel Prize in economics for historical work, and indeed the only one at all for what one might call historiography of economic history. Certainly, the status and merits of that particular prize are disputed and with reason. But if one reads it rather as a sign of the recognition of one's accomplishments by an often-conservative discipline, wary of anything that smacks of musings about methodology or philosophy (or even history), it was no small feat to impress his colleagues sufficiently with a qualitative theoretical approach like the NIEH. His most influential technical innovations surely remain his clear distinction within institutions—formal and informal—and between institutions and organizations; as well as his view of the state as a historical process of building impersonal institutions by self-interested elites, rather than simply assuming its necessary existence as a unitary enforcer of rules. Beyond this, it has been the *direction* of his thinking that is the greatest contribution of the NIEH: his insistence that any aspect of institutional analysis in economics must be explicable through dynamic (path dependent) historical processes and on the basis of a fully socialized and cultural view of human society.

This has been an all the more radical and innovative approach given how close it has brought his NIEH to the tradition of the Old Institutionalist Economics (OIE), which has long been neglected by the economic mainstream for its alleged lack of 'theory' (Dugger 1995; Hodgson 2014). (This was also North's own attitude.) Some have seen therefore in this possibility of unification between OIE and NIE a reason to call the NIEH on its own terms a success (Groenewegen, Kerstholt, and Nagelkerke 1995; Brownlow 2010; Ménard and Shirley 2014a, b). Others have been more skeptical of this convergence, pointing out serious methodological differences that remain (Rutherford 2001; Hodgson 2017a). From my viewpoint, it is not so strange that such a convergence would seem to the general tendency of North's NIEH despite his pointed neglect of OIE thinking. After all, the significance of Karl Polanyi in economic thought could be said to rest on his position as a bridge between very different fields: economic anthropology, OIE, and related non-Marxist heterodoxy in economics, and debates on the applications of social science theory to comparative historiographical method.[1] All these aspects recur in North's own work with a vengeance: from the study of cultural and social variation, typical of social and economic anthropology, to the notion of institutions as historically path-dependent constraints of social form, the main implication of the OIE, to ultimately the NIEH's own *raison d'être* as an economic theory that can also do duty as a systematic comparative theory of history.

[1] See Dale (2010) for an overview. Of course, Polanyi's quest for a non-Marxist approach to the topic of comparative institutional analysis with historical differentiation should not be taken to imply that Marxism had no effect on his thinking. Like North's early engagement with Marxism, it formed for him a foil for his own approach.

Having said this, however, we are still confronted with the question whether North really succeeded sufficiently in his aim to answer Polanyi's challenge. As Sally Humphreys described it at the time, Polanyi sought to answer "fundamental questions of the method needed for the comparative study of economic institutions in their social context" with the aim of founding a "new science of comparative economics" (Humphreys 1969: 182, 207). His foundation for this was the notion that this required an approach outside 'formalism' and 'modernism', a rejection of the transhistorical application of the conventional economic models of his time that were based on assumptions of universal self-regarding rational action.[2] For Polanyi, the embeddedness of economic behavior and institutions in wider sociocultural contexts meant that a new economics was needed, as the old one would never be able to address such topics, wedded as it was to scarcity, competition, market-centric thinking and rational self-interest (Humphreys 1969). North's task then was to provide such a theory without giving up on economics altogether: in other words, to prove that the discipline of economics—suitably provided with a more institutionalized and historicized theory—can provide the kind of socially 'embedded' comparative theory of variation in economic institutions that Polanyi sought to develop.

The answer to the question must be that North's NIEH did not succeed. It did to some extent answer Polanyi's point, but primarily by proving him right. Insofar as North was forced to considerably revise economics in the direction of a theory of embeddedness and variation in historical time, he in fact contributed to developing such a 'new theory of comparative economics'. But as we have seen, the effort was incomplete and incoherent on the whole, precisely because of North's inability to sever the umbilical cord connecting him to the premises that made post-war mainstream economics what it still is: individual rational choice (however bounded), self-regarding preferences, scarcity, prices as information, and finally an enduring faith in the virtues of competition as expressed through well-ordered markets. Polanyi had rejected the applicability of these to premodern economic formations.

[2] I will return to the significance of these concepts below.

While in 1977 North acknowledged that this dispute was too theoretical to resolve at that level, he had set out to demonstrate that the NIEH approach would produce testable propositions and theoretical elaborations that would prove that all these concepts could be applied to the kind of comparative research program Polanyi intended (North 1977: 707). In fact what we observe is that time and again, the direction of North's own thinking pushes him *away* from this micro- and macroeconomic orthodoxy and toward more Polanyian-type ideas.[3] The orthodoxy even so recurs in North's theory until the end, but precisely as an orthodoxy: a set of assumptions smuggled in through the back door and a set of claims about economic mechanisms that are either not or very poorly defended. Insofar then as the NIEH became more like Polanyi, it made great strides in developing NIE theory beyond its previous confines, and it brought together theoretical and methodological resources for comparative economic history in a way not seen before. However, insofar as the NIEH remained resolutely within economic orthodoxy, it has had to rely on shoddy methodological scaffolding, ad hoc claims about markets, incentives, and economic performance that are nowhere defended, and a long series of *petitio principii* maneuvers intended to safeguard those conclusions that North had already decided on in advance. We must therefore conclude that North's NIEH, understood as a rebuttal to Polanyi, failed in its mission. As a contribution to Polanyi's own aims, however, it has been at least moderately successful.

Indeterminacy and the Neoinstitutionalist Turn

With that conclusion stated, I will now move on to discussing some implications of my critical interpretation of North's NIE for the NIE and the neoinstitutionalist turn in social science. The first such theme I want

[3] That is to say, ideas closer to Polanyi's conception of what a new comparative economics would need to include. That does not necessarily imply an endorsement of Polanyi's specific claims about historical economies, which have remained controversial both at the methodological and empirical levels ever since he formulated them (e.g. Hejeebu and McCloskey 1999; Ogilvie 2001; Blyth 2004; Gemici 2008; Dale 2010; Jongman 2014; Hodgson 2017b).

to focus on is the problem of indeterminacy. I have already referred to this issue in a more summary way in chap. 5, but I will elaborate on it a little more here. Put (perhaps overly) simply, my concern about indeterminacy in the neoinstitutionalist turn is this. One of the reasons North's attempt to systematically revise the concept of rationality as a starting point for economic theorizing—and to simultaneously endogenize as much of the cultural, social, and institutional substrate of economic phenomena as possible—failed is because the more one deviates from the behavioral and methodological norms underpinning mainstream economic theory, the less determinate that theory gets. The mainstream approach in economics, based on conventional choice theory (whether boundedly rational with imperfect information or classic rational choice), is certainly lacking in realism, historicity, and socialization. In that sense it is undoubtedly an "undersocialized concept" of human behavior, disembedded from society and temporality (Granovetter 1985). However, there is a reason why this is so. As a well-established interpretive tradition in history and philosophy of economics shows, the *norms* of neoclassical economics arose as an attempt to model economics, and indeed all social behavior, as a form of 'social physics' of the Newtonian, deterministic type (Mirowski 1989). The norms therefore evolved as privileging tractability (i.e. transparency via, and applicability to, mathematical representation) by reducing choice to a straightforward interaction between beliefs and preferences over outcomes.

This means explicitly excluding psychology, culture, and any other *causes* of preferences, since what goes into the preferences was seen as unimportant for the outcome of the mechanism translating preferences—given beliefs—into behavior. Preferences themselves are already complete subjective evaluations for a given individual, again given beliefs, and therefore what comes before is of no importance except insofar as it is expressed in terms of such subjective evaluations, as part of them (Hausman 2012). Doing this allows for tractable representation of individual behavior, given beliefs (or a probability distribution of beliefs), and given a particular incentive structure posited by the constraints of the particular case study, in the form of a quantitative model. This form, quantitative modeling of individual behavior given such assumptions, is paramount to the self-image of mainstream economics as a discipline and survives when all other theoretical claims of the discipline are called into question (Rodrik 2015). The reason for this is that tractability leads to determinacy: the hope of modeling, as was the hope of rational choice theory itself, is that *if* one accepts the behavioral premises and *if* one takes either beliefs or preferences as known and *if* one knows the range of evaluated outcomes presented by a particular case, the behavior individuals should depict becomes absolutely determinate, in the sense that they can be *deduced from the model* as predictions.

The exclusion of psychology, history, institutions, and culture is therefore justifiable insofar as one accepts the norms of tractability and modeling representation as the sine qua non of scientificity, in other words as a norm for what counts as a scientific result or the answer to a question within the discipline of economics. Only what presents itself as translatable into the terms of revealed preference counts as evidence for economics, in this view, and in this sense economics is a completely separate science (Hausman 1992).[4] Of course, it has been observed many times that this 'pure' version of economic theory does not completely hold. Choice theory itself is simply too incomplete to function as a completely independent evidence-processing mechanism, and both it and the discussion of its implications in the form of welfare economics require auxiliary information and theory to function, including the sources of preference (Caplin and Schotter 2008; Schipper 2010; Hausman 2012). It is also a familiar observation from behavioral (as opposed to behaviorist) economics by now that experimental evidence disproves the strict implications of rational choice versions of choice theory, especially for the standard assumption where expected utility is expressed in the form of material reward (e.g. Gintis et al. 2005; Ainslie 2015; see also chaps. 4 and 5). One can of course always revise utility maximization to include preferences of any other kind, including altruistic or nonmaterial ones, since one can trivially 'explain' anything as optimization of *something*. This process, however, adds no new information.

---

[4] For a particularly stark, and therefore helpfully explicit, defense of 'mindless economics' in these terms, see Gul and Pesendorfer (2008). See also Satz and Ferejohn (1994) on rational choice as a nonpsychological theory. This argument goes back to the behaviorist, antipsychological foundations of postwar economics; see Bruni and Sugden (2007), Hands (2014).

In one of the few works to systematically study the problem of indeterminacy in economics, Yanis Varoufakis has described the commitment to closed systems modeling on the part of the economics mainstream as the "dance of the meta-axioms" (Varoufakis 2014: 1–19). As he points out, on its own choice theory is too incomplete to be deterministic. And yet determinacy is desired, so theoretical incoherence is chosen instead. This leads to a constant back-and-forth motion in mainstream economics. The attempt to close neoclassical economics as a system based on rational choice theory is impossible (at least without assuming wildly unrealistic parameters), as demonstrated for microeconomics by the Allais Paradox and other problems of preference (Allais 1953; Ellsberg 1956, 1961) and for macroeconomics by the extreme restrictions of the Sonnenschein-Mantel-Debreu conditions for general equilibrium (Sonnenschein 1972, 1973; Mantel 1974; Debreu 1974; Rizvi 2006) and the Cambridge capital controversy (Cohen and Harcourt 2003). The result is that economists look for ways to relax the strict axioms of choice theory, for example by bounded rationality and imperfect information, and seek refuge in additional tools like game theory and evolutionary approaches. But the more they pursue this path, the further away from the determinacy guaranteed by general equilibrium they get. The result is that at some point the trajectory of the research hits the 'wall' of indeterminacy and is flung back to its original position. The problem of indeterminacy pervades choice theory itself, and if one follows Varoufakis' argument, it makes sense to understand the specifically neoclassical form of it—and its disciplinary normative success—as the most secure attempt to pin it down, at the cost of accepting a great deal of methodological incoherence. Choice theory inherently has its conceptual trade-offs.

North's own motion, what I have described as his strange 'two steps forward, one step back' characteristic, has something in common with this "dance of the meta-axioms". This is, I think, because North's attachment to the norms of the economics discipline forces him to retrace many of these same steps: from ever further endogenization, to confronting indeterminacy, and then a hasty return to more strict behavioral premises that will guarantee some determinate equilibrium state. What differentiates North's NIEH, however, is that he is not *directly* concerned with closing his system. North makes no attempt at providing closed quantitative models of his analysis of agency, and does not really seem to care whether his NIEH as a whole is closed and deterministic in the way that economists would expect. From my viewpoint, this is commendable rather than condemnable. It is only when North realizes he is straying far from the prerequisites for his theory to be complementary to the neoclassical approach (North 1990: 4) that he suddenly makes a sharp turn. There is a lesson here for the neoinstitutionalist turn: both about the reality of tradeoffs between determinacy and coherence (as well as realisticness) inherent in choice theory, and about the perils of constraining one's investigation by disciplinary norms in advance.

My argument is therefore not meant as a defense of neoclassical economic methodology in its pure form per se, or as a defense of the way it is sometimes justified. Rather, it is to suggest that there exist nonetheless serious trade-offs that NIE theorists, and those who wax enthusiastic about the turn to institutions in the social sciences, need to take seriously. The first trade-off is between adherence to the disciplinary criteria of economics in terms of scientificity, through tractability and modeling, and the ability to revise behavioral principles. Put more crudely, at a certain point the institutionalist movement will have to confront the fact that either you can be 'scientific' according to the prevailing norms in economics of what it means to have given an answer to a question—namely, providing a model with deterministic predictions—or you can have behavioral foundations that take psychology, ideology, culture, and so forth seriously, and take each of them as some kind of input into an overall behavioral theory. The latter approach is not likely, at least with present methodological tools, to allow for modeling in the style familiar to economics, let alone models that have clear implications for what kind of observation *should* be observed given particular parameters.

This is nothing new: it is precisely why economics and other social sciences have been such noncommunicating fields, because the former relies on choice theory and the latter on the much broader (and more vague) constellation of sociological inputs into behavior sometimes loosely called 'social theory'. These have very different criteria for what counts as an explanation, and that makes them unable to accept each other. The institutionalist turn in social science will not be able to avoid making hard choices where to situate themselves along this axis. As I have sought to illustrate in this book using the case of North, one cannot have *both* adherence to the criteria of scientific results prevalent in mainstream economics *and* also want to incorporate all the substantive theories of cognitive science, psychology, sociology, anthropology, and biology. I suspect it is recognition of this fact that has made most NIE theorists, from Oliver Williamson to Avner Greif, choose to stay well within the bounds of rational choice theory and comparative statics, whether via rational choice models of transaction costs or the use of standard game theory. My personal preference is for the neoinstitutionalist turn to go in the other direction, pursuing a similar path of unification as sought by behavioral economics and by sociobiology, but the choice does have to be made.

The second trade-off, related to the first, is that between realism (here again 'realisticness') and determinacy. Again, the crude version of the argument is this: the more one endogenizes, the fewer predictions about behavior or outcomes actually follow from the model—especially so for the kind of qualitative model, like North's NIEH, best suited for such an operation. I suspect it has been a long-standing source of frustration for both economists and other social scientists when they exchange the usual accusations, with the sociologist or anthropologist accusing the economist of having a wildly reductive and unrealistic idea about human society and behavior, and the economist retorting that none of the sociologist or anthropologist's favored social theories have ever predicted any outcome or been testable in any way. (Working as a philosopher of economic history for several years at an anthropological research institute, I myself have observed this phenomenon many times.) It is therefore all the more curious and significant that North began by arguing Polanyi's theses needed to lead to testable propositions, and resolving to produce these, and yet he subsequently focused more and more on the critique of neoclassical economics as insufficiently realistic. As he did so, the scientific criterion of testability in the sense of economics—providing determinate predictions about behavior deducible from mathematical models—fell by the wayside, and was quietly and unobtrusively replaced by the scientific criterion of realisticness of assumptions and outcomes, which is often in direct conflict with the former.

North was undoubtedly right in these criticisms of neoclassical orthodoxy. The neoinstitutionalist turn, I suspect, is based for an important part on researchers trained in economic thinking being dissatisfied with the inability of orthodox methods to address the social and historical problems they are confronted with. I do not think that this development, toward a more historicist and institutionalized, in other words less 'undersocialized' view of agency and society is a bad one. But I do think we have to be honest about what it entails. It is my impression that there prevails still the widespread idea that one can simply add NIE theory to historical or social analysis of some sort and thereby have one's cake and eat it: one can have both the (alleged) rigor and tractability of economic analysis and also the ability to study the kind of institutional, cultural, or social topics that the economic historian, economic anthropologist, or economic sociologist is interested in. But this will not do. The result is simply that anything and everything becomes an 'institution' and that institutionalist theory is presumed to explain anything simply by virtue of calling something institutional. The applicability of NIE theory is assumed, not demonstrated, and the result is an enormous proliferation of institutional analyses where it is not clear how and why NIE theory is supposed to add to the explanatory value of the case study in question.

For one, such methods often ignore North's essential institution-organization distinction as a way of preserving a workable separation of structure and agency. But more fundamentally, researchers engaging with the neoinstitutionalist turn have to understand that rational choice NIE theory can do what it does *because it is a form of rational choice*, not because they invoke the magic word 'institution'; and, conversely, if one wishes to reject rational choice theory on the grounds of realism or because one wants to incorporate the kind of 'embedded' behavioral phenomena rational choice analysis is poorly suited to, one *cannot* then make use of theories whose methodological justification rests on behavioral assumptions at odds with what one is trying to do. North's NIEH as an effort at providing a nonrational choice–based NIE theory, precisely for the purposes of studying such kinds of deeper level ideological, cultural, and evolutionary causes of historical differentiation, has floundered precisely because of the unwillingness to be explicit about what behavioral premises are accepted and for what reason. North smuggles rational choice ideas back into the mix in an ad hoc fashion whenever it suits him, and equally explains this by reference to institutions (cultural, legal, and social norms) and their non'rational' causes whenever it suits him, and calls it a day. But this is a very insecure foundation on which to build a new form of social scientific integration. Many researchers in economic thought since him have replicated the same error, often without being aware they have done so.

What is needed is rather more serious attempts at integration at the level of methodology, not just at the object level of analyzing the workings of particular institutions. Even if there is complete agreement about what an institution is, for example based on North's definition, there would still be incoherence if there is no agreement about what the use of institutional analysis implies for what kinds of explanations are valid results, in other words what it takes for some form of institutional analysis to count as an explanation. Right now, we are confronted with a situation where an institution can be anything one wants and also does not constrain the explanatory model in any way. This allows the researcher a great deal of flexibility, but one should openly acknowledge that this comes at the expense of the determinacy of the model: nothing essentially follows from the analysis, and nothing is predicted or even retrodicted by it. There is no way of telling whether the use of institutional analysis has added anything to the explanation.

If the neoinstitutionalist turn is not just an academic fashion, but its aim is—as I hope—to contribute to better integration between the social and historical sciences including economics, we will need some clear analytical foundations that contribute to constraints on possible types of explanation and therefore to the determinacy of particular models or findings. I think the direction North himself took toward the end of his career is a promising one. Some form of behavioral economics, combined with the methods of historical analysis, the more analytically tractable concepts and theories from anthropology, and the contributions from sociobiology might very well represent a joint foundation more suited to the analysis of institutional embeddedness than the tautologies of choice theory. I am hopeful in that regard, but we are still very far from achieving methodological clarity across these different fields. If it is the case, as I also suspect, that biology will be the 'model science' for social science in the twenty-first century in the way physics has been for the twentieth, further research in this direction would seem to be particularly promising.

It would take the neoinstitutionalist turn beyond the dichotomy of either economics imperialism, in the form of simply reducing all sociocultural phenomena to rational responses to market failure, or indeterminacy, in the form of redescribing already-known social phenomena as 'institutions' and acting as if this has added explanatory value.

Polanyi and the Neoinstitutionalist Turn

One final observation is necessary before ending the present discussion. For this I will return once more to Polanyi. I would not consider myself a 'Polanyian', but I think the figure of Polanyi and the problems he attempted to confront will prove to be more important to the development of the neoinstitutionalist turn in the social sciences than is now often recognized. North wrote about how Polanyi's ghost haunted the New Economic Historians without them realizing it; I would say the same about those who take inspiration from the New Institutionalism. The reason is this: what makes Polanyi such a key figure in the history of economic thought is his position on the crossroads of two debates. One is about the applicability of economic theory to wider historical and social-institutional problems, and has become known as the 'formalism-substantivism' debate. 'Formalism' used in this sense reflects the presumed universality of economic methods based on choice theory, as opposed to Polanyi's own substantivism which sought to develop different methods specific to the different 'modes of integration' of different historical economies into their respective institutional orders. The other debate concerns the way one should think about the institutional differentiation itself. The question here was whether premodern economies (the most popular case study being the classical Mediterranean) were, because of their different institutional arrangements, in some sense fundamentally different in their economic functioning from modern capitalist societies, or whether the economies of the premodern world should simply be seen as embryonic, partial, and underdeveloped versions of subsequent phenomena. This came to be known (somewhat pejoratively) as the 'primitivism-modernism' debate. The two are closely related, but not identical (Amemiya 2007: ch. 5).

Polanyi's own views on these topics, which supported substantivism—which he himself developed—and primitivism, which predated him and which he supported (Bücher 1893; Finley 1973), have come under much criticism and have been occasion for many debates in especially ancient economic history since. There is no need to review their implications here. Instead, I want to focus on the meaning of these debates themselves for the neoinstitutionalist turn. It is my working hypothesis, if you will, that while these old debates have been thought to be essentially *passé* for decades now, the neoinstitutionalist turn represents in fact a revival of the same problems. This is in a sense a corollary of the problem of indeterminacy, but at the historiographical rather than economic theory level. The more the institutional order underpinning and (re)producing particular economic phenomena is seen as *the* relevant causal variable in the comparative study of economies across space and time, the more the questions Polanyi engaged with will return with a vengeance. If institutions, rather than 'getting the prices right', are really what explain historical differentiation, then can one apply the same methods to understanding these different institutions or do we need more specialized theories or models for different types of institutional orders? If we accept that institutional variation is real, at what point does the difference between past and present institutions become significant enough that we are willing to speak of a qualitative difference? An old-fashioned Marxism might have asked: At what point does quantity here turn into quality?

North's NIEH represents an ambitious attempt at answering these questions by providing a single model of institutional variation, building on transaction cost economics and bounded rationality and expanding from there with a series of auxiliary theories. If my analysis in this book is correct, this attempt has not been successful enough to qualify as a satisfactory answer to these questions. Given the above observations about the limitations of choice theory itself, and the problems of indeterminacy faced by anyone who seeks to revise or relax that approach for the purpose of building a more flexible unitary model, we may well doubt whether economics as a discipline is capable of providing all the necessary tools for such a single model. In that case two options seem to remain. One is choosing the path of primitivism, and viewing premodern institutional arrangements as *sui generis* different ones, requiring specific theories or models applicable only to them (although they may still be grouped or clustered in particular ways). The other is to choose the path of substantivism, and inquire whether disciplines like anthropology might not provide the necessary tools for the comparative investigation. Of course, anthropology was Polanyi's choice, and this is not predetermined. North's own intuition toward biology may well turn out to pay off just as much, once the constraints on applying evolutionary theory to social phenomena are better understood. Or one might choose a combination of both, as I would favor.

The alternatives do not look sustainable in the long run, however superficially appealing they may seem as present as a means to avoid the straitjacket of neoclassical ahistoricity and asociality. Either one simply relies on received economic theory and places 'institutions' on top, in the style of rational choice NIE, and then one reproduces all of the problems of indeterminacy involved in the institutionalization *and* all of the limitations of rational choice itself. Or one lets institutions stand alone as the explanatory variable of relevance. Here, an infinite regress emerges: to explain why a particular institution emerged, or persists, one would have to explain that institution by reference to another (previous) institution, and that one by another, and so forth. Unless some deeper level theory exists about why and how institutions come to be as they are at particular times and places, their ability to explain anything is very limited, even if the concept could be well defined.

Conclusion

As the economic anthropologist David Graeber puts it, "It is one thing to say 'societies' have different ways of distributing goods. It is another to explain what particular members of the society in question think they're doing when they give gifts, or demand bridewealth, or exchange saffron for ivory in a port of trade" (Graeber 2001: 11). It is the great merit of Polanyi that he recognized this as a serious problem that arises, and must arise, as soon as one permits institutional variation to exist in the model of economic behavior. In this sense, Polanyi's challenge goes further than even North recognized. For North, the significance of Polanyi rested in his demand that the historical variation or differentiation in institutional orders be explained: If economics really had an adequate and closed theory of economic behavior, why should there be any historical differentiation at all, and why should nonmarket institutions and organizations (including elites and states) even arise? But Polanyi's work, in its role as signpost on the crossroad of the two great economic debates, also points to the consequences of relaxing the behavioral strictures of neoclassical economics to make room for such comparative institutional analysis. The result is that the presumed universality of choice theory, and its deterministic power as a closed system, has to be explicitly given up. Now as the many heterodox and internal critics of microeconomics have pointed out, choice theory even in its most straightforward form as perfect rational choice fails to actually close as a system. But to acknowledge this, and therefore reject its strictures, is also impossible. It violates the much stronger disciplinary norm in economics against indeterminacy. Such boundary crossing leads to the shadowy realms of 'social theory', and there be dragons. Most economists, therefore, have chosen to live with the safety of incoherence over the dangers of indeterminacy (Varoufakis 2014).

It is to North's lasting credit that, while he wavered from time to time on the road, he at least pointed the way for economists and economic historians toward the land of danger and adventure and away from such complacency. But he dared not venture far enough to really answer the challenge of Karl Polanyi. If my analysis in this work is at all correct, the implications of the fundamental inconsistencies in North's NIEH are that the debates about the relationship between economic theory and historical reality, implicit in the debates about substantivism-formalism and primitivism-modernism, have not gone away and *cannot* go away as long as their source remains. That source is the contradictory aims implicit in the neoinstitutionalist turn in social science itself. The aim of the neoinstitutionalist turn appears to be to cloak oneself in the norms and prestige of the discipline of economics, and yet at the same time to pursue substantive research questions that are impossible to resolve with the methods of that discipline and with the premises on which that (supposed) rigor and prestige are based. North's NIEH shows that one simply can't have one's cake and also eat it in this fashion.

References

Ainslie, George. 2015. The Cardinal Anomalies That Led to Behavioral Economics: Cognitive or Motivational? *Managerial and Decision Economics* 37 (4–5): 261–273.

Allais, Maurice. 1953. Le Comportement de l'Homme Rationnel Devant le Risque, Critique des Postulats et Axiomes de l'École Americaine. *Econometrica* 21: 503–546.

Amemiya, Takeshi. 2007. *Economy and Economics of Ancient Greece*. Abingdon: Routledge.

Blyth, Mark. 2004. The Great Transformation in Understanding Polanyi: Reply to Hejeebu and McCloskey. *Critical Review* 16 (1): 117–133.

Boldizzoni, Francesco. 2011. *The Poverty of Clio: Resurrecting Economic History*. Princeton: Princeton University Press.

Brownlow, Graham A. 2010. Structure and Change: Douglass North's Economics. *Journal of Economic Methodology* 17 (3): 301–316.

Bruni, Luigino, and Robert Sugden. 2007. The Road Not Taken: How Psychology Was Removed from Economics, and How It Might Be Brought Back. *The Economic Journal* 117 (516): 146–173.

Bücher, Karl. 1893. *Die Entstehung der Volkswirtschaft. Sechs Vorträge*. Tübingen: Laupp.

Caplin, Andrew, and Andrew Schotter. 2008. *The Foundations of Positive and Normative Economics: A Handbook*. Oxford: Oxford University Press.

Cohen, Avi J., and Geoffrey C. Harcourt. 2003. Retrospectives: Whatever Happened to the Cambridge Capital Theory Controversies? *Journal of Economic Perspectives* 17 (1): 199–214.

Dale, Gareth. 2010. *Karl Polanyi: The Limits of the Market*. London: Polity Press.

Debreu, Gérard. 1974. Excess Demand Functions. *Journal of Mathematical Economics* 1 (1): 15–21.

Dugger, William M. 1995. Douglass North's New Institutionalism. *Journal of Economic Issues* 29 (2): 453–458.

Ellsberg, Daniel. 1956. Theory of the Reluctant Duelist. *The American Economic Review* 46: 909–923.

———. 1961. Risk, Ambiguity, and the Savage Axioms. *The Quarterly Journal of Economics* 75 (4): 643–669.

Finley, Moses I. 1973. *The Ancient Economy*. Berkeley: University of California Press.

Gemici, Kurtuluş. 2008. Karl Polanyi and the Antinomies of Embeddedness. *Socio-Economic Review* 6 (1): 5–33.

Gintis, Herbert, et al. 2005. *Moral Sentiments and Material Interests: On the Foundations of Cooperation in Economic Life*. Cambridge, MA: MIT Press.

Graeber, David. 2001. *Towards an Anthropological Theory of Value: The False Coin of Our Own Dreams*. Basingstoke: Palgrave.

Granovetter, Mark. 1985. Economic Action and Social Structure: The Problem of Embeddedness. *American Journal of Sociology* 91 (3): 481–510.

Groenewegen, John, Frans Kerstholt, and Ad Nagelkerke. 1995. On Integrating Old and New Institutionalism: Douglass North Building Bridges. *Journal of Economic Issues* 29 (2): 467–475.

Gul, Faruk, and Wolfgang Pesendorfer. 2008. The Case for Mindless Economics. In *The Foundations of Positive and Normative Economics: A Handbook*, ed. Andrew Caplin and Andrew Schotter, 3–42. Oxford: Oxford University Press.

Hands, D. Wade. 2014. Paul Samuelson and Revealed Preference Theory. *History of Political Economy* 46 (1): 85–116.

Hausman, Daniel M. 1992. *The Inexact and Separate Science of Economics*. Cambridge: Cambridge University Press.

———. 2012. *Preference, Value, Choice and Welfare*. Cambridge: Cambridge University Press.

Hejeebu, Santhi, and Deirdre McCloskey. 1999. The Reproving of Karl Polanyi. *Critical Review* 13 (3–4): 285–314.

Hodgson, Geoffrey M. 1999. *Economics and Utopia: Why the Learning Economy Is Not the End of History*. London: Routledge.

———. 2014. On Fuzzy Frontiers and Fragmented Foundations: Some Reflections on the Original and New *Institutional Economics*. *Journal of Institutional Economics* 10 (4): 591–611.

———. 2017a. Introduction to the Douglass C. North Memorial Issue. *Journal of Institutional Economics* 13 (1): 1–23.

———. 2017b. Karl Polanyi on Economy and Society: A Critical Analysis of Core Concepts. *Review of Social Economy* 75 (1): 1–25.

Humphreys, Sally C. 1969. History, Economics, and Anthropology: The Work of Karl Polanyi. *History & Theory* 8: 165–212.

Jongman, Willem M. 2014. Why Modern Economic Theory Applies, Even to the Distant Roman Past. In *TRAC 2013: Proceedings of the Twenty-Third Annual Theoretical Roman Archaeology Conference*, ed. H. Platts et al., 27–36. Oxford: Oxbow Books.

Mantel, Rolf R. 1974. On the Characterization of Aggregate Excess Demand. *Journal of Economic Theory* 7 (3): 348–353.

Ménard, Claude, and Mary M. Shirley. 2014a. The Contribution of Douglass North to New Institutional Economics. In *Institutions, Economic Growth, and Property Rights: The Legacy of Douglass North*, ed. Sebastian Galiani and Itai Sened, 11–29. Cambridge: Cambridge University Press.

———. 2014b. The Future of New Institutional Economics: From Early Intuitions to a New Paradigm? *Journal of Institutional Economics* 10 (4): 541–565.

Milonakis, Dimitris, and Ben Fine. 2007. Douglass North's Remaking of Economic History: A Critical Appraisal. *Review of Radical Political Economics* 39 (1): 27–57.

Mirowski, Philip. 1989. *More Heat than Light: Economics as Social Physics, Physics as Nature's Economics*. Cambridge: Cambridge University Press.

North, Douglass C. 1977. Markets and Other Allocation Systems in History: The Challenge of Karl Polanyi. *Journal of European Economic History* 6 (3): 703–716.

———. 1990. *Institutions, Institutional Change and Economic Performance*. Cambridge: Cambridge University Press.

Ogilvie, Sheilagh. 2001. The Economic World of the Bohemian Serf: Economic Concepts, Preferences, and Constraints on the Estate of Friedland, 1583–1692. *Economic History Review* 54 (3): 430–453.

Rizvi, S. Abu Turab. 2006. The Sonnenschein-Mantel-Debreu Results After Thirty Years. *History of Political Economy* 38: 228–245.

Rodrik, Dani. 2015. *Economics Rules: The Rights and Wrongs of the Dismal Science*. New York: W.W. Norton.

Rutherford, Malcolm. 2001. Institutional Economics: Then and Now. *Journal of Economic Perspectives* 15 (3): 173–194.

Satz, Debra, and John Ferejohn. 1994. Rational Choice and Social Theory. *The Journal of Philosophy* 91 (2): 71–87.

Schipper, Burkhard C. 2010. *How Mindless Is Standard Economics Really?*. Working Papers 917, University of California, Davis, Department of Economics.

Sonnenschein, Hugo. 1972. Market Excess-Demand Functions. *Econometrica* 40 (3): 549–563.

———. 1973. Do Walras' Identity and Continuity Characterize the Class of Community Excess-Demand Functions? *Journal of Economic Theory* 6: 345–354.

Varoufakis, Yanis. 2014. *Economic Indeterminacy*. Abingdon: Routledge.

8

Conclusion: The Future of the Neoinstitutionalist Turn

In this book, I have attempted to give an overview of the development, structure, and implications of the New Institutionalist Economic History of Douglass C. North. In contrast to existing literature on this topic, I have attempted to interpret the work as a whole, in and through its manifold transformations and changes of direction. I have tried to explain how and why it originated, what kind of questions led to its formulation as a distinct research program, and in what ways these questions have driven the virtually unprecedented expansion of interdisciplinary scope entailed by the NIEH. Central to the way I have formulated this investigation is the concept of the challenge of Karl Polanyi (North 1977). North's interpretation of, and subsequent response to, Polanyi captures in a nutshell the curious combination of 'outside' and 'inside' perspective (relative to mainstream economics) inherent in the NIEH. It still represents the best formulation of North's overarching disciplinary aim to preserve the prestige of economics and its anchoring in 'economic analysis', while simultaneously enabling it to explain institutional variation and embeddedness in historical time. It is the best means of explaining not just how, but *why*, North's theory developed in the way it did and why North's work

M. Krul, *The New Institutionalist Economic History of Douglass C. North*,
Palgrave Studies in the History of Economic Thought,
https://doi.org/10.1007/978-3-319-94084-7_8

throughout retained its curious spiral trajectory, its movement showing 'two steps forward, one step back'.

Moreover, the challenge of Karl Polanyi is also a challenge to the neoinstitutionalist turn itself. North's far-seeing intellect and his willingness to push the possibilities of his own theory to the limit show the potential boundaries of all NIE theory that seeks to follow him down this path. In being institutional, historical, and embedded, but also formalist, modernist, and committed to the disciplinary norms of orthodox economics, the neoinstitutionalist turn itself will end up reinventing the primitivism-modernism and formalism-substantivism debates in which Polanyi played such a key role. The less conscious its practitioners are of this fact, the less likely it is that they will spend the requisite time thinking about the methodological and historiographical implications of their work, and therefore the greater the risk of a repetition of old moves instead of an advancement beyond these debates. That is the meaning of the challenge of Karl Polanyi for the NIE as a whole and the institutionalist agenda it has inspired.

In my interpretation of North's work, I have sought to steer a middle course between the two extremes most prominent in the literature on the NIEH so far. Most commentary on North's work is largely or even overwhelmingly supportive and sees his work as producing the necessary theoretical advances to make the NIE—and the neoinstitutionalist turn—work for the future of the 'new mainstream' in economics (and elsewhere). Others do not go so far, but do think North offers new opportunities for reconciliation between NIE and OIE, or between economics and other social sciences, or between economic theory and historical analysis. Even those who sound the occasional critical note tend to see his work as largely productive and successful, even if it retains some theoretical incompleteness. By contrast, another literature on North, mainly originating in more heterodox sectors of economic thought, views his work very negatively. For this school, North's work is primarily an attempt at making some necessary adjustments to economic theory in order to allow its rapacious expansion, at the expense of heterodox economics or other social theory, to proceed more smoothly. North's stated differences with neoclassical economics, on this view, mask the fact that his historical and institutional analysis is really but the same economics imperialism of the neoclassical paradigm extended into new domains.

In my view, both of these approaches have some truth to them. But both also have significant drawbacks. The enthusiasts' interpretation fails to observe the serious incoherence inherent in the NIEH project itself, an incoherence which originates at a deep level in the very attempt to make conventional economics do what it is methodologically not equipped to do. Even if North's NIEH is institutional, nonergodic, skeptical of rational choice, and so forth, this by no means guarantees that the substitute framework offered by North is capable of carrying the vast explanatory weight the author placed on it. North's admirers are absolutely right to praise his ambition and efforts in this direction, but those virtues should not be mistaken for the actual success of the enterprise itself in its own terms. I think the enthusiasts tend to underestimate how unlikely it is that a theory, seeking to be nothing less than a "conceptual framework for interpreting recorded human history", can carry this burden and simultaneously justify the ways of economics to the outside world. The supporters also often fail to observe that what North says he is doing, or is committed to doing, and what actually ends up happening within his theory are rather different things. They rightly approve of the direction North attempted to move economics, but fail to observe that the means he used to do so were inadequate to his purpose.

The critics, on the other hand, observe many of the serious theoretical problems a project like North's NIEH faces. They see that the very desire to be 'in between' economics and the other social sciences, to fulfill the demands of both, requires methodological innovations that are simply not yet to hand. However, they do not give North sufficient credit for the sincerity of his efforts. They overlook how useful the attempt itself has been at revealing precisely how far the NIE project can be taken before it collapses under its own weight. By focusing on the limitations of the theory, they risk forgetting that the NIEH has nonetheless provided a sketch as well as some new tools for imagining what a reconciliation between economics and the historical social sciences would look like. That represents a very respectable advance, one that can be used and built upon by those who have different ideological and disciplinary commitments than North did. If in the present work I have tended to the critical side, it is all the more important to stress this feature of North's NIEH as well.

Above all, North is Janus-faced. There is the North who rejects neoclassical theory, and the North who sees agency as the rational pursuit of material incentives. There is the North who rejects simplistic free market policy solutions, and the North who assumes that a more liberalized version of American society would be an enduring ideal for all economies, an 'end of history' that would make Francis Fukuyama (1992) blush. There is the North who sees the foundation of human sociality in culture, learning, and belief systems, and views human progress as a groping toward knowledge under changing circumstances, and the North who sees societies as flawed and fallible attempts at Hobbesian social contracts for the reduction of violence and the promotion of trade. There is a North for whom institutions and beliefs in some fashion are inputs into preferences, and there is a North for whom institutions and beliefs are constraints on a given preference set. There is a North for whom agency is strategic action, and a North for whom agency is a collective process of cooperation and learning at societal level, where the familiar problems of collective action are overcome through socialization. There is a North for whom societies are like organisms competing to adapt in changing environments, and a North for whom societies are institutional orders designed—with various degrees of success—to promote economic growth and to 'capture the gains from trade'. For each North, there is an equal and opposite North.

My hope for this book is twofold. Naturally, I hope it will prove a useful and enduring contribution to the understanding of North's most significant contribution to economic thought, one which earned him his Nobel Prize. No doubt more literature on and more reading of North's work will follow after this one, and it may not remain the sole monograph about his NIEH. But my hope is that it will remain useful especially in the way the subtitle suggests, as a critical interpretation: one where both of those aspects are equally stressed. Owing jointly to my research interests and competencies and to the already-abstract nature of North's own writings, my critical interpretation has focused on philosophical and theoretical problems rather than empirical questions or issues involved in application. Inevitably, this has meant a high degree of abstraction. As a result, it may not be the most forgiving or accessible read, for which I apologize. (At least if you are reading this, the warning to this effect in the preface has not fazed you, for which I am grateful.) I hope nonetheless that it will prove to be worthwhile both for specialists interested in philosophy of economics as it relates to the NIE paradigm and for newcomers who want to know what North is all about.

My other aim with this book has been to demonstrate, if possible, that the neoinstitutionalist turn in the social sciences is in dire need of more grounded and systematic methodological reflection. On the whole I think it is likely that from the viewpoint of economics imperialism the neoinstitutionalist turn will have a salutary effect compared to the previous situation, where the available options seem to have been either accepting the dominance of rational choice neoclassicism or simply having no productive communication between economics and other social sciences at all. But an improvement over such a sorry condition should not be seen as a great leap forward in its own right. The risk remains that in explaining everything by institutions we will end up explaining nothing, and that the fashion itself will merely function as a vehicle for exporting the methodological crisis (or crises) in economics to other fields.

I do not mean to discourage working historians, sociologists, or other social scientists, naturally. In any case, the experience of many decades of modern philosophy of science suggests that very few practitioners in any field are particularly inclined to listen to arguments concentrating on philosophy, methodology, or disciplinary identity. The virtue of using North's NIEH as a case study in problems of New Institutionalism, however, is that precisely the immensity of his theoretical vision reveals a limit case for that paradigm. In pointing to this limit, I hope to at least give people working with New Institutionalist theory reason to pause and consider in what way and on what foundations they import institutional analysis into their own research problems. I sincerely think that a better grasp of the serious methodological problems contemporary economics faces—despite the frequent pretense of having bypassed them through some fashionable step in the 'dance of the meta-axioms'—will aid researchers in all the social and historical sciences in avoiding some of the pitfalls into which it tempts the unwary. In that regard, the task of philosophy of social science is now as it has always been. In John Locke's celebrated terms, "It is ambition enough to be employed as an under-labourer in clearing the ground a little, and removing some of the rubbish that lies in the way to knowledge" (Locke 1975 [1689]: 6).

References

Fukuyama, Francis. 1992. *The End of History and the Last Man*. New York: Free Press.

Locke, John. 1975 [1689]. *An Essay Concerning Human Understanding*. Ed. Peter H. Nidditch. Oxford: Oxford University Press.

North, Douglass C. 1977. Markets and Other Allocation Systems in History: The Challenge of Karl Polanyi. *Journal of European Economic History* 6 (3): 703–716.

Glossary[1]

Bounded rationality A form of choice theory in which agents are assumed to have limited rationality owing to cognitive constraints and limited time for decision-making. Boundedly rational agents are sometimes, following Herbert Simon's pioneering work, called 'satisficers': that is to say, they behave as if to satisfy a particular given norm over outcomes rather than optimizing, by using heuristics instead of evaluating each situation fully.

Choice theory Also called decision theory. In this book, choice theory is distinguished from rational choice theory, in that the latter is a subset of the former. Choice theory in general is the framework of analyzing individual behavior as consisting of a combination of beliefs and preferences, disregarding the inputs into those beliefs and preferences and assuming them stable for the relevant period. In contrast with *rational choice theory, forms of choice theoretical analysis are possible that do not assume perfect rationality or perfect information, though potentially at the cost of indeterminacy.

[1] For convenience, I provide here a brief glossary of terms. It contains both the abbreviations regularly used in this book in order to avoid dull repetition, and some definitions of technical terms that recur in the work for reference in the following discussion. A more complete overview of terms used can be found in the index.

M. Krul, *The New Institutionalist Economic History of Douglass C. North*,
Palgrave Studies in the History of Economic Thought,
https://doi.org/10.1007/978-3-319-94084-7

Cooperation In economics, cooperation is the interaction of agents to mutual benefit. It contrasts with conflict. Often market exchange is seen as a form of cooperation, but collective action is also a prevalent form, much more difficult for economic theory to explain.

Evolutionary game theory Evolutionary game theory uses the methods of game theory within an evolutionary framework. Since the 'selfishness' of the replicators in evolution is much less controversial than in social theory, it allows the study of how and whether particular ethological or social phenomena might have evolved.

Game theory The mathematical modeling of strategic action and conflict by rational agents. It extends the rational choice framework to multiagent interactions. See also *evolutionary game theory.

IICEP *Institutions, Institutional Change and Economic Performance*. North's 1990 monograph.

Indeterminacy The failure of a model to 'close', in other words the failure of a model of behavior to give an expected outcome (to be observed in the real world) for any or all permitted inputs into the model. In *neoclassical economics, indeterminacy is avoided by imposing unrealistic constraints on the model.

Institutions For North, institutions are the 'rules of the game'. They are distinguished from agents, and provide the agents with social structure within which behavior occurs. They come in two types: formal, meaning laws and regulations, and informal, meaning social norms and conventions.

Methodological individualism As discussed in the book, there are various definitions of this term in the literature. It generally means either the explanation of all higher-order phenomena as the aggregate result of individual choice behavior or the explanation of all higher-order phenomena as the result of the interaction between individuals combined with their aggregate choice behavior. In this book, I consider the question to what extent North is a methodological individualist by these (differing) definitions.

Neoclassical economics For North, neoclassical economics is defined by the use of rational choice theory with perfect information, rendering institutions and history irrelevant. Other definitions of neoclassical economics exist, both in terms of explicit modeling assumptions and in terms of methodology. In the rare cases where I am not referring to North's definition in this work, I will use Yanis Varoufakis' definition of neoclassical economics at the level of methodology: "methodological individualism, methodological instrumentalism and methodological equilibriation", with the third being the most decisive where they conflict.

NIE New Institutionalist Economics. Contrasting with the *OIE, the New Institutionalist Economics uses *transaction cost theory and models of imperfect information to explain the significance of economic institutions and organizations.

NIEH New Institutionalist Economic History. The application of *NIE to economic history in the long run. Primarily known in the form presented by North, although other authors could be placed in the same tradition even if they do not use the term themselves, such as Avner Greif or Daron Acemoglu. Nonergodicity: See *path dependence.

OIE Old Institutional Economics (sometimes 'Original Institutional Economics' or the 'American school'). The prewar school of institutional economics that combined an evolutionary approach to social structure with an analysis of the role of institutions, habits, and conventions in shaping the nature of modern economies. It tended to focus primarily on the United States, and did not have a larger historical focus. *Neoclassical and *NIE tradition has generally dismissed it as lacking in theory (meaning, lacking in determinate models). It was indirectly influential on the work of Karl Polanyi, who is sometimes counted an OIE theorist. In recent years there have been attempts at revival, especially within the school known as evolutionary economics.

Organizations For North, organizations are agents and 'players of the game' in their own right. He assumes that people will naturally form organizations to more effectively pursue their aims in a given institutional environment.

Path dependence For North, the existence of constraints on the possibility of institutional change in a given period, and the inheritance of institutional orders via cultural learning, creates historical trajectories that are nonreversible and depend on variations in the original state. North also calls this, with reference to equilibrium theory in *neoclassical economics, a *nonergodic approach. (Ergodicity is defined as zero probability that any state will never recur, meaning that one can in principle return from any state to the equilibrium state.)

Public choice theory The application of neoclassical economic tools of analysis to the study of politics. In essence, public choice theory extends rational choice neoclassicism to the domain of political science, including voting, bureaucracy, party formation, and so forth. The public choice tradition is known for its skeptical attitude toward government organizations, since it assumes behavior within them is rationally self-interested.

Rational choice theory A form of choice theory in which any individual is assumed to have a complete and transitive self-regarding preference ordering over all possible states of the world and to have perfect information about all such states. Using rational choice theory, behavior can be interpreted as maximization of expected utility, that is, optimization given the set of preferences and beliefs of the individual.

Self-regarding preferences In canonical choice theoretical models, preferences are assumed to concern only the individual who has them. So the individual may have a preference ranking concerning any elements in the world, but *not* a preference ranking concerning states affecting agents other than herself. Put crudely, you can rank outcomes by how much you want to experience them—regardless of what they are—but not by how much you want others to experience them. However, attempts at models of other-regarding preferences have been made, at the cost of greater indeterminacy.

Sociobiology The application of biological theory, particularly evolutionary theory, to the study of human society.

Transaction costs Costs inherent in using the process of market exchange itself. Ronald Coase in 1937 defined them as "the costs of using the price mechanism". For North, the main such costs are measurement and search costs, enforcement costs of rules in the marketplace, costs imposed by small market size, and bargaining costs (influenced by ideology).

UPEC *Understanding the Process of Economic Change*. North's 2005 monograph.

VSO *Violence and Social Orders*. North's 2009 collaboration with John Joseph Wallis and Barry Weingast.

Index[1]

[1] Note: Page numbers followed by 'n' refer to notes.

M. Krul, *The New Institutionalist Economic History of Douglass C. North*, Palgrave Studies in the History of Economic Thought, https://doi.org/10.1007/978-3-319-94084-7